Kitchen Remodeling

TAUNTON'S

FOR PROS BY PROS ®

BUILDER-TESTED | CODE APPROVED

Kitchen Remodeling

EDITORS OF

Fine Homebuilding

The Taunton Press

The Taunton Press
Inspiration for hands-on living®

The Taunton Press, Inc., 63 South Main Street, PO Box 5506, Newtown, CT 06470-5506
e-mail: tp@taunton.com

Editor: Christina Glennon
Copy editor: Candace B. Levy
Indexer: Jim Curtis
Interior design: Carol Singer
Layout: Laura Lind Design
Front cover photographer: Patrick McCombe, courtesy of *Fine Homebuilding*, © The Taunton Press, Inc.
Back cover photographer: Chris Ermides, courtesy of *Fine Homebuilding*, © The Taunton Press, Inc.

Fine Homebuilding® is a trademark of The Taunton Press, Inc., registered in the U.S. Patent and Trademark Office.

The following names/manufacturers appearing in *Kitchen Remodeling* are trademarks: 1006 Navy®, ABET Laminati®, Accuride®, Adura®, Aged Woods®, Amana Tool®, Amtico®, Architect®, Armstrong®, AutoChef™, Basic® Coating, Blanco®, Blum®, Bona® Prep™, Bosch®, Broan®, Bruce®, Bruck®, Cali Bamboo®, Cheng Design®, Congoleum®, Corian®, Cover Guard®, Crossville® Inc., Dacor®, Daltile®, Discovery™, Domino®, EcoTop®, Electric Glide™, Elkay®, EnduraWood™, Energy Star®, Evolution™, Expanko®, FastCap®, Festool®, Fil-O-Wood™, Formica®, Franke®, Frigidaire®, GE®, Green Mountain Soapstone®, Häfele®, Halo®, Home Ventilating Institute®, Hoover®, Hubbardton Forge®, IceStone®, IKEA®, iPhone®, Jenn-Air®, Kichler®, KitchenAid®, KitchenMate™, Knape and Vogt®, Kobe®, Kohler®, KraftMaid®, Kreg®, Lie-Nielsen®, Lithonia Lighting®, Mannington®, Marmoleum®, Mohawk®, National Kitchen & Bath Association℠, NuTone®, Ovis®, PaperStone®, Pergo®, Pionite®, Quick-Step®, Ramboard™, Rejuvenation®, Rev-A-Shelf®, Richlite®, Rockler®, Sea Gull Lighting®, Silestone®, Silgranit™, SketchUp®, Smith & Fong Plyboo®, Stabila®, Sub-Zero®, Swanstone®, Teragren®, ThinkGlass™, Timbermate®, Titebond II®, TyKote®, UltraGlas®, US Floors®, Vent-A-Hood®, Viking®, Waterlox®, Wellborn Cabinet Inc.®, West System®, Wilsonart®, Windex®, Zephyr®, ZipWall®

Library of Congress Cataloging-in-Publication Data

Kitchen remodeling / editors of Fine homebuilding.
     pages cm
 Includes index.
 ISBN 978-1-62113-806-8
 1. Kitchens--Remodeling. I. Fine homebuilding.
 TH4816.3.K58K582115 2013
 643'.30288--dc23

PRINTED IN THE UNITED STATES OF AMERICA
10 9 8 7 6 5 4 3 2 1

ACKNOWLEDGMENTS

Special thanks to the authors, editors, art directors, copy editors, and other staff members of *Fine Homebuilding* who contributed to the development of the articles in this book.

Contents

The editors of *Fine Homebuilding* have a long-standing and heated breakroom debate about which kitchen countertop material is best. In the spirit of a good argument, and one that has lasted years, I have probably made a case for all of the common countertop materials at one point or another.

I like the aesthetics of wood and concrete. I can make these types of counters myself and even add custom elements like a drain board to personalize my kitchen. Soapstone has a rustic, natural appeal and can also be worked with the common tools that I already own. Laminate is certainly cost-effective; if I use this material, I can also upgrade my appliances. But the fact is, I have never seen a granite countertop that looked old or worn. Though it's expensive, you can spill wine or place a hot pot on a polished granite top and not worry about the consequences.

But before I was able to rest my argument on granite, our newest editor pointed out that this kind of durability might be irrelevant, because most kitchens are remodeled every 10 to 15 years. And so, the debate goes on.

This, however is not a book about countertops, it is about kitchen remodeling. Countertops are only one of the many materials that you will have to choose if you decide to remodel your kitchen. They're important and expensive, so you must choose wisely, but you won't have years to consider your options. You'll need to get on to choosing other things like cabinets, flooring, lighting, fixtures, and appliances. You'll need to resolve these decisions with your floor plan, your storage strategies, and your budget. And, ultimately, you'll have to get out the prybars and safety glasses, demo your old kitchen, and build your new one.

This book is about getting it done. That's our mission at *Fine Homebuilding*: to help our readers design, build, and remodel their homes, making smart decisions along the way. Whether you'll be doing the work yourself or hiring professionals, this book will allow you to feel confident that the results will be everything you want your kitchen to be.

Build well,

Brian Pontolilo, editor, *Fine Homebuilding*

Planning

How Much Will My Kitchen Cost?

BY JOHN MCLEAN

"How much will it cost?" is almost always one of the first questions that clients ask. And it's a good question, because the true costs of their dream home—or in this case, dream kitchen—may not jibe with their budget. Uncovering any disparity before design begins is a good idea.

To the surprise of some people, kitchen remodels are one of the most expensive building projects. They may have seen a kitchen that they liked on television or at a neighbor's house but were left with unrealistic impressions of what it cost. What you see when you visit a new kitchen often doesn't reflect the complexity of construction. The cabinets, countertops, and floor in one house can cost more or less than the same items in another. The difference may be based on a number of factors from difficulty of demolition to region of the country (see "Regional Cost Adjustments," p. 12).

For these reasons, I often use the following charts to project the initial cost of a kitchen remodel at the first meeting with new clients (see "The Checklist: How to Use It," p. 6). When I arrive at an estimated

cost for the potential remodel, we compare it with the client's budget. If we're over budget and the client can't or doesn't want to spend more money, we take a look at each item and try to cut costs. If the estimate is less than anticipated, we may consider upgrades, or the client simply may appreciate the savings.

In my experience, the cost of new construction and the cost of remodeling are similar. Therefore, these charts are viable whether renovating an existing kitchen or building a new one.

Once you've arrived at an estimated cost per square foot, multiply it by the total square footage of your kitchen. Changes to adjacent spaces need to be considered as well. For example, if you are removing a 10-ft. wall between a kitchen and a dining room, you likely will incur collateral costs for moving outlets and switches or patching the floor or ceiling in the dining room. To incorporate these costs into the estimate, I consider at least 2 ft. into affected adjacent spaces in the total size projection. For the example I just mentioned, I would add 20 sq. ft.

THE CHECKLIST: HOW TO USE IT

THE CHECKLIST CONSISTS OF THREE CHARTS. Each focuses on a chapter in a kitchen remodel, from demolition to fixture installation. The items in the chart affect the cost of a remodel in different ways. For each item listed in the left-hand column, five project levels are listed in the columns to the right. They progress from the simplest construction and least expensive materials to the most complex construction and most expensive materials. To use the chart, highlight the choices that most closely match your situation and preferences. Total the number of choices in each column, and move to the next chart. If a term is unfamiliar, skip it until you can get an explanation. If an item doesn't apply, don't highlight any level of that particular item.

To illustrate the charts in action, I've highlighted items for a kitchen remodel in San Francisco: a 235-sq.-ft. second-story kitchen in the back of the house. The room has two exterior walls that need new windows, one interior wall to be removed, and one to be given a 7-ft.-wide opening, adding 65 sq. ft. of collateral costs to the size of the reno-vation (now 300 sq. ft.). The new kitchen will have cabinets along both exterior walls and an island with a breakfast bar that seats three.

CEILING REMOVAL
Low ceilings and flat ceilings are easy to reach. Removing plaster is messy and requires diligent dust protection.

WALL CHANGES
Working with interior partition walls is almost always less expensive than working with load-bearing walls. Exterior wall openings require flashing and exterior finish work.

NEW WINDOWS
Fixed and sliding windows are less expensive because they are simpler to fabricate than casement and double-hung windows. Choose standard sizes and common colors to keep down costs.

NEW EXTERIOR DOORS
Standard-size aluminum and clad-wood swinging and sliding doors are produced in large quantities, are readily available, and often fit existing openings. Larger doors may require new framing and exterior finish work.

NEW INTERIOR DOORS
Standard-size prehung doors keep down costs because they require the least time to install. Prefinished doors tend to cost less than site-finished doors. Custom doors take much more time and money to build and install.

NEW CEILINGS
Ceilings are expensive when additional framing is needed, which is why drywall ceilings attached to existing rafters or joists are the least expensive option for both flat and sloped ceilings. Curved and plaster ceilings take longer to build.

KITCHEN ACCESS
Direct access to the kitchen from a parking/loading area speeds debris removal and material delivery.

FLOORING REMOVAL
Sheet flooring is light and usually easy to remove. Tile and wood take longer to pry up and dispose of. Removing strong adhesive is labor intensive.

WALL REMOVAL
Removing load-bearing walls is expensive, requiring temporary support and a new post-and-beam system.

CHART 1: DEMOLITION AND STRUCTURAL CHANGES

| ITEM | **EASY AND INEXPENSIVE** | | | **HARD AND EXPENSIVE** | |
	1	2	3	4	5
KITCHEN ACCESS	Direct; less than 3 ft. above grade	Direct; one story above grade	Indirect; less than 3 ft. above grade	*Indirect; one story above grade*	Indirect; more than one story above grade
FLOORING REMOVAL	Flooring to remain	*Remove sheet vinyl or linoleum*	Remove tile on mortar bed	Remove wood flooring	Remove any floor installed with tenacious adhesive
WALL REMOVAL	All walls to remain	1–2 partition walls	*1 load-bearing wall replaced with beam below ceiling*	2 load-bearing walls replaced with beams below ceiling	1–2 load-bearing walls replaced with beams above ceiling
CEILING REMOVAL	Ceiling to remain	Remove 8-ft. to 9-ft. drywall ceiling	Remove sloped or tall (more than 10 ft.) drywall ceiling	Remove flat wood or complex drywall ceiling	*Remove plaster ceiling*
WALL CHANGES	No changes	1 opening in interior partition wall	*1 opening in interior load-bearing wall or new partition*	1–2 openings in exterior wall or a new curved partition wall	More than 2 openings in or 2 new exterior walls
NEW WINDOWS	None or 1 new aluminum slider, mill finish	1–2 new aluminum or economy-grade white vinyl	1–2 white vinyl or inexpensive wood in standard sizes	2 good-quality wood, standard sizes, primed or clad color	*More than 2 top-quality clad wood or steel*
NEW EXTERIOR DOORS	*No new doors*	1 site-finished wood or metal; or aluminum slider, mill finish	1 prefinished door, wood or metal; or wood slider, primed	3-panel wood slider; or 1 pair site-finished French doors	2–3 pairs French doors; premium hardware
NEW INTERIOR DOORS	None or 1 paint-grade, hollow-core prehung	1 stain-grade, hollow-core prehung	1–2 paint-grade, solid-core wood doors	*1–3 paint- or stain-grade, frame-and-panel doors*	1–3 custom frame-and-panel or glass doors
NEW CEILINGS	None or an 8-ft. flat drywall ceiling	9-ft. flat drywall with soffit above cabinets	*10-ft. flat or sloped drywall attached to rafters*	Sloped drywall at different angle from roof rafters	Multiangle or curved drywall, or flat plaster
SUBTOTAL	1	1	3	2	2

PLUMBING CHANGES

Moving water and drain lines is inexpensive until the framing has to be modified; then cost rises quickly. New plumbing vents must extend to the roof, so unless the line is placed on an exterior wall, a new vertical space (a chase) has to be built. A second sink requires a second set of drain and vent lines.

HVAC CHANGES

Changing supply-register positions is not expensive as long as the new duct run serving the register does not entail extensive framing changes. It may be cost-effective to install a new small furnace close to the new kitchen being served. Updating the entire heating system is generally not cost-effective for just a kitchen.

ELECTRICAL CHANGES

If an existing panel has sufficient capacity, the cost of adding kitchen circuits is minimal. Bringing an old kitchen up to modern codes may require new circuits, and increased load on an electrical system may require a new panel or subpanel.

LIGHTING CONTROLS

Automated and electronic lighting controls are innovative, convenient, and very expensive. Dimmers for incandescent lights are readily available and less expensive than those for fluorescent lights. Dimmers for the latter must be high quality to be reliable.

LIGHT FIXTURES

Replacing surface-mounted fixtures with similar fixtures may require only a new junction box in the wall or ceiling. Standard-voltage recessed fixtures, while relatively inexpensive to buy, may require framing, mechanical, or plumbing changes. Low-voltage fixtures, requiring step-down transformers, are more costly.

CHART 2: MECHANICAL CHANGES, SURFACE FINISHES, AND TRIM

EASY AND INEXPENSIVE

ITEM	1	2	
PLUMBING CHANGES	None	Relocate sink and dishwasher supply and drain lines less than 3 ft. from present location; use existing vent pipe	
HVAC CHANGES	None	*Relocate 1 supply-air register and duct within 3 ft. of present location; connect to nearby supply duct from furnace*	
ELECTRICAL CHANGES	None	Minor wiring to relocate 1–2 switches and/or receptacles close to existing locations	
LIGHTING CONTROLS	Use existing switches	Replace switches with decorator-style (rocker) switches; install 1 new rotary or slide dimmer for incandescent fixtures	
LIGHT FIXTURES	No changes	Replace surface-mounted ceiling fixtures with new midrange-quality surface-mounted fixtures	
FLOORING	No new flooring	Vinyl or linoleum sheets or tiles; floating laminate flooring	
WALL FINISH	½-in. drywall with medium or heavy texture	½-in. drywall with light texture or sufficiently smooth for flat paint	
CEILING FINISH	½-in. drywall with medium or heavy texture	½-in. drywall with light texture or sufficiently smooth for flat paint	
TRIM AND DETAILING	Common paint-grade moldings for door casings; drywall-cased window openings; vinyl baseboard	Common paint-grade moldings for door casings, window casings, and baseboard	
SUBTOTAL	**0**	**1**	

FLOORING

More flooring options are available at better prices. Installation costs, though, remain unchanged, which explains the high cost of tile and hardwood floors. Floating floors and sheet flooring can be installed quickly.

WALL FINISH

High-gloss paints and smooth surfaces require better craftsmanship because they show imperfections much more than flat finishes. Textured wall finishes are less expensive and help to hide poor framing and drywall work. Tile and wood wainscot and plaster are expensive and complicated to install.

3	4	5
Relocate sink and dishwasher supply and drain lines more than 3 ft. from present location, with new vent pipe in existing vertical chase	Add new sink and dishwasher supply and drain lines and new vent pipe in existing vertical chase	Add supply, drain, and vent lines for 2 sinks and dishwasher, requiring considerable reframing of walls and floor; construct vertical chase
Relocate 2 supply-air registers and ducts more than 3 ft. from present location; connect to nearby supply duct from furnace	Add new supply-air registers, duct, and return-air grille and duct to and from new furnace; add cooling capability to heating system	Replace or supplement existing heating system with new hydronic radiant-floor system; install solar-heating system
Wiring for up to 6 new switches, receptacles, and/or light-fixture junction boxes with 1–2 new circuits from existing panel	*Wiring for more than 6 new switches, outlets, and/or light-fixture junction boxes, requiring 3 or more new circuits from existing panel*	Replace all existing wiring; install new panel; upgrade electrical service to higher amperage
Replace all switches with rotary or slide dimmers for incandescent fixtures	*Install new touch dimmer controls (incandescent and fluorescent types) and motion detectors*	Install programmable electronic light-control system
Replace surface-mounted ceiling fixtures with midrange-quality recessed ceiling fixtures	*Install new low-voltage recessed fixtures and undercabinet task lighting*	Install new low-voltage recessed fixtures, wall sconces, cove lighting, and undercabinet task lighting
Engineered wood, solid-wood parquet, or floating linoleum	Prefinished or site-finished hardwood	*Ceramic or stone tile*
½-in. drywall with smooth finish for any paint gloss level	*⅝-in. drywall with smooth finish; painted wood wainscot*	Full-height plaster finish; ceramic- or stone-tile wainscot
½-in. drywall with smooth finish for any paint gloss level	*½-in. drywall with smooth finish on many ceiling planes*	Plaster with cove detail or clear vertical-grain wood
Common stain-grade moldings for door casings, window casings, baseboard, and crown	*Paint-grade, built-up moldings for door casings, window casings, baseboard, and crown*	Custom stain-grade trim details including wainscot; or contemporary minimal trim with reveals to separate adjacent flush surfaces
1	6	1

CEILING FINISH

Working overhead is difficult. Thin, light drywall is the easiest ceiling material to install. Installing wood paneling or a coffered ceiling is labor intensive. In any case, the complexity of the ceiling increases the cost.

TRIM AND DETAILING

A trim package can be as simple as stock door casings, drywall around window openings, and vinyl baseboard. Wood molding profiles used alone or in combination increase installation time and cost. Stain and clear finishes require more expensive wood. Wainscot, built-up casings, and crown molding increase material and installation cost. Contemporary details (without surface trim) require detailed planning and precise craftsmanship.

CABINET CONFIGURATION

Galley-style kitchens may not be the most efficient working arrangements, but straight runs of cabinets are easy to install. Inside-corner cabinets have less convenient storage, are more expensive to purchase, and may require undesirable spacers between adjacent cabinets.

CABINETS

Prices are based on case and finish material, construction type, and the quantity and quality of hardware. Large manufacturers offer economy-grade cabinets. Custom cabinets are appropriate for unusual kitchen configurations and unique owner preferences.

COUNTERTOP AND BACKSPLASH

Plastic laminate is inexpensive to buy and easy to install. Stone is expensive, requires careful fabrication, and must be installed over an even, properly supported substrate. Color choice, thickness, and edge profile affect the price of solid surface.

PRIMARY SINK

Stainless-steel sinks rise in price as thickness and quietness increase. White cast-iron sinks are as much as 25% less expensive than neutral colors, and 45% less expensive than dark colors. Regardless of material, drop-in sinks are less complicated to install than undermount sinks.

SECONDARY SINK

These sinks are a good idea in large kitchens with multiple workstations or as a convenience. Because a secondary sink is often a significant distance from the primary sink, the two may not be able to share water, vent, and drain lines.

CHART 3: CABINETS AND APPLIANCES

EASY AND INEXPENSIVE

ITEM	1	2	
CABINET CONFIGURATION	Linear (galley) base- and wall-cabinet plan	L-shaped base- and wall-cabinet plan	
CABINETS	3-in. modular widths, economy-grade carcases and drawers, pressed-wood doors and drawer fronts with lipped (standard offset) design; prefinished; ¾-in. extension slides; exposed hinges; no cabinet accessories	3-in. modular widths, midgrade carcase and drawer construction, pressed-wood doors and drawer fronts, flush overlay; melamine finish; three-quarter ⅝-in. extension slides; concealed hinges with minimal adjustment	
COUNTERTOP AND BACKSPLASH	Plastic laminate with square edge; 4-in.-high splash	Plastic laminate with bullnose edge; 4-in.-high coved splash	
PRIMARY SINK	8-in.-deep single or double bowl, drop-in; 20-gauge stainless steel or white enameled steel	8-in.-deep single or double bowl, drop-in or metal frame; 18-gauge stainless steel or white enameled cast iron	
SECONDARY SINK	N/A	N/A	
FAUCET	Two-handle, swivel spout, brass construction, rubber washers, polished chrome, utilitarian design	Single control, swivel spout, brass construction, ceramic-disk valve, polished chrome, hand-spray, utilitarian design	
APPLIANCE GROUP	Bargain brand or economy line in white: small fridge with top freezer, electric range, recirculating hood, base model dishwasher, ⅓-hp disposal	Brand names in white: small fridge with top freezer, electric or gas cooktop, ventilating hood, wall oven, microwave, midrange dishwasher, ½-hp disposal	
SUBTOTAL	*0*	*0*	

FAUCET

A tall, swiveling faucet with an integral spray handle is a useful convenience that may outlast its inexpensive counterpart. Single-control valves are more expensive than dual controls, and finishes other than polished chrome add 15% to 50% to the cost.

APPLIANCE GROUP

Selecting white appliances with few bells and whistles usually provides the highest value. Extremely energy-efficient and quiet appliances tend to cost more initially. As the number of appliances rises, so does the cost of the necessary mechanical work.

3	4	5
U-shaped base- and wall-cabinet plan	U-shaped base- and wall-cabinet plan with raised eating counter	*Perimeter base- and wall-cabinet plan with island cabinet in center*
3-in. modular widths, midgrade carcase and drawer construction, wood frame-and-panel doors and drawer fronts, flush overlay; clear finish; full-extension slides; adjustable concealed hinges; some accessories	Custom widths, screwed plywood and fiberboard carcases, slab or frame-and-panel doors and drawer fronts, flush overlay; full-extension slides; fully adjustable concealed hinges; many accessories	Custom widths and heights, screwed plywood carcases, slab or frame-and-panel doors and drawer fronts, frameless or inset; special finishes; top-quality hardware and cabinet accessories
Solid-surface material in neutral color with 1-in.-thick square edge; 4-in.-high splash	Solid-surface material in dark color with full 1½-in. bullnose edge; 4-in.-high coved splash	*Stone, quartz, solid surface, concrete, or stainless steel with slab or tile backsplash more than 6 in. high*
10-in.-deep double bowl, drop-in or undermount; 18-gauge stainless steel or neutral-color enameled cast iron	10-in.-deep double or triple bowl, undermount; 18-gauge stainless steel or dark-color enameled cast iron	Triple bowl, commercial-type work center; undermount or apron front; 16-gauge stainless steel, any color enameled cast iron, bronze, or copper
N/A	*Bar sink, 18-gauge stainless steel or neutral-color enameled cast iron*	10-in.-deep single bowl; 18-gauge stainless steel or any color enameled cast iron
Single control, angled swivel spout with pullout spray, ceramic-disk valve, finish other than polished chrome	Single control, high-arch swivel spout with pull-down spray, washerless ceramic valve, finish other than polished chrome	Single control, very-high-arch swivel spout with pull-down adjustable spray, washerless ceramic valve; or articulated long-reach spout
Brand names in most colors: side-by-side fridge, electric or gas cooktop with ceramic or glass top, 300-cfm hood (or downdraft), convection wall oven, microwave and dishwasher with presets, ¾-hp disposal	Quiet, excellent-grade stainless-steel appliances with electronic controls: side-by-side fridge, 5-element or -burner cooktop, 600-cfm hood, double wall ovens, microwave and dishwasher with presets, quiet ¾-hp disposal	Quiet, commercial-grade stainless-steel appliances with electronic controls: 24-in. by 36-in. fridge, 6-burner range, double convection ovens, 1,200-cfm hood, large microwave, 2 dishwashers, 1-hp disposal
4	1	2

TOTALS

ONCE YOU'VE HIGHLIGHTED THE APPROPRIATE BOXES, you can add up the subtotals from all three charts. Chances are, all your choices haven't landed in the same project-level categories. Find the average by following the equation demonstrated below.

PROJECT LEVEL						
	1	2	3	4	5	
EXAMPLE	1	2	8	9	5	Total items 25
Total items × Project level	1 × 1 = 1	2 × 2 = 4	8 × 3 = 24	9 × 4 = 36	5 × 5 = 25	
Item values	1	4	24	36	25	Total item value 90

Divide the total item value by the total items: 90 ÷ 25 = 3.6. Now find the unadjusted square-footage cost in the chart below. In our example, the item value average is 3.6, putting it at the high end of $450 to $600 per sq. ft. We'll figure $600 per sq. ft. (remember, these are San Francisco prices). Next, we make an adjustment to the cost by subtracting $75 per sq. ft. from our projection because the homeowner is using a small, two-person construction company. Our adjusted ballpark number is $525 per sq. ft., bringing our reality-check cost projection to 300 sq. ft. × $525 = $157,500.

PROJECT COST PER SQUARE FOOT					
	1	2	3	4	5
SQUARE-FOOT COST	< $300/ sq. ft.	$300–$450/ sq. ft.	$450–$600/ sq. ft.	$600–$900/ sq. ft.	≥ $900/ sq. ft.
ADJUSTMENTS TO COST					
Kitchens > 300 sq. ft.	N/A	N/A	N/A	Subtract $50/ sq. ft.	Subtract $100/sq. ft.
Kitchens < 100 sq. ft.	N/A	N/A	N/A	Add $50/ sq. ft.	Add $100/ sq. ft.
Small crew	N/A	Subtract $50/sq. ft.	Subtract $75/sq. ft.	Subtract $100/sq. ft.	Subtract $125/sq. ft.

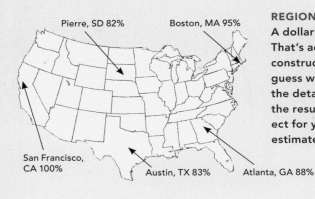

Pierre, SD 82%
Boston, MA 95%
San Francisco, CA 100%
Austin, TX 83%
Atlanta, GA 88%

REGIONAL COST ADJUSTMENTS

A dollar's worth of building in San Francisco would cost 82¢ in Pierre, S.D. That's according to HomeTech, an information service that keeps tabs on construction labor and material costs. You can customize your educated guess with the help of its website, www.costestimator.com. Simply key in the details of a project with San Francisco's ZIP code (94102), and print out the results. In a new browser (very important), key in the exact same project for your ZIP code. Divide the number for your area by the San Francisco estimate. The result is your regional adjustment percentage.

Ten Ingredients of a Great Kitchen

BY DAVID EDRINGTON

I've been designing kitchens for more than 30 years now, and I've made a career-long study of the reasons why some kitchens are so much better than others. I have seen kitchens with nearly identical budgets and the same amount of floor space, yet one perfectly suits its owners while the other one doesn't even come close. Here's what I've learned about where things go right.

Great kitchens have a lot of things in common that don't necessarily jump out at you. It's not one detail that separates a great kitchen from a not-so-great one; it's getting all the details right and making sure they work together. The relationships between various functions in the kitchen and how the space is connected to the house and its surroundings emerge as most important.

I offer the following 10 elements as points to consider when creating your own kitchen. As you study the accompanying photographs, you'll note that these elements don't exist in a vacuum. They all fit together, and you'll see many of them at work, side by side.

FOOD PREP. This big island and the countertop flanking the stove provide plenty of surface space to get food ready.

BRING IN THE LIGHT. The combination of full-size and transom windows in this kitchen brings in lots of light and provides a connection to the outdoors.

1 Natural Light

Sunlight wakes us up in the morning and makes us feel good all day long. A great kitchen has generous windows on at least two and preferably three walls. Ideally, some of them face east or southeast to catch morning sun. The windowsills should be 4 in. to 6 in. above the countertops (lower where there are no counters). If the ceiling is at least 9 ft. high, the windows should include transoms above. A shelf between the transoms and the windows is a wonderful place to display treasured objects.

2 Central Location

A great kitchen is at the heart of family activity, so it should be at the crossroads of circulation through the house—but it shouldn't have one of those roads going through it. Rather, the kitchen should be tangent to where the main circulation paths intersect. Ideally, the kitchen's location has a view of the main entrance and a view of the main garden or outdoor room.

CENTRAL BUT NOT GRAND CENTRAL. This kitchen is located adjacent to the main path through the house but is set back enough to keep it out of the flow of traffic.

CLEANUP. This sink is located at the pass-through from the kitchen to the dining room and next to the dishwasher, making after-dinner cleanup a breeze.

3 Zones for Cleanup, Food Prep, and Storage

Kitchens are only as good as they are functional. The best kitchens are subtly divided into three zones for different types of work, each with its own counters, cabinets, and equipment for a specific function. Arranging these zones incorrectly is probably the most critical mistake in kitchen design.

The cleanup zone has a counter or a pass-through for staging dirty dishes that have come back from the dinner table and a big sink for scraping and rinsing pots, pans, and plates before they go in the dishwasher. This area is also the place to store dishes, glasses, cups, and flatware, particularly if they can be stored between the dishwasher and the table. This zone contains recycling bins and a compost bucket, too.

The food-preparation zone should have a large cutting surface, a prep sink, and a stove. When designing kitchens for new homes, I typically locate this zone in a space that includes an island and a portion of the adjacent counter. This zone also contains storage space for all cutting, mixing, and cooking tools, along with counter space for arranging food on plates before bringing them to the table.

The food-storage zone houses a pantry for dry storage and a refrigerator for cold storage. To be most efficient, the pantry and the refrigerator should be 6 ft. to 7 ft. tall. Group them together so you can gather ingredients without affecting any of the other zones.

EASY ACCESS. Lots of accessible storage is key to a good food prep area.

STORAGE. A refrigerator and pantry provide all the food-storage space this kitchen needs.

4 High-Quality Equipment and Finishes

When creating a great kitchen, the most fundamental economy is to buy equipment and finishes that endure. They should last 20 years minimum, longer if possible. For this reason, I prefer commercial or commercial-style equipment for sinks, faucets, refrigeration, dishwashers, fans, and ranges. I like solid wood for cabinets; oil-based enamel for painted surfaces; and the patina of a clear, oil-based polyurethane varnish on woodwork when a clear finish is called for. I recommend faucets that are guaranteed for the life of the house, simple cabinet-door hinges that look good whether the door is open or closed, and doorknobs and drawer pulls that grow more beautiful with the patina of age.

LONG-LASTING. This commercial-style range and tile countertop and backsplash will stand the test of time.

5 The Farmhouse-Kitchen Table and the Modern Island

No great kitchen is complete without a place for visiting. For centuries, the kitchen table was where you could sit down for a conversation over a cup of coffee or just to rest a moment. Children could do their homework there, too. At seasonal benchmarks such as harvest time, the table became an extended workplace for canning, baking, or putting up preserves. Modern kitchens, for the most part, have lost that table; it has been replaced by the kitchen island. If designed properly, however, an island can serve many of the same functions.

THE NEW KITCHEN TABLE. This large island can serve many of the same functions as the traditional farmhouse-kitchen table.

6 A Mix of Countertops

A great kitchen has counters made of different materials, at a variety of heights and depths. For any counter to be considered an effective work area, it should be at least 48 in. long.

A 33-in.-tall counter is useful for kneading dough. This countertop should be a cold stone such as granite, soapstone, or a quartz composite. Another counter is for cutting and chopping at a comfortable height, usually 36 in. This countertop is typically maple block treated with food-grade oil or wax. The counter near the stove should be a heat-resistant surface such as stone or stainless steel. If you can spare the space, make this counter a little deeper than usual, say 30 in., to fit bottles of olive oil, vinegar, and spices. The countertop near the cleanup sink can be a softer dish-friendly surface such as linoleum, plastic laminate, or even maple.

7 The Garden Connection

A view of the garden is so important that if you don't have one, I urge you to plant a garden next to the kitchen; even a window box or a few potted plants are better than nothing. This outdoor connection expands the kitchen visually. French doors opening onto a sunny, wind-protected garden, complete with table and chairs, can extend kitchen function outdoors. The yard even can include another place to cook.

The door to the garden should be placed along the edge of the room, or between the kitchen and its adjacent eating space, not in the middle of the kitchen.

BRING THE OUTDOORS IN. A bank of windows and large sliding doors (to the left) give the cook a view of the garden and make for convenient outdoor dining.

NO LOST CONDIMENTS. A pull out drawer on full-extension slides means your ketchup won't languish in the back of a cabinet.

A CLEAR VIEW. Cabinets with glass doors and glass sides make this kitchen feel open and filled with light.

8 Glass Doors and Lots of Drawers

More and more, the kitchens I design don't have upper cabinets. The storage load that they typically handle is taken up by drawers instead. Drawers are far more convenient than cabinets with doors anyway, as long as the drawers, which should be on full-extension slides, are a variety of widths and depths to store different items: dishes, pots, pans, and silverware; recycling bins; table linens; mixers, blenders, and toasters; and condiments and spices. Narrow drawers can be side-loaded rather than top-loaded (see top left photo above).

A great kitchen does have at least one upper cabinet for glasses, teacups, and coffee mugs. It should feature glass doors; if the cabinet is on an outside corner, it also should have glass sides (see top right photo above). Glass doors not only show off attractive glasses and mugs but are also a lighter alternative to solid upper cabinets, which can bring in the walls of a kitchen, making it feel smaller and more cramped.

9 Seating Areas

A kitchen table or a bar at the island is one kind of sit-down spot that every kitchen needs. The other kind is the soft, sit-way-back places that can be provided only by an easy chair, a sofa, or a window seat. I'm especially fond of the latter, which should be placed next to big windows with low sills overlooking the garden. The key is to place the window seat between work zones, not in the middle of one of them.

A breakfast nook that is almost in the kitchen is also beneficial. Visually and acoustically entwined with the kitchen, the nook is nevertheless off to the side with built-in benches that take up a minimum of space.

10 Lighting and Personality

A great kitchen fits the character of the house. It has some regional characteristics in its detailing and use of materials, and it doesn't look like it's from a foreign country or another galaxy. The colors and the lighting should be on the warm side. Uniform lighting isn't necessary, however; some areas of a

A COZY NOOK. A built-in breakfast nook allows diners to be part of the action without being in the way.

kitchen are clearly meant to be brighter than others. I use incandescent lighting, xenon undercabinet lighting, and occasionally halogen accent lighting. When I use compact fluorescent bulbs, I make sure they are inside a warm-glass globe or shade. The light fixtures that are visible are a joy to see.

Finally, a great kitchen contains keepsakes: platters from a favorite potter, framed menus from special dinners, or labels from long-gone vintage wines. Put them on display, where they will infuse the space with your life.

Opening up a Small Kitchen

BY JERRI HOLAN

Remodeling a small kitchen without adding square footage can be frustrating: too many tasks to fit into a limited space. However, a small kitchen can function well and include interesting elements if you open the kitchen to larger spaces and keep the layout simple.

Make It Feel Spacious

The first step toward making a small kitchen feel larger and more open is to improve its relationship with any adjoining rooms and outside spaces.

A kitchen surrounded by four solid walls can feel downright claustrophobic. To improve the space, you can open the walls between the kitchen and any supporting rooms, such as a dining room, a breakfast nook, or a family room. By opening the wall and allowing the sightlines to expand beyond the kitchen, you create the perception of more space without the cost of creating more square footage.

Depending on the circumstances, the wall might be removed entirely or be replaced with a peninsula countertop, a high counter, or a half-wall. Even a simple pass-through window helps if other options are not feasible.

A popular solution when space is at a premium is a peninsula that serves both the kitchen and an adjacent space. This allows open sight lines between the two rooms and adds counter space and storage on both sides (see the top "After" plans on p. 22).

A separate high counter above a transitional counter requires more space but replaces a table in a highly efficient manner. If the high counter will be a breakfast bar for morning coffee, it should be 12 in. to 15 in. wide. Bump the width to between 18 in. and 24 in. if it will be the place for all your informal meals. (A counter-height peninsula can be used as a primary eating area by adding 6 in. to 12 in. to the typical 24-in. counter depth.)

Regardless of depth, make sure it's long enough for the number of people using it. Each person should have at least 24 in. of space, although 30 in. will be more comfortable.

Pay Attention to the Transition

Once the kitchen is opened up, you can detail the opening depending on how you wish to treat the transition from the kitchen to the adjoining space. If you remove a wall to connect the kitchen with another room, part of the enlarged space can be dedicated to food preparation and part to eating, socializing, reading, or watching TV (depending on whether the kitchen now adjoins a dining area, a living area, or a family room). A design element at the ceiling—an arch, a beam, a series of lights, a change in ceiling height—can define the two areas as effectively as a peninsula. An overhead element such as an arch above a transition counter helps ink the two spaces by repeating elements in one or both of the rooms.

Sometimes drawing a distinction between the two spaces with a half-wall makes sense. Extending 8 in. to 12 in. higher than the countertop, a half-wall screens the kitchen counter without taking up as much floor space as an eating counter (see "Remove Walls to Improve Sight Lines," above). To display vases of flowers, the half-wall's cap should be between 8 in. and 12 in. wide; to hold serving plates, plan on 10 in. to 12 in. Remember that the cap is a transitional element, so the material, the shape, and the style should relate to both spaces.

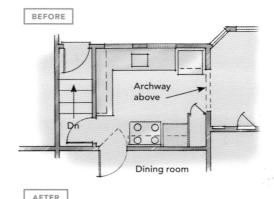

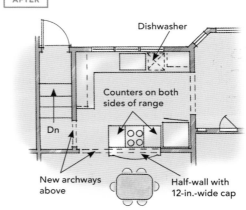

REMOVE WALLS TO IMPROVE SIGHT LINES

This small kitchen had too many doors, a dysfunctional range area, and a pantry that was too deep to be usable. Removing the wall between the kitchen and the dining room was the best way to enlarge the kitchen without adding space.

With an archway and a half-wall separating the kitchen from the dining area (see the drawing on the facing page), the two rooms are perceived as one large room, greatly improving the relationship between the spaces. The high counter serves as a staging area for formal dinners and as an informal place to hang out at other times, keeping diners out of the small kitchen while still encouraging them to converse with the cook.

An additional window over the sink and open archways instead of doors enhance the spacious feeling. Using a smaller range made room for counter space on each side of the stovetop and a safer, more comfortable cooking arrangement.

Add Natural Light

Take advantage of exterior walls by adding windows and doors. When you can see the landscaping, it becomes part of your kitchen. If a garden or yard borders the kitchen, add a French door or two to allow access and big views.

If a door isn't possible, add as many windows as you can. When exterior-wall space is limited and you have to choose between an extra upper cabinet

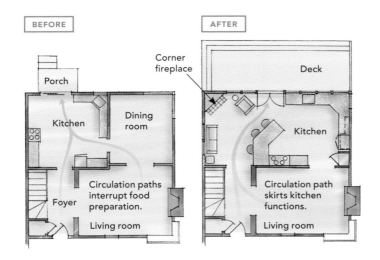

BEFORE

AFTER

Corner fireplace

Porch

Kitchen

Dining room

Deck

Kitchen

Foyer

Circulation paths interrupt food preparation.

Circulation path skirts kitchen functions.

Living room

Living room

DIRECT FOOT TRAFFIC AWAY FROM WORK AREAS

This small kitchen suffered from too many circulation routes, which disrupted its three main activity areas. Also, the dining room was rarely used.

The solution was to combine the two rooms into one spacious family room/kitchen that suits an informal lifestyle. The large new peninsula counter defines the main circulation route to the new deck, and it separates and marks the transition between family room and kitchen activities. Opening the rear wall with a gang of windows and French doors incorporates the backyard. A cozy corner fireplace enhances both kitchen and family-room functions.

and a window, choose the window. Corner windows are especially effective for opening views and outside relationships. Even if there's no view, a translucent or stained-glass window can brighten the space with natural light and lend an airy feeling to a tight room.

Simplify the Space

Maximize kitchen square footage by relocating functions not directly related to preparing and eating meals. The more regular or square a kitchen's floor plan, the more functional its space will be. For example, many older homes have laundry areas or closets between the kitchen and the backyard (see

"Before" below). Moving the laundry to a small closet adds space and reduces traffic through the kitchen while gaining an exterior wall for windows and doors.

Make sure circulation patterns through the kitchen aren't disruptive. This might mean eliminating some doorways and relocating others. If you must have multiple doorways in the kitchen, try to group them in one area to confine circulation to one or two routes. For example, relocate a back door next to the dining room door to consolidate foot traffic. Rooms that aren't related to the kitchen shouldn't connect to the kitchen.

TAKE ADVANTAGE OF EXTERIOR WALLS

This small kitchen had little natural light, an awkward circulation path to the deck, and a laundry room with great garden views. Not only did the kitchen lack counter space, the home also lacked a dining area.

By relocating the washer and dryer upstairs, a dining room could occupy the desirable space overlooking the backyard. Three new windows and a pair of French doors complete the outdoor connection. The guest room door was relocated, and continuous counters were installed for a functional, yet compact, kitchen.

The small peninsula's extra depth serves as a coffee counter in the morning and as a preparation/staging area for large dinners.

BEFORE

Deck

Laundry room

Guest room

Kitchen

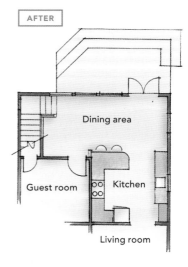

AFTER

Dining area

Guest room

Kitchen

Living room

Getting Appliances to Fit

BY DAVID GETTS

Over 10 years ago, I wrote an article for *Fine Homebuilding* on getting appliances to fit kitchen cabinetry. The basics of installation have remained the same since that time, but appliance options, configurations, and trends have changed. This has greatly affected kitchen design and the way cabinets should be constructed.

Getting appliances to fit properly ensures a space that functions well, looks good, and operates safely.

What you'll learn here is invaluable, but don't stop with this information. I've installed dozens of appliances through the years and still encounter new issues, even for appliances I've worked with before. Develop a good relationship with a local appliance distributor, especially if you are part of a kitchen design or installation team. A distributor will become one of your best sources for installation-specific information in the ever-evolving market of kitchen design.

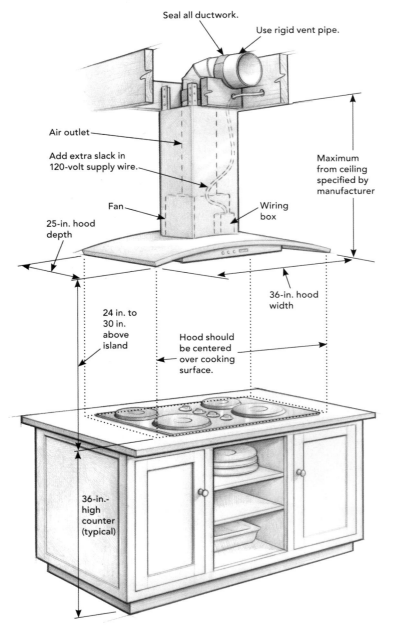

Seal all ductwork.

Use rigid vent pipe.

Air outlet

Add extra slack in 120-volt supply wire.

Maximum from ceiling specified by manufacturer

Fan

Wiring box

25-in. hood depth

24 in. to 30 in. above island

36-in. hood width

Hood should be centered over cooking surface.

36-in.-high counter (typical)

Island Ventilation Hoods

Island hoods hang independent of cabinetry and must be located directly over the cooktop for best performance. To line things up properly, you'll need to use a plumb bob or, preferably, a laser level.

The hood is suspended and fully supported from the ceiling, so solid blocking needs to be installed between the joists above the island for the steel support framework to be bolted to. The rigid vent pipe, which is commonly 8 in. dia. but is sized according to the manufacturer's specifications, fits inside the frame support.

Because the motor is located on the hood itself, simply run the nonmetallic sheathed cable—which will be hard-wired into a 120-volt dedicated circuit— down the same shaft. The finish material, usually a stainless-steel flue, is attached to cover up the frame.

AVOID THESE MISTAKES

POOR DUCT LAYOUT. It's easy enough to vent a hood straight through the roof, but that's not always an option. Wall exits require careful manipulation through joist bays that may or may not be filled with electrical and plumbing utilities. Take the time to consider duct routing well before installation time.

NOT ENOUGH WIRE. Make sure the electrician leaves enough wire in the ceiling to reach the appliance. Take care not to pinch the wire when attaching the framework.

UNHEALTHFUL VENTILATION. Seal and insulate all the ductwork in unconditioned spaces to reduce condensation and the potential for mold growth.

USING FLEXIBLE PIPE. Always specify rigid-metal vent pipe, which is more durable and performs better.

Dishwasher Drawers

In my opinion, the dishwasher drawer is one of the best improvements made among all kitchen appliances. Pulling out an elevated drawer to load dishes is a lot more convenient than bending down to load a standard washer.

Dish drawers can be stacked on top of each other—to occupy a similarly sized space as a standard washer—or purchased as separate units and placed on each side of the sink. Separate, single drawers require a cabinet box to sit on and demand two separate plumbing supply and waste lines. A single 120-volt duplex outlet supports two separate dish drawers. Just make sure it is centrally located. Like standard dishwashers, a dish drawer is secured to the counter above or to the cabinetry on each side.

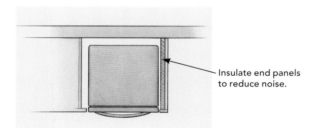

Insulate end panels to reduce noise.

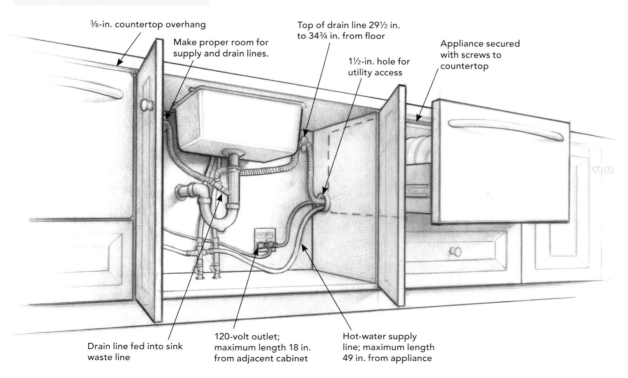

⅜-in. countertop overhang

Make proper room for supply and drain lines.

Top of drain line 29½ in. to 34¾ in. from floor

1½-in. hole for utility access

Appliance secured with screws to countertop

Drain line fed into sink waste line

120-volt outlet; maximum length 18 in. from adjacent cabinet

Hot-water supply line; maximum length 49 in. from appliance

INACCESSIBLE KITCHEN. A built-in refrigerator is the largest and heaviest appliance. Many of these units barely make it into the house. Before purchase and installation, make sure the fridge will fit into the intended space.

AN APPLIANCE THAT WOBBLES OR HAS AN UNEVEN REVEAL AROUND THE CABINETRY. Built-in refrigerators usually have a good leveling system accessible from the front of the appliance, but for floors that are really bad, you may not have enough adjustment. Check the floor before installing so that you can be prepared to shim the appliance if needed.

IMPROPER UTILITY PLACEMENT. You don't want to slide the big beast into place and have it cover up the water-supply line for the icemaker.

DAMAGING ADJACENT SURFACES UPON INSTALLATION. Cover the floors with something flat and rigid like hardboard. Refrigerators will easily shred a floor finish when pushed into place.

Built-In Refrigerators

Although expensive, a built-in refrigerator has many options that make it worth its hefty price tag. Some are designed to fit into a standard 24-in.-deep cabinet. Flush inset units require a deeper cabinet but don't project out farther than any other piece of cabinetry; for the largest appliance in the kitchen, this is significant. These units are now designed to be fully integrated with overlay wood panels that match the rest of the cabinetry.

Once considered the eyesore of the kitchen, the refrigerator can now disappear. With a top-mount compressor, you'll still see the vent grille, but if you choose a refrigerator with a bottom-mount compressor, even the venting unit can be disguised.

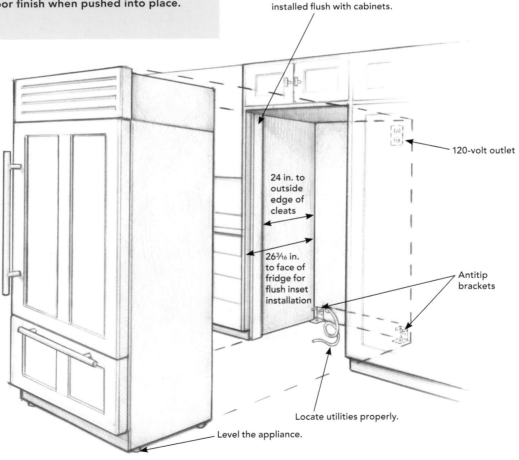

This 3-in. by ¼-in. cleat serves as a stop and creates a shadow line around units installed flush with cabinets.

120-volt outlet

24 in. to outside edge of cleats

26³⁄₁₆ in. to face of fridge for flush inset installation

Antitip brackets

Locate utilities properly.

Level the appliance.

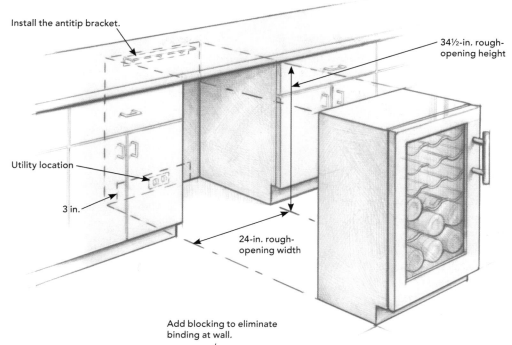

Install the antitip bracket.

34½-in. rough-opening height

Utility location

3 in.

24-in. rough-opening width

Add blocking to eliminate binding at wall.

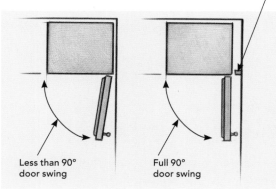

Less than 90°
door swing

Full 90°
door swing

Under-Counter Refrigerators, Wine Coolers, and Ice Makers

Many people are including smaller appliances, such as small refrigerators and ice makers designed to fit under a countertop, in their main kitchen or outdoor kitchen designs because they take up little space. There are few differences between these appliances from an installation standpoint. They are all roughly the same size and have similar electrical demands. Even though they are small, they still need to be secured to the adjacent cabinets and/or countertop above with screws and a bracket.

AVOID THESE MISTAKES

NOT FOLLOWING MANUFACTURER CABINET SPECS PRECISELY. Nothing looks worse than one of these small units shoved into a cabinet opening that's too big. Build the cabinet with tight tolerances in mind.

IMPROPER PLUMBING AND ELECTRICAL ROUGH-IN. Locate the electrical and plumbing in the exact spots recommended by the manufacturer. If you don't, you may have issues getting the appliance to fit in the opening. This can be a real problem in islands where the opening may not be as deep.

PREPPING FOR THE WRONG ELECTRICAL DEMAND. The appliance will come with a pigtail ready to be plugged into an outlet. Be sure you have an outlet installed during rough-in, not a loose wire for a hard-wire application.

INADEQUATE SPACING. Installing the fridge too close to a wall can result in door binding and wall damage. Space the appliance out from the wall with blocking, and cover with matching trim.

UNSTABLE APPLIANCE. Don't forget to install the antitip bracket that comes with the unit.

Warming Drawers

Just like dishwasher drawers, warming drawers use the popular drawer feature for their ease of access. They're most commonly placed under a countertop near the oven, but these appliances can be placed at any location where there is enough room to pull out a drawer.

Warming drawers come with a wide variety of options, but their main purpose is keeping food or dishes warm, not cooking. Therefore, they require a dedicated circuit with only a 120-volt outlet (the appliance generally comes with an attached pigtail). Mount the outlet in an adjacent cabinet to the appliance as specified by the manufacturer. Different-size units are available, so verify that the model fits into the recommended opening.

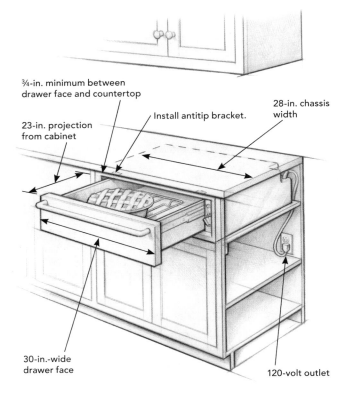

¾-in. minimum between drawer face and countertop

23-in. projection from cabinet

Install antitip bracket.

28-in. chassis width

30-in.-wide drawer face

120-volt outlet

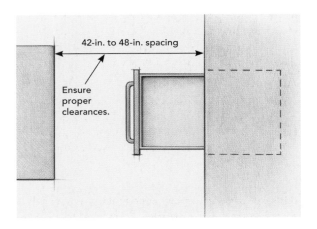

42-in. to 48-in. spacing

Ensure proper clearances.

AVOID THESE MISTAKES

AN APPLIANCE THAT WON'T FIT BECAUSE OF IMPROPER ROUGH-IN WORK. An outlet located in the wrong place at rough-in can keep the appliance from sitting properly. Double-check the layout to ensure that all electrical outlets and wires end up in the right location.

INCORRECT CLEARANCES. Make sure adjacent cabinets don't interfere with the safe operation of the warming drawer as it is opened and closed.

AN APPLIANCE THAT'S UNSTABLE WHEN THE DRAWER IS FULLY EXTENDED. Install the antitip bracket to keep the unit stable under heavy loads.

TEN TIPS FOR THE SEAMLESS INSTALLATION OF ANY APPLIANCE

1. READ THE INSTRUCTIONS—REALLY.
Unless you install appliances for a living, it's good to review the instructions, even if you've installed the appliance before. Specifications can change.

2. OBTAIN THE APPLIANCE SPECIFICATIONS BEFORE CABINET FABRICATION OR LAYOUT.
To avoid problems down the road, I require this of all my clients. There's nothing worse than preparing an opening for a particular unit and then finding out later that the client bought something else that won't fit.

3. ALWAYS GET HELP.
Appliances are heavy and expensive, which means it's easy to damage them and the surrounding areas. Having an extra set of hands to maneuver appliances around tight spaces is critical.

4. ADEQUATELY PROTECT SURROUNDING SURFACES AND THE APPLIANCE ITSELF.
Always protect the floor and any surface that's close to the appliance when setting it in place. If there is a protective coating on the appliance, don't remove it until the unit is installed.

5. CAREFULLY PREP UTILITIES FOR RETROFITS.
When retrofitting an existing kitchen for a new appliance, carefully survey the space before drilling holes, modifying the opening, or cutting cabinetry. It's a lot easier to make a mistake than to fix one.

6. IN A RETROFIT SITUATION, YOU MAY NEED TO MODIFY MATERIAL YOU'RE NOT FAMILIAR WITH.
If it's out of your comfort zone and expertise, call a professional. For example, attempting to enlarge the cooktop opening on an existing slab stone counter can have disastrous effects. One errant tap can crack the counter.

7. ALWAYS CHECK FOR INADEQUATE CABINET CLEARANCES AND INTERFERENCE WITH OTHER APPLIANCES.
Clearance and interference issues are typically a direct result of improper planning. Check for these before beginning the work to avoid any rework to make it right.

8. ROUGH-IN GAS, ELECTRICAL, OR VENT PIPES IN THE RIGHT SPOT.
You don't want to install an appliance toward the end of a job only to discover that the rough-in is incorrect or that there isn't sufficient clearance to run ventilation through the ceiling. Don't lock yourself in to a rough-in location if you're unsure about the layout.

9. CREATE ADEQUATE SPACE WITHIN APPLIANCE CABINETS.
The utilities that appliances need to operate require space inside the cabinet. Sometimes an adjacent cabinet won't house the utilities, and you'll need to use the back wall. Make sure there is sufficient depth in the cabinet before installing the appliance.

10. PREPARE THE JOB SITE FOR APPLIANCE DELIVERY.
This seems obvious, but some of these appliances are so large and heavy that you really need to have a strategic plan. Whatever you can do to get the appliance into the space safely will make the entire process flow more smoothly, even if it means removing doors and door stops.

Kitchen Remodeling for Any Budget

BY PAUL DEGROOT

Most kitchen remodels that I design turn out to be major affairs. The homeowners have lived with cramped, outdated kitchens for so long that cosmetic updates just aren't enough. Your kitchen may be at a better starting point. If you have enough storage and counter space, a functional cleanup area, and sensible traffic flow, gutting your kitchen may not be necessary. By focusing on key upgrades, an old kitchen can come to back life with a smaller investment.

Either way, kitchens are the most expensive room to remodel, so it's easy for even a modest wish list to outpace funds. Because it's my job to help homeowners make remodeling decisions, I've put a lot of thought into when you should splurge, how you can save, and what you should never do.

Cabinets Are the Heart of a Kitchen

Unlike the standard dimensions of stock cabinets, custom cabinets make the most of every inch of a kitchen. Made of cherry, mahogany, oak, maple, or Douglas fir, custom cabinets are typically built with furniture-grade details by a local cabinetmaker. When splurging on stain-grade (clear-finished wood) cabinets, make sure the cabinetmaker uses clear lumber culled of knots, mineral streaks, and sap-wood, and insist on color and grain direction that are consistent throughout. In this price range ($500+ per linear foot in 2009 prices), you should expect durable, solid-wood drawer boxes with dovetail joints, solid-wood door and drawer fronts, full-extension undermount slides, and top-quality hinges.

You can save by ordering painted, semicustom cabinets from a national manufacturer. These cabinets are more affordable ($300 to $400 per linear foot) because the wood doesn't have to meet the higher standards of appearance that stain-grade cabinets do. Drawers are more expensive than doors with shelves behind them, so ask for fewer drawers if your budget is tight. And skip the dovetail joints for drawer boxes. An interlocking pinned or doweled joint can last for decades. If you can't afford undermount drawer slides, choose side-mounted ball-bearing drawer slides. You'll appreciate their fair cost and smooth operation.

Don't buy the cheapest cabinets you can find to save money. Cabinets are the heart of a kitchen, and entry-level cabinets are likely to have components made from particleboard, which can lead to sagging shelves and hinge screws that pull out. They're also apt to have poorly made door hinges, drawer boxes, and drawer slides that cannot be expected to hold up to years of use. If your budget's tight, you will be better off saving in other areas.

BIG SAVINGS AFFORD BIGGER APPLIANCES

BUDGET: $30,000

The homeowners splurged to create a better floor plan with a walk-in pantry. Part of a bigger remodel, the kitchen budget was limited, so the homeowners chose to save money on finishes and countertops, knowing these items can be upgraded easily later. They also saved on fixtures and plumbing with an inexpensive drop-in sink in the same location as the old sink. Splurges beyond construction were mostly for professional-style appliances.

SAVINGS

- Painted cabinets: $300 per linear foot
- Plastic-laminate countertops: $10 per square foot
- Ceramic subway-tile backsplash: $10 per square foot
- Mexican Saltillo floor tile: $5 per square foot

SPLURGES

- Stainless-steel vent hood: $1,500
- Pro-style dual-fuel stainless-steel range: $5,000
- Sub-Zero® refrigerator/freezer, complete with wood panels to match the cabinets: $6,000

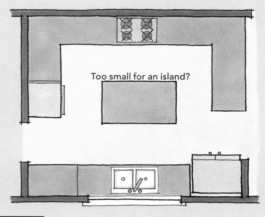

Too small for an island?

BEFORE

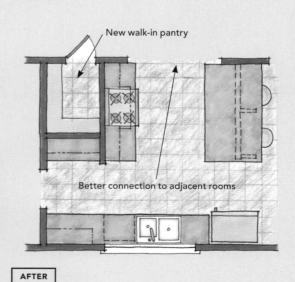

New walk-in pantry

Better connection to adjacent rooms

AFTER

STRETCHING THE BUDGET (4 FT.)

BUDGET: $50,000

These homeowners earned a tax deduction by donating their old kitchen to Habitat for Humanity. Because they wanted to add on to the house anyway, they decided to splurge on stretching the kitchen 4 ft. Stainless-steel appliances were another splurge, but a combination microwave/convection oven speed cooker served up some savings. Keeping the sink location and matching (instead of replacing) the existing sink window also saved the budget.

SAVINGS
- Matched instead of replaced existing kitchen window
- Painted drywall above 4-in.-high granite backsplashes: $20 per linear foot

SPLURGES
- Deep-bowl undermount stainless-steel sink: $900
- Granite countertops: $65 per square foot
- Oak flooring to match original floors in house: $12 per square foot

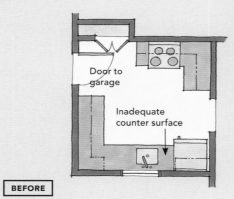

Door to garage

Inadequate counter surface

BEFORE

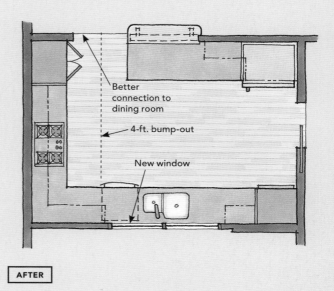

Better connection to dining room

4-ft. bump-out

New window

AFTER

Durability Rules the Countertop

Although they can cost well over $65 per square foot, natural stone, quartz composites, and recycled glass are the most sought-after countertop materials today because they are durable, are available in large slabs, and are pretty enough to be a kitchen's centerpiece. If you have to have stone counters but don't have thousands to spend, look for slabs used by high-volume builders in your area. These slabs are less expensive due to limited color choices, but they are widely available. Choosing simple edge profiles can save money, too. If you're looking to upgrade your counters, contact a company that resurfaces existing counters, such as Granite Transformations (www.granitetransformations.com).

For an artistic effect, you can splurge on concrete countertops. Their shape, color, and finish are limited

SAVINGS IN SWEAT EQUITY

BUDGET: $70,000

For my own kitchen remodel, I saved considerably by doing a good bit of the work myself, starting with the demolition. But even this thrifty weekend warrior was wise enough to realize that he couldn't do it all alone. With a contractor's help (and a bit of splurging), I bumped out the space 3 ft. into the backyard and raised the ceiling height in a dramatic way.

SAVINGS

- Efficient fluorescent cove, can, and undercabinet lighting for long-term savings
- Stainless-steel backsplash installation, cabinet finishing, backsplash sealing, painting, trim carpentry, and many other tasks performed by homeowner, for an estimated sweat-equity savings of: $4,000

SPLURGES

- Clerestory: $3,500 for construction and materials
- Cable lights and mini-pendants for bright task lighting: $1,200
- Two separate built-in wall ovens: $2,800
- Custom quartersawn-maple veneered cabinets: $400 per linear foot
- Prefinished, engineered pecan flooring: $15 per square foot

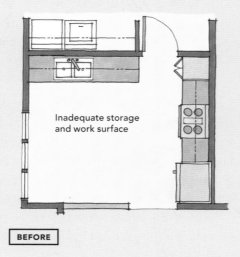

Inadequate storage and work surface

BEFORE

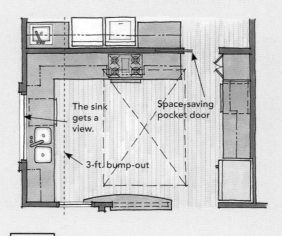

The sink gets a view.

Space-saving pocket door

3-ft. bump-out

AFTER

only by your imagination. Stainless-steel tops can add a modern look to your kitchen, and maple butcher block is a beautiful way to contrast painted cabinetry.

Available for under $60 per square foot, solid-surface countertops from manufacturers like Corian® and Avonite are a more affordable option. These counters are nonporous, heat tolerant, and scratch resistant, with consistent color all the way through. Even more reasonably priced are tile and plastic laminate. Tile is available in a range of sizes, colors, patterns, and finishes, but my recommendation is to stick with dense ceramic or porcelain, which are impervious to moisture. Plastic laminate is nonabsorptive and heat and stain resistant but can be scratched. Because countertops are an easy upgrade and because plastic laminate is so inexpensive, it is a great entry point if you need to save now but will have more to spend later.

In general, you should avoid wood countertops around sinks unless you're meticulous about wiping up splashes. Messy folks should shy away from marble, travertine, and limestone slabs. They can be stained easily by wine, lemon juice, and the like. Think twice about tiles with tumbled or otherwise uneven edges that require wide grout joints. And don't use cheap glazed wall tile on a countertop. Heavy metal pots and pans can scratch it.

Stretch Your Backsplash Bucks

Backsplashes can cost a lot or next to nothing (the price of a quart of paint). Splurge on durable, easy-to-clean, and decorative materials, including stainless steel, stone, tile, and glass mosaics. Remember, grout should be kept to a minimum and must be well sealed. You can avoid grout joints altogether by choosing the same stone slab used for the counters.

Save backsplash bucks by choosing larger mass-produced tiles. If tile is not the look you're after, a simple 4-in.- or 6-in.-high backsplash made from the countertop material is cost effective and practical, especially if it's laminate. Or simply paint the wall with a durable finish. Avoid rough or porous backsplashes that will be difficult to clean where you most anticipate splatters. Wood backsplashes even-

tually show moisture damage. Keep in mind that shiny materials below upper cabinets show reflections of undercabinet lights. I prefer honed, matte, or satin finishes.

Flooring Choices Are Hard (or Soft)

When it comes to flooring, you can spend a lot of your budget on a kitchen floor by laying down oak, maple, cherry, pecan, Douglas fir, or reclaimed longleaf pine. Traditional wood flooring is ¾ in. thick and is sanded, stained, and finished after installation. Durability varies among species, but a professional floor finisher should be able to make even the softest wood species look good for a long time.

MY TOP 10 KITCHEN-REMODELING DON'TS

1. Don't choose tile for countertops unless you are willing to scrub grout joints often.

2. Don't settle for cheap drawer slides. They're noisy and flimsy.

3. Don't install a light-gauge stainless-steel sink. It will flex, dent, and scratch easily.

4. Don't buy cheap cabinets to save a penny. They won't last.

5. Don't skimp on lighting. A dim kitchen is dreary and can be unsafe.

6. Don't install wood floors in an active family kitchen unless you won't mind refinishing them occasionally.

7. Don't be stingy with counter space next to the sink, cooktop, or refrigerator.

8. Don't buy a cheap dishwasher. Most likely, it will clean poorly and loudly.

9. Don't use halogen undercabinet lights. They're too hot.

10. Don't install hard-to-clean backsplash materials such as porous stone, brick, or stucco.

Premium-grade engineered wood is a more immediate alternative; you can walk on it as soon as it is installed. And forget the rumors that you can't sand and refinish these floors. They can be lightly sanded (called screening) and refinished when they begin to show wear. For flooring without water worries, consider porcelain tile. If porcelain is too austere, try tiles cut from slate, limestone, granite, or marble.

Save without sacrificing character or durability by using stained and sealed concrete. Where concrete slabs are common, this can be an economical route because the slab is simply given an attractive finish. A multitude of affordable ceramic floor tiles are available as well.

If you want to save on flooring but prefer a softer surface, consider cork, linoleum, or vinyl. An added benefit is that not everything you drop will break. Floating laminate and inexpensive engineered floors such as bamboo rest on a thin foam underlayment, so you can keep standing in the kitchen longer.

Before buying a wood floor, know that a water leak in the kitchen can cause the boards to swell and buckle. If you are prone to dropping things, check to see how easily the wood dents. (Try this test with a sample board: Drop a can of tuna or tomato paste from 3 ft. up, and see what happens.) If you have dogs, their nails can scratch the finish. (Try scratching the sample with the tip of a ballpoint pen.) In high-traffic kitchens, avoid using light grout colors on a tile floor, and avoid highly polished floors that are slippery when wet.

Put Some Coin into Convenience

Well-designed fixtures can make cleanup less of a chore, they can add style to a kitchen, and they should last as long as any other material. I don't advise buying the least expensive faucets and sinks you can find, but you won't have to spend a lot to get a lot, either.

Splurging on a faucet means paying for improved functionality, stylish design, and top-quality materials and finishes. Acknowledging the trend for pro-style fixtures, manufacturers offer tall faucets with pull-down sprayers that share the solid brass or stainless-steel body materials that make up the core of all premium faucets.

FEWER CABINETS, BETTER VIEWS

BUDGET: $75,000
This family had too many cabinets in their kitchen and no views of the backyard pool. The remedy? Swap out wall cabinets for windows. With plenty of space on the interior walls for cabinets, the loss of upper cabinets on the exterior walls was not a deal-breaker. Along with reusing their existing appliances, it was one of the ways this family saved.

SAVINGS
- Drop-in sink, kept in the original sink location: $500
- Ceramic subway-tile backsplash: $10 per square foot
- Painted cabinets: $300 per linear foot
- Porcelain floor tile in a simple pattern, without borders: $7 per square foot

SPLURGES
- Electric hot-water dispenser at the sink: $400
- Low-voltage mini-pendant lights flanking the range: $800
- Quartz-composite engineered slab countertops: $60 per square foot

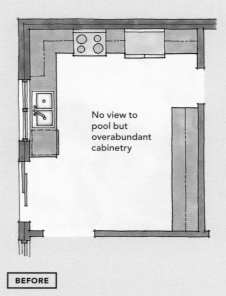

No view to pool but overabundant cabinetry

BEFORE

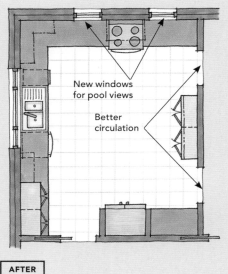

New windows
for pool views

Better
circulation

AFTER

You can save money by opting for a faucet with tubular-brass construction. Basic finishes and standard designs cost less too, as do fixtures bought online (www.kitchensource.com, www.sinksgallery.com, www.faucet.com, www.faucetdirect.com) or at a home center. Don't buy a faucet online without seeing it in person first, though. Visit showrooms and home centers to do your homework.

High-end sinks are made from several sturdy materials and come in many sizes and configurations other than the common one- and two-basin models. Add convenience to cleanup with an oversize single-basin sink, or a three-bowl model with different basin depths for different functions. An integral drain board keeps counters drier. If you want to make a statement with your sink, order one carved from granite or soapstone ($1,000+), or integrate a custom-designed concrete sink into the countertop. If you're sticking with stainless steel, you'll appreciate the stiffness and quiet of 16-gauge metal.

Save on sink installation by choosing a drop-in sink. You can find plenty of attractive, durable drop-in sinks that don't cost a bundle (under $250), from 18-gauge stainless steel to solid surface. And don't overlook the venerable workhorses made from vitreous china (aka fireclay) and enameled cast iron.

Avoid thin stainless-steel sinks (22 gauge is very thin) because they are noisy and dent easily. Be aware that a heavy pot can chip enameled and vitreous-china sinks. If your back is sensitive, make sure you're comfortable washing dishes in a deep sink before purchasing one. Finally, make sure the size, shape, and configuration of an undermount sink are completely to your liking before the installers cut a big hole in your countertop.

Appliances Cost Money and Space

If you have a big kitchen and you cook a lot, it might make sense to splurge on appliances. But when you choose new appliances, keep in mind that this is a good place to save both money and space. In fact, many of my clients save by sticking with their existing kitchen appliances.

If you decide to splurge, consider restaurant-style models that boast high-Btu cooking power, extra burners, and extra oven capacity. Keep in mind that these models consume a lot of space with gas cooktops and convection ovens as wide as 48 in. and 30 in., respectively. High-Btu cooking also requires the installation of a powerful hood fan.

Save space and money with a slide-in range. Use a "microhood," which is a vent hood and microwave oven in one (make sure it vents outside the house). Another combo is a speed cooker that can function as a baking oven and a microwave. Appliances with white or black enamel finishes cost considerably less than stainless steel.

You can save over time by choosing energy-efficient dishwashers, refrigerators, and freezers certified by Energy Star®. And remember, smaller ovens heat up faster, which also saves energy.

NEW BLACK APPLIANCES MATCH THE OLD DISHWASHER

BUDGET: $80,000
Splurging on a breakfast-nook bump-out and raising the ceiling by 1 ft. added much-needed space to this remodel, which required stripping the kitchen down to the studs and starting over. With more floor space, the remodeled kitchen has room for a center island that doubles as a prep and serving station.

SAVINGS
- Efficient fluorescent cove, can, and undercabinet lighting for long-term savings
- Countertop microwave oven in a cabinet cubby rather than an expensive built-in model: $100
- Black appliances and reuse of the existing black dishwasher
- Porcelain floor tile that looks like stone: $8 per square foot

SPLURGES
- Custom white-oak cabinets: $400 per linear foot
- Stainless-steel vent hood: $1,200
- French-limestone backsplash tile with matte finish: $15 per square foot
- Polished-granite countertops: $70 per square foot

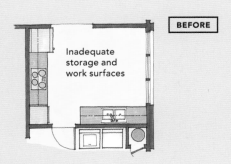

Inadequate storage and work surfaces

BEFORE

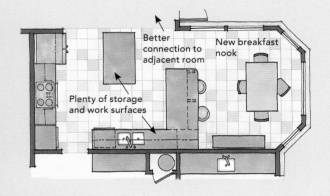

Better connection to adjacent room

New breakfast nook

Plenty of storage and work surfaces

AFTER

GETTING IT ALL INTO A GALLEY

BUDGET: $55,000

Only the window above the sink is original to this kitchen. Even the pantry closet, with its 2×4 walls, was removed and rebuilt as a pantry cabinet, gaining a few inches of precious storage space. Likewise, a brick wall next to the old 24-in.-wide wall ovens was removed to allow room for 27-in.-wide ovens. These homeowners splurged considerably, but made sure to stay within the existing footprint to tame already-high construction costs.

SAVINGS
- Refinished rather than replaced oak flooring: $800
- Worked within the existing footprint to minimize construction costs

SPLURGES
- Terrazzo countertops with recycled-glass chips: $100 per square foot
- Deep-bowl, undermount, heavy-gauge stainless-steel sink: $1,200
- Custom, quartersawn-maple cabinets: $425 per linear foot
- Pot filler next to the cooktop: $600
- Glass-tile backsplash: $25 per square foot

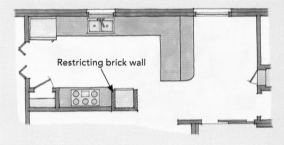

Restricting brick wall

BEFORE

More convenient pantry

AFTER

Avoid bargain-priced dishwashers. They are likely to be noisy and probably won't clean well. Also be aware that most counter-depth refrigerators cost more but have less storage volume than full-depth models. Resist the temptation of hip stainless-steel finishes if there are little sticky fingers about.

Don't Underlight Your Kitchen

The goal of lighting a kitchen is to integrate layers of adjustable light so you can see well enough to dice an onion or dial in the right mood for a party (see "Kitchen Lighting Design," on p. 187). Decent kitchen lighting can be achieved with nothing more than well-placed recessed lights and dimmers. Including trim and baffle, these lights range from less than $25 to $125 per fixture.

Two areas where can lights fall short, however, are countertop illumination and style. So consider splurging on undercabinet lighting ($45+ for 24-in. fixtures), and choose at least one decorative fixture to add style. You can also save by choosing energy-efficient fixtures and bulbs.

The most important mistake to avoid is underlighting the kitchen. A poorly lit kitchen is impractical and potentially dangerous. If you use recessed cans, skip the budget-grade white plastic trim and baffles; they will yellow over time. Know that halogen undercabinet lights can heat up the cabinet above. Opt for cooler LED, fluorescent, or xenon instead.

A Note on Prices*

Are you wondering why this article says that custom, stain-grade cabinets cost $500+ per linear foot while two of the case studies show these cabinets for about $100 less? Because they're frameless versions with slab doors and drawer fronts of veneered medium-density fiberboard (MDF). Nailing down prices is hard. In every instance, a range of variables from construction style to geographic region affects price considerably. With that in mind, a few comments: Cabinet prices include uppers and lowers; most materials, excluding fixtures, appliances, and lighting, reflect installed costs; and the case studies show rounded numbers. Finally, it's important to realize that spending $20 per square foot on a backsplash might be a splurge for one homeowner and a savings for another.

＊Please note that prices were current in 2009.

A Kitchen for Cooks and Kids

BY MICHAEL PEKOVICH

We used to have a love/hate relationship with our kitchen. Our house was built in 1937, and a mid-1970s remodel added 75 sq. ft., a bank of windows, and a skylight adjacent to the kitchen. This effort created a large, light-filled space, which sold us on the house, but like many poorly planned renovations, the added space lacked purpose and efficiency. It had a small work area along one wall, with some sagging bookshelves inset between the studs over a radiator.

We filled the open space with a table and some chairs, adding an obstacle to traffic flow into and out of the house. In a display of useless redundancy, our seldom-used dining room a few feet away held another table and a set of chairs (see the floor plan on p. 43).

When our second child arrived, we felt our house begin to shrink. We had to find a way to open the rooms to one another and create a sense of spaciousness. And we needed to make better use of the spaces we already had, especially the sunny, underused corner by the kitchen.

HAVING IT ALL. This remodeled kitchen with a 1930s look finds room for sit-down meals, cooking lessons, and homework sessions, all at the same time.

THE KITCHEN/DINING CONNECTION.
Opening up the wall between the kitchen and the dining room extended the views from one to the other. The countertop between the two rooms serves as a buffet for dinner parties. Like the views, the cabinet drawers open into both the kitchen and the dining room. Photo taken at B on floor plan. Photo on p. 41 taken at A.

FROM JUST OK TO INTERNET CAFÉ. A computer workstation tucked into the corner and a bar-height dining counter turned inefficient spaces into hardworking places. Photo taken at C on floor plan.

Long Sight Lines Add Space without Adding More Room

Our first move was to open the kitchen to the dining room (see the left photo above), creating a view that extends across the house. The once-lonely and underused dining table is now visually connected to the kitchen and serves frequently as a homework, craft, or sewing table where someone can have a little more space to work yet still partake in kitchen banter.

A new peninsula extends partway across the opening to the dining room. Its cherry counter acts as a built-in sideboard for the dining area. The cabinet below houses table linens, place settings, napkins, and other paraphernalia, along with all of the kids' art supplies.

The peninsula countertop wraps around the opening into the kitchen and steps down to create a desk above the radiator. The family computer is stationed here, serving as a homework and gaming center for the kids and as handy Internet access for anyone in need of a recipe. I took out the sagging shelves, which spanned more than 5 ft., and replaced them with a combination of open shelves for cookbooks and a cabinet for enclosed storage.

Our little kitchen table was now a bigger obstacle than ever. It had to go, but we still wanted a place to sit in the kitchen for breakfast, snacks, and week-night dinners. So we extended the kitchen counter beyond the cabinets, into the previously open territory, creating a dining area. This move also extended the work area of the kitchen to almost its entire length and made a rational pathway from the back door to the rest of the house (see the floor plan).

In addition to being a place for meals, the dining counter is a prime homework location where student and cook can keep each other company. The barstools are also a favorite gathering spot for guests when we entertain.

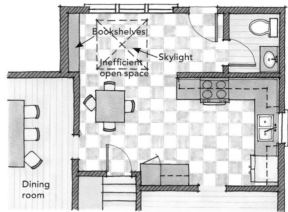

NEW EDITION OF AN OLD ADDITION

Before: Lost Opportunity, but Plenty of Daylight

A long, narrow 1970s-era addition to the back of the house included a powder room, a back door leading to the garage, and a big skylight over an open space. Unfortunately, though, the space lacked purpose.

COOL STONE COUNTER, WARM WOOD TABLE. Soapstone counters to the right of the stove are the primary food-prep surfaces. Because of its soft, talc-based composition, soapstone can be shaped with woodworking tools. The author sealed this counter with boiled linseed oil for a hard, lustrous finish that isn't oily to the touch. To the left of the stove, a cherry counter extends beyond the cabinets into a tabletop that's warm to the touch.

After: A Kitchen an Efficiency Expert Could Love

Enlarging the opening between the kitchen and the dining room created long sight lines along two axes and provided room for a sideboard with drawers accessible from both sides. To streamline traffic flow, kitchen seating changed from a table to a counter; a door added to the den passageway also cut down on through-kitchen traffic. And the new storage cabinet and computer station are much more useful than the original set of sagging shelves.

Photos taken at lettered positions.

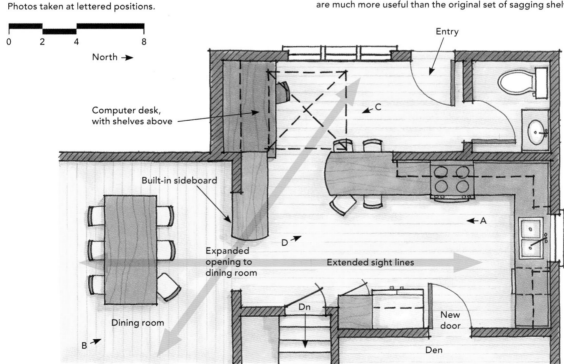

FEEDBACK FAUX OAK FLOORING

As much as I would have loved a hard-wood floor in the kitchen, it was beyond our means. Our main priority, then, was finding a floor covering that looked reasonably like hardwood and was extremely durable. We chose Adura®, a vinyl plank flooring by Mannington®. The 3/16-in.-thick planks have a fairly random pattern and a satin finish. We chose Essex Oak Honeytone, but a variety of wood patterns are available in multiple color options. The 5-in.-wide by 48-in.-long planks are glued to the subfloor, so seams aren't an issue. We use a damp mop to keep the floor clean. It's holding up well, and more than a few people have mistaken it for the real thing. (Photo taken at D on floor plan.)

Simple Refinements for Cabinets and Countertops

In designing the kitchen, my aesthetic goal was to keep it consistent with the house's vintage and modest sensibility. I kept things simple, with white-painted cabinets and nickel-plated hardware. I built the cabinets myself and couldn't resist adding a few details to distinguish them from the factory-made variety. For example, I wanted the upper cabinets to extend to the ceiling, but I was worried about the tall, skinny doors that would result. To solve that problem, I added small, glass-paneled doors along the tops of the cabinets. The glass fronts also let us display our collection of 1930s California pottery.

To keep the cabinets consistent with the period, I eliminated the toe kick, bringing the face frames to the floor. The exception to this detail is the arched cutout at the sink, where toe space is most appreciated.

When it came to counters, we dallied. We had intended to use manufactured stone because of the low maintenance, but it was too artificial looking. Granite and marble seemed too extravagant for our dwindling budget, so we chose soapstone, which is softer than granite yet denser and more stain resistant. Because soapstone can be worked with woodworking tools, I was able to fabricate and install the counters myself, saving a lot of money.

As much as we liked soapstone, we thought it would be too cold and uninviting for a dining surface. We used cherry for that portion of the counter instead. To protect the wood surface, I brushed on three coats of Waterlox®, a tung-oil-based varnish. After extended use, the finish is holding up well.

The Hate Is Gone from the Kitchen Relationship

Our kitchen is not just good-looking; it's hardworking too. Relocating the refrigerator rewarded us with another 3 ft. of counter space and created a more efficient work triangle. Two slide-out cutting boards flanking the stove add utility and the unexpected advantage of providing a lower work surface for the kids. There is plenty of room for multiple cooks.

My biggest regret was not insisting on a vent routed to the outside for the stove's exhaust fan. Instead, we're stuck with a recirculating fan that practically rules out any serious grilling action on the stove. Other than that, the love/hate relationship we used to have with our kitchen is history.

SOURCES

MANNINGTON
www.mannington.com
Adura vinyl plank flooring

HOUSE OF ANTIQUE HARDWARE
www.houseofantiquehardware.com
Hardware

HAMPTON BAY
www.hamptonbay.com
Pendant light

DESIGN WITHIN REACH
www.dwr.com
1006 Navy® counter stool

WATERLOX
www.waterlox.com

NICKEL-PLATED ACCESSORIES. Cupboard latches, bin pulls, and hinges are right in keeping with the style of the house.

Cabinets

Four Quick Cabinet Upgrades

BY GARY STRIEGLER

AFTER

Kitchen remodels are a priority for many of my clients, but some budgets won't allow me to gut the kitchen and install all new cabinets, fixtures, and appliances. So I've developed methods to give clients improved function and a style upgrade without breaking the bank. The concept is simple: Give the existing cabinets an overhaul. By adding new doors and drawers, upgrading storage, dressing things up with trim, and then applying a glazed paint job, I can tie the new components in with the old ones for a seamless face lift. Upgrading these cabinets took me six days and cost about $600 in materials. The backsplash cost about $225 and took another day to install. I hired out the granite

BEFORE

AFTER THE DOOR-FRAME STOCK IS CUT TO WIDTH and rabbeted to receive the panel, rout the other edge with a ⅜-in. beading bit.

A PAIR OF POCKET SCREWS (Kreg® micro jig) at each miter creates a tight joint. The holes are then plugged and sanded flush.

A HINGE-BORING JIG (www.eurolimited.com) makes quick work of preparing each door to receive the new concealed hinges.

CUT THE OLD DOORS DOWN to the appropriate size to become panels, and cut a matching rabbet around each so that it will sit about ¼ in. below the front face of the frame.

countertop and the painting, which cost $1,400 and $1,000, respectively (2010 prices).

There are a couple of prerequisites. First, the cabinet boxes need to be in sound condition. Adding new doors and drawers to poorly constructed boxes makes about as much sense as building a new house on a crumbling foundation. Second, the existing materials and style of construction are a big factor. The kitchen shown here had site-built face-frame cabinets made with a combination of solid wood and plywood, common in older houses. If the cabinets had been made from particleboard or didn't have face frames, the process would have been more complicated, and the return on investment less promising.

Solid Doors Become Framed Panels

On this project, the existing cabinet doors were made from ¾-in. mahogany plywood. The plywood was in decent condition, so I wanted to find a way to reuse it. Most flat-panel cabinet doors tend to be made with ¼-in.- to ½-in.-thick plywood panels, which are lightweight and inexpensive but also feel cheap in terms of quality. I decided to use the old doors as panels, setting each in a new frame to create a more substantial cabinet door. If I hadn't been able to use the doors for the new panels, I would likely have chosen MDF, which is extremely stable and takes paint well.

For the door-frame stock, I chose poplar, a relatively inexpensive closed-grain hardwood that looks excellent in paint-grade cabinetry. Other hardwoods like maple and oak are good choices for stain-grade door frames as well. In terms of cost and durability, though, poplar can't be beat. The door construction is simple. It's crucial, however, that all of the wood be milled, that the rabbets be cut, and that beaded profiles be routed before the stock is cut to final size, or the cuts may not match up properly.

New Drawers in an Hour

The existing drawers in this kitchen were made from 1× pine and assembled with glued rabbet joints reinforced with nails. Decades of use had loosened the

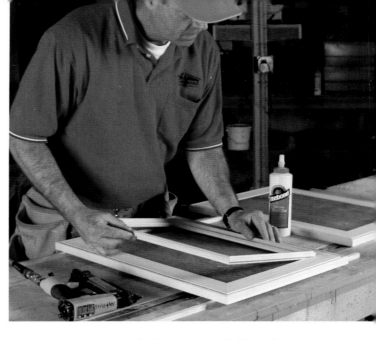

THE PANEL MOLDING, which also gets a shallow rabbet before assembly, is used to secure the panel in place and hide the joint.

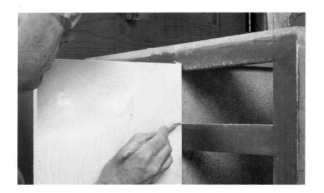

AFTER CUTTING A BACKER BOARD equal to the interior width of each cabinet, use the face frame as a template to mark the drawer-slide mounts before nailing the panel into place at the back of each cabinet.

ATTACH THE BRACKETS AND DRAWER SLIDES to a plywood cleat, and install each preassembled unit as one piece.

SLIDE THE DRAWER BOX INTO PLACE, and use a straightedge to adjust the slides until the drawer box is flush with the face frame. Then drive the screws to secure the assembly.

USING A SPACER JIG to establish a consistent height above the cabinet doors, secure each drawer front from the inside of the drawer box with screws.

DOORS AND LARGER DRAWER FRONTS are routed with the bead profile before the stock is cut to length and assembled. Smaller drawer fronts can be made from solid poplar dressed up with a mitered bead detail installed separately using glue and pin nails.

drawer boxes and left the aluminum drawer slides sticky or falling apart.

This kitchen (and its budget) didn't warrant a high-end drawer with dovetail joints and hidden self-closing drawer slides. Instead, I built the drawers in this project from birch plywood. They are just as strong as the boxes found in high-end kitchen cabinets, and each takes me less than an hour to complete.

The construction of each drawer—butt joints, pocket screws, and a bottom panel captured in a dado—is simple. Installation is a bit more complicated, however, because site-built cabinets don't typically have back panels, so a plywood backer is needed for solid attachment of the drawer slides.

BASE CABINETS WITH DOORS DON'T OFFER much accessibility. Either build a pullout shelf (above left) or divide up the space with drawers by adding new rails with pocket screws (above).

Fixed Shelves Become Adjustable

Site-built cabinets typically have shelves set into dadoes, so they can't be moved up or down to accommodate items of different sizes. I like to rip out these old fixed shelves and then install new painted side panels that cover the dadoes and allow for adjustable shelving.

YOU CAN MAKE YOUR OWN SHELF-PIN DRILLING TEMPLATE, but a self-centering bit and a compatible drilling guide (www.eurolimited.com) make the job go much faster.

TO REMOVE THE OLD SHELVES, drill a hole in the rear center of the board (left), then cut up to the hole with a jigsaw so the shelf can be removed in two pieces (above).

INSERT THE NEW SIDE PANEL into place over the old inside of the cabinet, and secure it with finish nails.

Trim Takes It from Plain to Pretty

If I were building cabinets from scratch, I would install the boxes and add the molding on site. An old kitchen isn't much different because what you have is a bunch of plain boxes ready for molding.

Old-style cabinets were typically designed for utility, not so much for elegance. The addition of molding helps balance the look of the new doors and drawer fronts, adds depth and shadow lines, and most important, gussies up the whole installation. For a job like this, I typically add band molding at the bottom, crown molding at the top, and picture-frame molding wherever end panels will show.

DEPENDING ON THE SPACE REMAINING below the cabinet doors, another nailer may be necessary to provide solid backing for the band molding. Some extra blocking may be necessary at the top too. On this job, the author added a valance to provide solid nailing for part of the crown molding. If the cabinets don't extend to the ceiling, a nailer may be necessary at the top edge of the cabinet as well.

THE BEST APPROACH FOR END PANELS is to preassemble the picture-frame molding and install it as one piece. Use spacers to center the molding, and then attach it using nails that won't penetrate into the cabinet interior.

A Buyer's Guide to Kitchen Cabinets

BY SCOTT GIBSON

Cabinet manufacturers from all over the country roll out their best stuff for the kitchen and bath industry's annual springtime trade show. When I last attended, kitchen cabinets of every style were sprinkled among booths showcasing bathtubs and appliances. Every style from Arts and Crafts in quartersawn oak to modern in Macassar ebony was available. Wellborn Cabinet Inc.® alone offered nearly 1,500 different combinations of finish and door styles.

Yet for all this diversity, every cabinet is made from the same basic components. Where they differ, and why prices vary so widely, can be traced to what's under the hood: materials, hardware, and construction techniques. Although manufacturers offer such a wide price range that they can cater to budgets of any size, spending more money usually means greater durability, better hardware, a nicer fit and finish, and more flexible designs.

A competitive scramble among stock and semicustom cabinet manufacturers gives buyers more choices than ever. Stock cabinets, the most economical, are still essentially an off-the-shelf commodity with the fewest options in finish and materials. Semicustom cabinets allow buyers to specify most but not all features. Prices vary accordingly.

While cabinet sizes in both categories tend to be standardized (available for the most part in 3-in. increments), manufacturers have tried to make it easier for buyers to order the options they want even on a modest budget.

Custom cabinets can be whatever a buyer is willing to pay for, usually with the longest lead time and the highest prices. In the end, how a cabinet is made is a lot more important than what it's called. The essential elements to consider are box construction, drawers, doors, hardware, and finish.

DOVETAILED DRAWERS

SOFT-CLOSE HINGES

FULL-EXTENSION DRAWER SLIDES

DESIGN WITH YOU IN MIND

THE SAME KITCHEN DESIGN doesn't work for every homeowner, so a new generation of designers have sharpened their pencils to match their products with the lifestyles of potential buyers. Whether you're a first-time homeowner or a retiree, someone has been thinking about you.

In fact, Heather Argo, a designer for the cabinet manufacturer KraftMaid®, invented "Edward" to help design a kitchen for Gen-Y buyers. A 20-something lawyer in Philadelphia, Edward likes games and electronics, doesn't cook much, and needs lots of storage for bottled water and ready-to-eat food. The result? A modern kitchen with a clean, white finish, contemporary hardware, a big TV cabinet, and a raised circular counter for eating or playing cards.

KraftMaid's layout for "active seniors" includes a built-in desk with an adjacent full-height pullout for office and cleaning supplies (see the photo at right). Armstrong®, another manufacturer, has taken a similar "lifestyle solutions" approach. Among its offerings are a cabinet doubling as a children's play area (see the photo below) and a chef's zone that keeps cooking tools and other accessories within a couple of feet of the cooktop.

To Wellborn Cabinet's Kimberly Dunn, it's a question of providing "more customization on every level." Buyers are less likely to follow broad trends these days than they are to buy cabinets that suit their needs and tastes exactly. "Everybody wants what they want," she says, "not just what their neighbor just bought."

KITCHEN OFFICE. A desktop flanked by a full-height rollout by KraftMaid provides storage for office supplies and space for paying bills.

PLAYTIME. With toys and a writing surface close at hand, Armstrong's play center can be a part of kitchen activity, but not underfoot.

Go for Plywood Boxes, Even if You'll Never See Them

A box, or carcase, is the foundation of any kitchen cabinet. Hidden behind face frames and end panels, the box is often unseen, but everything depends on its structural integrity.

Where you'll find significant differences is in the materials that go into the sides and back of the box. Economy cabinets usually are made of particleboard covered with a thin layer of vinyl printed with a wood-grain pattern. Particleboard is inexpensive, which helps keep the cost of the cabinets down, but it doesn't hold screws as well as plywood, and it is susceptible to water damage. If the vinyl surface tears or becomes delaminated, there's no way to repair it.

Melamine is a type of pressed wood-fiber panel that's often used for cabinet boxes because the plastic layer on top is easy to keep clean. It's heartier than the vinyl-covered particleboard in economy cabinets, but the surface can chip if it's abused.

Plywood costs more, but it's inherently more robust. Screws that attach hinges, drawer slides, and other hardware are less likely to be pulled out over time, and the surface can be repainted or refinished if it's damaged.

Cabinet sides range in thickness from ½ in. to ¾ in. Thin walls can make a cabinet feel cheap, and they offer less meat for shelf pins and hardware screws to grab. Plywood a full ¾ in. thick makes a solid, long-lasting box that can support heavy counters without complaint.

Cabinet backs aren't that important. Even good-quality cabinets might have backs made of ¼-in. material. There is a structural purpose—the back prevents the cabinet from racking—but unless the countertop is unusually heavy or drawer hardware is to be mounted directly to the back, a panel that's ¼ in. thick shouldn't be a drawback. Still, plywood is a better choice than hardboard.

Face frames also help make the box sturdy. They are usually made from the same hardwood as the drawer faces and doors. Look for gap-free joints between the pieces that make up the frame. When inside edges around door and drawer openings are sanded smooth and joints are tight, it's an indication the frame was made with care. In frameless cabinets (also known as European cabinets), doors and drawers hide the front of the box completely. Without a frame to help keep the box rigid, it's more important than ever to buy a cabinet made of high-quality ¾-in. material.

Dovetails Are Stronger, so the Drawers Last Longer

Hardwood drawer sides that are ⅝ in. or ¾ in. thick are a good idea on all but the lightest and smallest drawers. Material that's only ½ in. thick, especially if it's particleboard, is not as dependable.

Drawer bottoms are often ¼ in. thick, and again, plywood is a better choice than particleboard or hardboard. On cabinet pullouts that carry a lot of weight, a ⅜-in. or even a ½-in. plywood bottom is less likely to sag over time.

Well-made dovetail joints make the most-durable drawers. A poorly made dovetail, on the other hand, is no better than a poorly made anything else. There should be no gaps in the interlocking parts, and the joint should be sanded and finished carefully. Particleboard drawers are typically glued and stapled at the corners and don't stand up well to heavy use.

Wood drawers are by far the most common, but metal-sided drawer boxes like Blum®'s Tandembox

GOING GREEN

A SIGNIFICANT NUMBER OF CABINET manufacturers have won "green" certification from the Kitchen Cabinet Manufacturers Association's environmental stewardship program. If you're interested in sustainable options for your kitchen, go to www.kcma.org.

YOU GET WHAT YOU PAY FOR

IKEA READY-TO-ASSEMBLE

- **Box:** ¾-in. frame-less melamine
- **Drawers:** Metal sides, melamine front and bottom
- **Doors:** Melamine
- **Hardware:** Adjustable cup hinges, integral drawer slide
- **Finish:** Plastic
- **Price:** $127*

WELLBORN STOCK

- **Box:** ½-in. particleboard sides, ¾-in. hardwood face frame
- **Drawers:** Stapled ¾-in. particleboard
- **Doors:** Hardwood frame and panel
- **Hardware:** Euro cup hinges, epoxy-coated drawer slides
- **Finish:** Stain with clear coat
- **Price:** $245

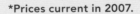

PARTS THAT FIT. Thanks to careful machining, the precut and predrilled cabinet parts go together easily. Assembly of the 24-in. base unit took about 90 minutes.

EURO HINGES RULE. Many manufacturers supply cabinets with cup hinges, borrowing an idea that started with European cabinets. Although cup hinges are a little bulky, they are easy to adjust to keep cabinet doors aligned.

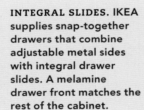

INTEGRAL SLIDES. IKEA supplies snap-together drawers that combine adjustable metal sides with integral drawer slides. A melamine drawer front matches the rest of the cabinet.

BASIC DRAWERS. Particleboard drawers that have been stapled together are a potential weak spot. These epoxy-coated drawer slides are three-quarter extension and make access to the back of the drawer difficult.

*Prices current in 2007.

---

or IKEA®'s ready-to-assemble cabinets have a sleeker, more contemporary look. They're well adapted to frameless cabinets, and some come with integrated full-extension drawer slides and a soft-close feature. They can be paired with a variety of dividers and organizers.

Solid Wood Doesn't Always Make the Best Door

Cabinet doors come in two basic types: frame and panel or slab. Frame-and-panel doors are the traditional choice with face-frame cabinets and are avail-

able in dozens of styles. The frames are typically made of solid wood, while the panels might be solid wood or veneered medium-density fiberboard (MDF).

Veneered panels are flat and stable, and furniture history proves there is nothing structurally inferior about them. However, they might age differently than a solid-wood frame, resulting in a contrast between the two. This is an issue only with woods that change dramatically with age, such as cherry, but the concern is worth considering. Solid-wood panels are more likely to shrink and expand with

ARMSTRONG SEMICUSTOM

- **Box:** ½-in. plywood, ¾-in. hardwood face frame
- **Drawers:** Stapled ½-in. hardwood sides, plywood bottom
- **Doors:** Hardwood frame and panel
- **Hardware:** Adjustable cup hinges, epoxy-coated slides
- **Finish:** Stain with catalyzed clear top coat
- **Price:** $300

PLAIN & FANCY CUSTOM CABINETRY

- **Box:** ½-in. plywood, ¾-in. face frame
- **Drawers:** Dovetailed ⅝-in. hardwood
- **Doors:** Frame and panel
- **Hardware:** Pin hinges, full-extension undermount drawer slides
- **Finish:** Antiqued paint
- **Price:** $1,200

PLYWOOD UPGRADE. Plywood is stronger and more durable than particleboard. It's usually available as an upgrade.

STURDY CABINET BOX. Plywood components and wood glue blocks, rather than stapled plastic corner braces, are signs of a well-made, fully custom cabinet.

ROLLOUTS FOR CONVENIENCE. The cup hinges are standard, but the two rollouts on the inside of this cabinet offer more convenient storage than shelves.

OUT OF SIGHT. These undermount drawer slides allow the drawer box to roll all the way out. They're hidden beneath the drawer, so all you see are the drawer sides and the carefully machined dovetails.

changes in humidity, but won't show color differences and won't delaminate. Solid-wood panels are probably worth their slightly higher cost.

Slab doors are either glued-up solid wood or veneered MDF and are typically used with frameless cabinets. A substrate of MDF should help keep the door flat and free of warp. A solid-wood door that's 18 in. or 20 in. wide might cup or twist over time.

No matter what the style, look at the doors carefully. On frame-and-panel doors, the joints should be tight and free of gaps when the cabinets are new.

If the panels are glued up from solid wood, look for a good match in grain and color between adjacent boards. No cross-grain sanding marks should be visible on either the inside or the outside of the door, and the finish should feel soft and silky.

If the door has a glass panel, the fit between glass and wood should be neat, and you should not find globs of glue or caulk oozing out of the seam.

Hardware Should Stand up to Wear and Tear

Hardware manufacturers have pulled out all the stops to make cabinet interiors more functional and user-friendly. Most cabinet companies buy hardware from the same manufacturers, so no matter what brand of cabinet you buy, you should have a good menu of hardware to choose from.

Most drawers and pullouts ride on side-mounted ball-bearing metal slides. A variety of types are available as full extension or three-quarter extension, meaning the drawer either comes all the way out or stops with about a quarter of its depth still buried inside the cabinet. Full-extension slides are well worth the extra cost.

Slides are rated by the weight they are designed to carry, typically 75 lb. or 100 lb. Slides rated at 75 lb. should be fine for all but the largest and heaviest drawers, but roll-out pantry shelves or drawers for heavy pots and pans or appliances do better with beefier slides.

Undermount slides are becoming increasingly common. They are attached to the bottom of the drawer and are hidden by the drawer sides, making the cabinets look more like furniture.

Many cabinet companies now equip their drawers with a soft-close mechanism made by Blum called "Blumotion." It grabs the drawer near the end of its travel, slows it down, and then gently brings it to a stop—a great idea if you live in a house where people tend to slam drawers closed.

Good luck finding cabinets with traditional butt hinges. European-style door hinges, or cup hinges,

PANTRY IN A DRAWER. A wire organizer in an Armstrong base cabinet makes it possible to stow a great deal of supplies in a small space without losing track of anything.

FOLD-OUT STORAGE. This storage unit in an Armstrong base cabinet eliminates wasted space in the corner. Racks fold open and roll out from the cabinet on ball-bearing slides.

RECYCLING CENTER. DeWils Custom Cabinetry offers a revolving recycling center in this corner base cabinet, making good use of an often awkward space. The rack holds three plastic bins.

UP AND AWAY. These upper cabinet doors from Wellborn pop up to provide full access without conventional hinges.

ROUNDABOUT. A wire lazy Susan in this DeWils cabinet provides plenty of storage and better visibility than an organizer with solid shelves.

FLEXIBLE STORAGE. A full-height rollout from Kraft-Maid provides storage for office supplies on one side and cleaning supplies on the other, making the most of a narrow cabinet. (See the other side in the right photo on p. 56.)

SOURCES

ARMSTRONG
www.armstrong.com

BLUM
www.blum.com

DEWILS CUSTOM CABINETRY
www.dewils.com

IKEA
www.ikea.com

KRAFTMAID
www.kraftmaid.com

PLAIN & FANCY CUSTOM CABINETRY
www.plainfancycabinetry.com

WELLBORN CABINET INC.
www.wellborn.com

have taken over. They are available for both frameless and face-frame cabinets, and because they allow a variety of adjustments, these hinges make it easy to hang even finicky inset doors. The Blumotion soft-close feature is also available for hinges.

Fancy Finishes Are Durable, Too

Manufacturers devote a lot of energy to cabinet finishes, what might be the most fickle part of the business as designers try to gauge shifting buyer preferences. The tremendous diversity of painted, glazed, stained, and distressed finishes is a testament to the industry's effort to appeal to any taste.

In general, the least-expensive finishes are simple clear coats. The most expensive are multilayered glazes and paints, crackle finishes, and rub-through painted surfaces that take more time to execute at the factory. Painted surfaces are somewhat less durable than clear finishes and might show slight gaps

in joinery more readily. Glazed-paint finishes can help disguise these minor flaws.

For clear finishes, most manufacturers use a conversion varnish, a tough two-part catalyzed coating. Old-schoolers might prefer lacquer because it's more repairable, but catalyzed finishes are extremely durable and are now the norm.

Where you're likely to find differences is in the quality of application. The best finishes start with thorough surface prep, meaning you should see no sanding marks of any kind on the finished surface. Whether the surface is matte or glossy, it should be smooth and blemish free. Look along edges and inside doors, using your fingers as well as your eyes.

In the end, finishes are largely a matter of personal taste. Basic, no-frills finishes should provide a long service life, but if you want something more elaborate and are willing to pay for it, you have plenty of options.

Installing Stock Cabinets

BY RICK GEDNEY

My father started working in the kitchen industry in the early 1950s. I spent many of my high-school days making cabinet deliveries and installing appliances. In 1979, he and I opened a small business together, Kitchens by Gedney. In one way or another, I've spent nearly 35 years designing, installing, and managing the installation of high-end kitchens.

A lot has changed in the kitchen industry since those early days. (See "A Buyer's Guide to Kitchen Cabinets," on p. 54) What hasn't changed is the demand for flawlessly installed cabinetry, a standard we've been committed to for nearly two generations.

Over the years, I—along with our skilled installation crews—have developed an approach to installing cabinets that ensures accuracy and quality. Here, I'll explain how to organize the job so that it keeps moving forward, how to prep the site properly, how to achieve an accurate layout, and how to install correctly the three most common types of kitchen cabinets: base cabinets, wall cabinets, and tall units that serve as pantries or that often house refrigerators or ovens.

Have a Plan to Stay Organized

Whether in a remodel or a new home, the installation of kitchen cabinets involves high levels of stress and activity. In a remodel, you're occupying the space that makes the home habitable. Getting the job done as quickly as possible is almost always the goal. In new construction, you're working amid a host of other subcontractors, all vying for space. In either environment, the room for error is significant. We keep our jobs accurate and in order with communication, a plan review, and a systems approach to installation.

Communication is critical. Create an installation calendar so that everyone involved in the project knows what's happening in the kitchen and when. Be sure to have established contacts with the cabinet supplier so that if a question or error arises, you can make a quick call to the person who can remedy the problem.

Before a single cabinet is uncrated, review the plan with your designer or cabinet supplier to be sure all cabinets are on site. Be sure you understand the supplier's terminology, because most cabinetmakers have their own codes and product numbers. Then be sure that all the labels actually match the cabinets in each package. Nobody wants to demolish a kitchen only to realize that the new corner base cabinet is the wrong size and that the correct unit is on back order for four weeks.

Establish a repetitive system, from site prep through installation, to be sure the job progresses as it should. Having a systematic approach makes cabinet installation more accurate and also saves time. With this system and two people on the job, expect to install the cabinetry for a typical kitchen in about three days. Another three days will likely be spent applying moldings, installing appliances, and completing ventilation work.

Protect Finished Surfaces

Install the cabinets when the kitchen is in a nearly finished state. The kitchen flooring should be installed before any cabinets are put in place. Wood floors should have one or two coats of finish on them. You can see the floor beneath many of today's professional-style appliances and furniture-like cabinets, so

installing the floor first is smart. Also, the cabinets are finished, so it's foolish to try to maneuver a floor sander around the new units. The floor on this project is prefinished maple, so floor protection was critical. We've found success with products such as Ramboard™ and Cover Guard®. Be sure all the seams are taped. When connecting sheets of Ramboard, use Ramboard tape only. The adhesive is strong and nearly impossible to remove from tile, wood, and other finished materials. Use painter's tape to secure the edges of each sheet to the floor.

Ideally, the ceiling in the kitchen should be primed and painted. The walls should be primed and have one finish coat, if possible. You'll have to do some touching up, but at least you won't risk paint splatter on the new cabinets and appliances while cutting in or painting large wall and ceiling areas.

Working in a fairly finished environment demands substantial care and dust control, especially during a remodel. Lose the tool belt to prevent scratches, and ensure all saws and sanders are connected to vacuums. ZipWall® protection or other dust barriers should cordon off the kitchen. We place a dust collector outside the house and install a 12-in. flex duct in an open window. This creates negative pressure in the room and collects airborne dust. The unit is positioned far from the house, so everyone can talk or listen to music.

Work Smart

In the old days, it was common practice to start a kitchen installation with the wall cabinets so that you didn't have to lean over the bases. In today's complex kitchens, we start with the base cabinets for several reasons.

Many kitchen designs call for wall cabinets to sit atop the counter. Establishing the height of the base cabinets is critical to getting boxes to fit properly. The height of most wall cabinets can be adjusted easily, while the height of bases and tall cabinets can't.

The base corner unit, if there is one, helps establish the layout and determines how the upper and lower cabinets align. On this project, we started with the sink cabinet as our control. For the sink to line up perfectly with the middle stile of the window, the cabinet had to be dead center.

To expedite the project, countertop installers can come in as soon as the bases are put into place to make their templates. They can be working on the countertops while you're busy finishing the rest of the kitchen.

Finally, there isn't always an extra set of hands to help install the cabinets. Being able to prop a wall cabinet on a base unit to maneuver it into position is an easy, safe, and accurate way to work.

Lay Out the Base Cabinets

With plans in hand, draw the cabinetry layout on the wall. Layout lines not only serve as a template for the cabinet installation but also let you verify the plan. Be sure that vent, plumbing, and electrical locations are accurate. Mark stud locations during the layout phase to anticipate the need for extra blocking or additional cabinet support.

FIND THE HIGH POINT IN THE FLOOR. Measure the distance between the floor and a laser-level line about 4 ft. above the floor to find the high and low points in the floor (left). The high point dictates the height of the base cabinets; use shims to compensate for the low points in the floor.

MARK THE HEIGHT OF THE BASES. Measure the height of the cabinets, usually 34½ in., from the high point in the floor, and mark the wall (top right). Measure the distance between the cabinet height and the laser line. Mark off the cabinet height around the room by measuring down off the laser-level line. This takes the uneven floor out of the equation.

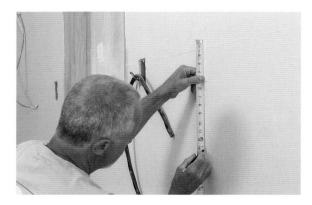

DRAW A LEVEL LINE ACROSS THE WALL. Connect the marks on the wall with a level to establish a line to hold the base cabinets to during installation. This technique is more accurate than snapping chalklines or using a laser-level line.

MARK CABINET LOCATIONS. Draw plumb lines on the wall to establish cabinet positions, taking care to be sure that cabinets such as the sink base align perfectly with the windows above.

Install the Base Cabinets

The first cabinet installed determines the placement of all the others. In most kitchens, it's important to start with a corner cabinet. If you save the corner cabinet for last and your layout is even the slightest bit off, it won't fit, and you'll be stuck waiting for a new, custom-built unit. Working away from a corner offers more flexibility. Instead of a cabinet, this kitchen has a sitting bench in the corner, so it offered some wiggle room. This project started with the next-most-critical cabinets in terms of layout: the sink base and the cabinet beneath the range hood that holds the cooktop.

PLUMB AND LEVEL THE CABINET. With the cabinet in position, use a 4-ft. level to check if it's plumb (above). Place another level across the top of the cabinet to determine if it's level. Make adjustments with cedar shims (left). An applied toe kick scribed to the floor will hide any shims and gaps.

MODIFY FOR SERVICES. Measure the distance from the cabinet layout lines on the wall to the services coming through the wall or floor. Transfer the vertical and horizontal measurements to the back or bottom of the cabinet, and cut a hole with a hole saw that's slightly larger than the size of the service line being accommodated.

THREE PLACES TO FASTEN. The first cabinet is screwed to the wall, but all other cabinets are flushed to their adjacent units, screwed together with 1¼-in. by #8 Twinfast screws, and then screwed to the wall. Exposed fasteners are covered with FastCap® covers. Screw cabinets to the wall through pilot holes in the hanging rail with 2½-in. by #8 Twinfast screws or a product with similar shear strength, but never with drywall screws. Shims prevent the cabinet from being pulled out of alignment. On end cabinets where a toe kick is present, toenail a screw into the bottom plate.

Scribe and Secure Tall Cabinets

Pantry and tall cabinets that typically house ovens or refrigerators demand extra work for correct installation. Their long side panels will expose every bump and dip in the wall if not scribed and cut to fit perfectly. Order these cabinets with end panels that are 3 in. to 4 in. wider than necessary to accommodate scribing. Having excess material offers a solid base for the saw to rest against when cutting to the scribe line and ensures plenty of play when fitting a cabinet against the most out-of-whack walls. These units typically stand proud of the other base cabinets so countertops can die into their side panels.

STRENGTHEN THE ATTACHMENT TO THE WALL. With the layout established on the wall, span studs with plywood reinforcement strips at the top of the unit. Screwing the unit to studs will be enough, but sinking a few more screws into the plywood offers insurance, especially when the cabinet is intended to house an oven that may have heavy doors.

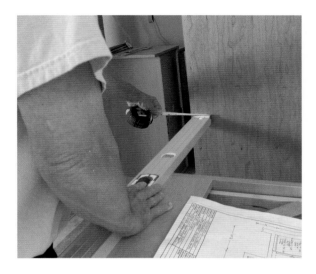

CALCULATE HOW MUCH TO TRIM. With the cabinet in place, use a level to represent the overhang of the counter on the adjacent base cabinet. The distance between the front edge of the level and the front edge of the cabinet determines how much material can be taken off the back of the cabinet's panels.

SCRIBE. With a compass and a sharp pencil, draw a continuous scribe line on each side panel of the cabinet.

CUT THE WASTE. Bulk material can be removed with a track-guided circular saw or a jigsaw. Follow the scribe line closely, but leave the pencil line.

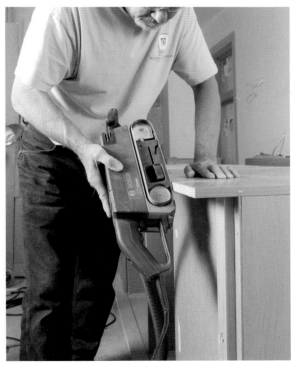

BEVEL THE EDGE. With a belt sander, remove the rest of the waste while giving the edge a bevel. Beveling the back of the panel ensures that the cabinet's outside edges will fit tight to the wall.

Hang Wall Cabinets Safely

Some kitchen installers gang wall cabinets together on the ground and raise them in place with a lift or lots of helping hands. Installing wall cabinets one by one is also fine and is much more manageable when working alone or with one helper.

USE A BOX AS A PROP. With the cabinet's layout on the wall, position the cabinet atop a sturdy plywood box and plywood strips. Shim the box until it's level before setting a screw through the top and bottom hanging rails and into studs.

CHECK FOR PLUMB. Before completely securing the cabinet to the wall, make sure it's plumb so that the doors will work properly.

Installing Cabinets in Tight Spaces

BY BRENT BENNER

One of the more enjoyable aspects of my work as a cabinetmaker is solving problems, especially those concerned with creating or maximizing space. Designing and building cabinets in the rectilinear worlds of computers and workshops is the simple part. Installing cabinets in the real world is usually a straightforward exercise too, but in a confined space like a pantry or a wet bar, it can be a challenge. The following is a procedure I've developed that reduces the frustrations.

To begin, I design the cabinet with three discrete parts: a base, a cabinet case, and a face frame. I use Festool®'s Domino® system or biscuits to register the face frame to the cabinet so that I can check the fit without having to move the entire cabinet. After the base is set, I drop in the cabinet, scribe the face frame to match the walls, and then permanently attach the face frame.

To scribe the face frame, I set up a plumb laser line centered in the opening. At vertical increments of a few inches, I take measurements from the laser line to the walls on each side at the point where the face frame will land. I transfer the measurements to the face frame, back-bevel the cuts, and leave the line. Then I test-fit and fine-tune with a handplane.

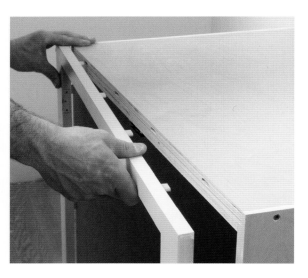

SEPARATE IS BETTER. Especially in an enclosed space, a separate base makes the job of setting the cabinet much easier. Once the base is leveled and attached to the floor, it's a good time to install the finished toe kick.

THE PLUG-AND-PLAY FACE FRAME. Before scribing, dry-fit the face frame to the case with biscuits or Festool's Domino system (shown here). After the carcase is on the base, the face frame can be scribed, test-fit, and still register accurately against the box's inside edge.

A REFERENCE LINE IN SPACE. Set up a laser level so that it casts a vertical plumb line through the exact center of the space. Next, mark the approximate depth of the cabinet on both walls, as measured from the back. Now measure from the centerline (above) to each side at vertical intervals of 4 in. to 6 in., and record the measurements.

After the face frame is scribed, I glue and clamp it to the cabinet. When I'm installing stock cabinets whose face frames are already attached, the process is the same, except that I have to jockey the entire unit in and out of position.

TRANSFER THE NUMBERS. At the same intervals used to measure the space, transfer the measurements to both sides of the face frame. Connect the dots and cut to the line, making sure to back-bevel the cut (below). Check the fit, and fine-tune with a block plane.

REUNITE FACE FRAME AND CARCASE. When the fit is satisfactory, install the cabinet case and attach the face frame in place with biscuits and glue.

PERFECT LINES EVERY TIME

LASER LEVELS HAVE A WIDE VARIETY of uses, but I've found a use that's not as common. When I'm installing cabinets, a laser can set a level reference line quickly, but its best feature is the ability to create a reference line in space. Where I would typically have to hold a plumb level with one hand and a tape measure with the other, a laser allows accurate repeatable measurements. The best models are self-leveling and accurate to approximately ¼ in. at 100 ft. I use a Stabila®.

A Faster, Easier Approach to Custom Cabinets

BY MIKE MAINES

When designed and constructed properly, built-in cabinets can bring both style and storage to many parts of a home. Over the years, I've refined my approach to constructing cabinets to decrease the time and tools it takes to build them while ensuring their strength and good looks. I used my technique to build the Douglas-fir kitchen island featured here for my home, but I've followed the same process to make stain- and paint-grade kitchen cabinets, bookcases, linen cabinets, pantries, desks, bathroom vanities, and storage cubbies.

Your Shop Is Where You Make It

The beauty of this system is that the setup is simple and doesn't rely on the space or tools found in big cabinet shops. Being able to set up shop in a driveway, a garage, or a small room has always been helpful in keeping my work on schedule.

The tools you need to construct these cabinets are likely sitting in the back of your truck. For cutting components to size, you need a miter saw, a portable tablesaw, a circular saw, an edge guide to cut sheet goods safely, and a portable thickness planer. To fasten the carcase and face frames together, you need a 16-gauge or 18-gauge finish nailer, a screw gun, a pocket-screw jig (www.kregtool.com; www. pennstateind.com), a bunch of screws, and some glue.

A Hybrid Design Makes Face-Frame Cabinets Better

Cabinets are typically designed in one of two ways: frameless or with face frames. Each has its merits. Face-frame cabinets are traditional and strong, and they can be scribed to fit seamlessly against a wall. Frameless cabinets are quicker to put together and can be used in conjunction with adjustable, hidden, and now soft-close hinges.

I've done a lot of historically informed work, and frameless boxes just don't provide the appeal of face-frame cabinets with inset doors. Although frameless cabinets allow a bit more space inside, their end panels tend to look tacked-on, crown molding is hard to detail properly, and filler strips are heavily relied on during installation. I use the benefits of both styles by building a hybrid cabinet. Flushing the inside of the carcase to the inside of the face frame allows me to use hardware designed for frameless cabinets while still providing the traditional look, ease of installation, and strength of face-frame construction.

CUT ALL THE FACE-FRAME COMPONENTS AT ONCE. When milling 1×6 face-frame material to size, I like to fine-tune its final width with a planer, not a tablesaw. I use a tablesaw to square all boards with rounded edges. Then I rip the face-frame stock ⅛ in. wider than I need on a tablesaw. Finally, I remove the last ⅛ in. with a planer. The planer produces more precise dimensions and smoother cuts.

PLANE SIMILAR PARTS TOGETHER. Instead of planing each board individually, plane all the end stiles, then inner stiles, and then rails to their exact width.

CHOP TO LENGTH. Armed with a fence and a stop made of scrap material and a cut list, chop all the face-frame material to its precise length. Stack all the material to make a complete face frame.

GOOD PROPORTIONS ARE NO ACCIDENT

ALTHOUGH MY BUILT-IN CABINETS are assembled easily, there's no guarantee they'll look good in a home. A cabinet constructed with wacky proportions won't look or function as well as it should. To start, make a scale drawing on paper of each piece you intend to build. Having this reference on hand will give you a clear idea of what you're building and will help you create a detailed cut list. I follow a few basic rules when it comes to designing cabinets.

- Built-in cabinets that will be used as workstations generally have countertops 36 in. above the floor, so boxes should be built to a height of 34½ in.

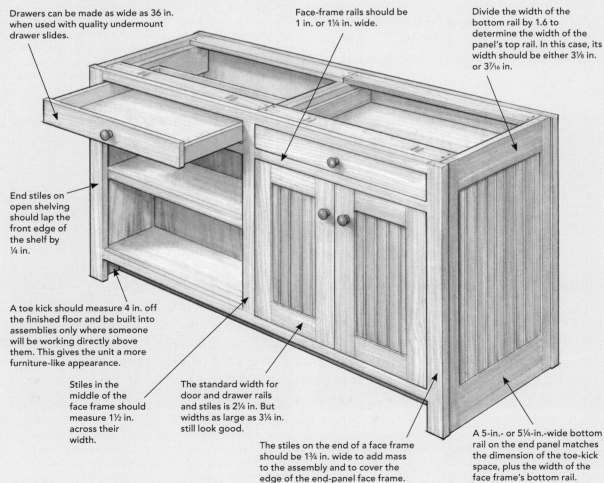

Drawers can be made as wide as 36 in. when used with quality undermount drawer slides.

Face-frame rails should be 1 in. or 1¼ in. wide.

Divide the width of the bottom rail by 1.6 to determine the width of the panel's top rail. In this case, its width should be either 3⅛ in. or 3⁷⁄₁₆ in.

End stiles on open shelving should lap the front edge of the shelf by ¼ in.

A toe kick should measure 4 in. off the finished floor and be built into assemblies only where someone will be working directly above them. This gives the unit a more furniture-like appearance.

Stiles in the middle of the face frame should measure 1½ in. across their width.

The standard width for door and drawer rails and stiles is 2¼ in. But widths as large as 3¼ in. still look good.

The stiles on the end of a face frame should be 1¾ in. wide to add mass to the assembly and to cover the edge of the end-panel face frame.

A 5-in.- or 5¼-in.-wide bottom rail on the end panel matches the dimension of the toe-kick space, plus the width of the face frame's bottom rail.

to 35 in., depending on the thickness of the countertop. Cabinets that aren't task oriented can be any size and are built without toe kicks. I distinguish these units by building the bottom rail taller or shorter than the house's baseboard. When in doubt of any proportions, I use the golden rectangle, a shape 1.6 times as high as it is wide. I also find the widths of components by dividing similar members by 1.6 as done with the end-panel rails.

■ When multiple cabinet boxes are lined up in a row, they appear more fitted when tied together with a single face frame. I connect the boxes by hiding a screw behind each door hinge. You can make all the face-frame components the same size, but that can make the rails look fat and the end stiles look skinny. Instead, I like to adjust their widths (see the drawing on the facing page) so that the built-in looks more balanced.

■ Doors should always be taller than they are wide and should never exceed 20 in. in width; otherwise they project too far into a space when opened. Even an 18-in.-wide door can be too large on certain units. Drawers should be left with a flat face when they're shorter than 4½ in., which is typical, and can be detailed to match frame-and-panel doors when they're taller.

Screws, Glue, and Quality Hardware Hold It Together

Traditionally, face-frame cabinets are constructed with dadoes, grooves, dowels, or mortise-and-tenon joinery to lock together each component. These techniques create strong assemblies but require a good bit of time.

I assemble face frames with fine-thread, 1¼-in. square-drive washer-head pocket screws and yellow glue. I tack the carcases together with finish nails and then drive 1⅝-in. drywall screws for strength. I've used drywall screws for years and have never had a cabinet fail, but it's important to use stronger screws when attaching a cabinet to the wall.

ASSEMBLE THE FACE FRAMES FIRST. I build all the face frames before I build their corresponding boxes. This not only saves room on the job site but also allows me to use the face frames for reference when a dimension comes into question during carcase construction. To start, dry-fit the face-frame components so their grain and color look best. Mark the boards to show their orientation in the assembly and where they'll be pocket screwed.

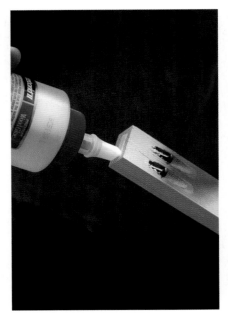

A POCKET-HOLE JIG MAKES ASSEMBLY EASY. Drill two pocket holes in the end of each rail and each inner stile.

SQUEEZE THE GRAIN TO ELIMINATE SPLITTING. Put a bit of wood glue on the board end before securing a locking C-clamp so that it exerts equal pressure on the grain of each component. The clamp should be placed in line with the pocket hole being screwed.

QUALITY CONTROL. Check to be sure that every component is aligned and secured properly before building subsequent frames. Accuracy here is crucial because the dimensions of the face frame might be used as a reference when building the boxes.

JIG TIP. I make a simple jig out of thin medium-density fiberboard (MDF) to orient shelf pinholes 1½ in. from the front and back of the box. I usually place the first hole 12 in. off the bottom of the box and drill holes in 1½-in. increments above and below.

BUILD THE BOXES. Box assembly is a relatively straightforward process. Before the sides of the boxes are fastened together, though, I drill pocket holes and the holes for shelving pins. Please note that full sheets of plywood should never be cut on a tablesaw. Instead, use a straightedge clamped to the sheet's surface and a circular saw with a fine-toothed alternate top bevel (ATB) sawblade.

DRILL POCKET HOLES IN GROUPS OF TWO. When preparing the sides of the carcase that will be joined with the face frame, drill two holes instead of one for each connection point. This extra step will come in handy when attaching the face frames.

Beyond box strength, cabinets are often measured by the quality of their hardware. The best hinge for this hybrid system is a 32mm cup hinge made by Blum (www.blum.com) or Mepla (www.mepla-alfit. com). Adjustable, self-closing, and quick to install, they are usually my first choice. In more historically accurate work when a visible hinge is preferred or when I don't want a hinge to intrude on storage space, I like to use Cliffside's 2-in. butt hinges (www. cliffsideind.com). I use a trim router to mortise the door for a single leaf and don't mortise the face frame at all, which helps provide just the right reveal between the door and the face frame.

I've used all three types of drawer slides in my cabinets, but when I have a choice, I opt for the Blum Tandem, an undermount full-extension unit that is forgiving to install and smooth to operate.

For adjustable shelves, I like to drill groups of three to five holes where I think the shelf should be.

TACK AND SCREW TOGETHER THE BOX PARTS. Nailing the box with 16-gauge finish nails makes it easier to keep pieces in place while they're locked together with 1⅝-in. drywall screws.

This allows some adjustability while avoiding the factory-made look of a continuous row of holes. Often, I use paddle-type supports installed in a 5mm hole. For heavy-duty applications, such as a bookshelf, I like an L-shaped pin in a ¼-in. hole.

Get Doors and Drawer Fronts That Fit the Second Time

I order or build doors and drawer fronts before the built-ins are complete so I can finish the job quickly. To be sure they fit the way I want them to, with the perfect reveal, I have them built to the exact size of the face-frame opening written on my plans. Once on site, I fit them tight into their openings. I reduce their size on all sides a heavy ¹⁄₁₆ in. by taking measurements from the face frame, not the door or drawer front itself, and rip them on the tablesaw.

SUPPORT THE BOX AND THE DRAWER SLIDES. On top of each box and below each drawer, ¾-in. plywood crosspieces add strength, a place to connect the face frame's top rail, and a surface to attach countertops and undermount drawer slides.

ATTACH THE FACE FRAMES TO THE BOXES. A face frame can be nailed to a box with 16-gauge finish nails. However, the holes still need to be filled, and the gun can scuff the face-frame surface. Another way to attach face frames is with biscuit joinery, a solid solution, but one that demands a lot of time and a massive arsenal of clamps. By attaching the face frame with pocket screws, I get an immediate, permanent connection while leaving the face of the cabinet clear.

PICK A HOLE, BUT NOT JUST ANY HOLE. Although I drilled groups of two pocket holes in the box, only one hole in each set needs to be screwed. The face frame should flush with the inside of the box perfectly, but if it doesn't, having multiple holes gives you the flexibility to push and pull the face frame into alignment.

DRESS UP AN EXPOSED END PANEL

BUILT-IN CABINETS usually have their sides buried in a wall. Sometimes, however, the sides and even the back are exposed to public view. I detail these areas to hide pocket holes in a couple of ways.

On my kitchen island, I used a stock of reclaimed Douglas-fir edge and center bead that had been collecting dust in my garage for years. I simply filled the face-frame opening with the boards, attaching them with an 18-gauge pin nailer. Held tight against the carcase, the ¾-in.-thick face frame would leave a ¼-in. reveal where it meets the end stiles of the front face frame. So I furred out the end panel with ³⁄₁₆-in. plywood strips to reduce the size of the reveal.

If I'm not going to use bead board on a built-in, I fill the face frame with ½-in. plywood to create a flat recessed panel. Alternatively, I cover the entire side of the carcase with a sheet of ¼-in. plywood that can be stained or painted to match the wood I've used, then glue and nail the face frame to it.

COVER YOUR TRACKS. To hide pocket holes and screws used to assemble the cabinet, wrap exposed faces with a decorative material, such as stain- or paint-grade plywood, bead board, or edge and center bead.

Build a Kitchen Island

BY RICK GEDNEY

The function of a modern kitchen island can be traced to the familiar kitchen worktable that's been helping families run the household and prepare meals for generations. An island's job is even tougher, though: A table from the eighteenth or nineteenth century didn't need to be a space for making pizza, checking email, or stir-frying. It also didn't have to integrate pipes, ducts, and wires.

I was recently called to a client's house for a full kitchen remodel. The young family wanted to renovate their existing, space-challenged galley kitchen, turning it into a wide-open room with an eat-at island. We looked at the available space and decided a single-level island with a farm sink made the most sense.

One often-overlooked item with island installations is how different floor coverings transition

WORK FROM THE END. With the position of the sink's overhead light as a starting point, use the kitchen designer's measured drawings to determine the end of the island. Measure from the wall cabinets to create a parallel line that the island will follow.

CENTER THE SINK. Using a pair of levels, transfer to the floor the location of the light fixture centered over the sink. This becomes the starting point for the layout.

FIND MIDDLE GROUND. Many installers find the highest point of the floor to reference cabinet height, and then shim up the cabinets that sit on low spots. A better option is to find a cabinet at average height and then shim the low cabinets up and plane the high cabinets down. Shimming and planing should be minimal.

around the cabinets. On this project, we had to make an attractive transition between the wide pine floors in the adjacent living areas and the new kitchen's tile floor. We opted to make the transition at the end of the island and run the wide pine under the eating area. This seemed like the most logical spot to transition between the two types of flooring.

The installation of this island was pretty typical, although the open ceiling in the basement made running pipes and wires to the island a little easier. In this case, the plumber and electrician decided it would be best to do their rough-ins after the cabinets were installed, although such a process varies from one job to the next. When I'm designing a kitchen island, I always get the general contractor and the subcontractors involved as soon as we have preliminary drawings because plumbing, ventilation, and electrical requirements can make some designs unworkable with a typical budget.

CHECK ACROSS THE GAP. Where there's a gap in the island's cabinet run for a dishwasher or other appliance, use a long level to ensure that both cabinets are at the same height. Check front and back to confirm that the cabinet tops are in the same plane. Also make sure the cabinets are spread at the proper distance and their sides are parallel.

Start with a Focal Point, Then Follow the Plans

Light fixtures are typically centered over sinks and appliances, so this is a logical starting point for establishing the cabinet layout. From there, move left and right according to the plans, accounting for discrepancies in floor height as you move (see the photos on p. 81). With the cabinets aligned, screwed together, and at a consistent height, they can be fastened to the floor.

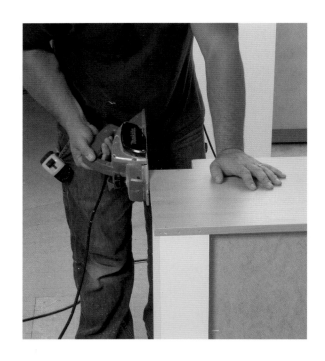

LOWER THE HIGH CABINETS. Using a level that spans from a high cabinet to one already at the correct height, center the bubble, and adjust your compass scribes so that they reflect the height difference. Use the same tool to mark the base of the cabinet for planing.

ADJUST THE HEIGHT. A few strokes with a power plane quickly remove enough stock to level the cabinet. This planer can remove about $\frac{1}{32}$ in. with each pass while providing a smooth finish. Deeper passes leave a rough surface. Planing should be limited to a maximum of about $\frac{3}{8}$ in.

CHECK ONE MORE TIME FOR INCONSISTENT HEIGHT. After the cabinet bottom is trimmed, put the cabinet in place, and check for level side to side and front to back. If necessary, make further adjustments with shims or planing until the cabinet is level in all directions.

FASTEN TO THE FLOOR. After two or three cabinets are screwed to each other, the cabinets are screwed to the floor. Drill pilot holes at an angle with a $\frac{7}{32}$-in. twist bit, and then use $2\frac{1}{2}$-in. square-drive screws to hold the cabinets to the floor.

Create a Seating Area

Rather than having extradeep or extrawide boxes, semicustom cabinets often have extended side panels for scribing to walls or other cabinets. These panels often work in conjunction with factory-finished plywood and solid hardwood to cover cabinet backs and empty cavities. The built-in eating area on this island is defined with a plywood panel that matches the cabinets. These additional parts are cut to size before they're fit and fastened.

TRIM FACTORY-FINISHED PANELS ON SITE. Using a track-guided saw, cut a plywood panel to form one side of the island's eating area (left). Cut it with a 45° bevel to correspond to a bevel on the cabinet's side panel.

GLUE MITERED JOINTS. The end and back panels meet with a mitered joint. A thick bead of wood glue prevents the mitered joint from opening with changes in humidity (left). While the glue dries, the joint is held together with 2-in.-wide masking tape (above).

BLOCKING REINFORCES THE PANEL. Use scraps of hardwood or plywood blocking to reinforce the eating area's plywood panels. Pocket screws are a strong, efficient way to make these connections. Previously installed cabinets make a great workbench for drilling pocket holes.

FASTEN THE BLOCKING. Using 1¼-in. coarse-thread pocket-hole screws, fasten blocking between the top of the plywood and the adjacent cabinet backs. The blocking prevents the plywood panel from warping.

TURN EACH LEG UPSIDE DOWN over where it will be installed so that it can be marked for trimming on a miter saw. Cut the long part of the leg to keep the top consistent.

LOCATE THE LEGS, AND CUT THEM TO LENGTH. A pair of legs support the eating area's overhanging countertop. Use a pair of levels as straightedges to position the legs in plane with the cabinets.

INSTALL AN APRON. Secured with pocket screws, a 2-in.-wide apron under the overhanging countertop supports the legs and provides a finished look. A 6-in. apron on the back of the island holds a receptacle.

ADD BRACING. Two-in.-wide stretchers attach the apron to the back of the cabinets, while angle braces keep the corners square. Both types of bracing are held in place with 1¼-in. coarse-thread pocket screws.

ATTACH THE LEGS TO THE FLOOR. After drilling a hole in the center of the leg, fasten the leg to a 2½-in. drywall screw that's been cut off with lineman's pliers (left). This anchors the leg in place without visible fasteners (below).

Finishing Touches

The finishing touches depend on the individual island, but most islands need drawer and cabinet pulls and some way to hide the obvious seams between cabinets. Appliances and fixtures may be installed now or after the top is in place, depending on the appliances. Once the cabinets are finished, it's time for the fabricator to measure for the countertop.

HIDE THE SEAMS AND SCREWS. The seam at the end of the island where the two cabinets meet is often hidden with a wine rack, bookshelves, or panels. This island has a pair of panels that mimic the cabinet doors (left). The seam between panels is offset from the cabinet seam, locking the cabinets together. Screws installed from the back side are hidden from view (above).

CUT THE FARM-SINK OPENING. Once the cleats that support the sink top are cut and secured to the sides of this cabinet, the installer cuts the blank panel at the front of the cabinet with a jigsaw (left) and cleans it up with a rasp (right). When finished, the sink will be flush with the cabinet.

TIME FOR TEMPLATING

WITH THE CABINETS IN PLACE, the eating area finished, and the farm sink installed, it's time for the stone fabricator to create a template of the countertop. Decisions about thickness, the way the top overhangs the cabinets, and edge treatments should all be decided by this point.

How to Install Inset Cabinet Doors

BY SCOTT GIBSON

Making and fitting cabinet doors takes time, and it has its occasional frustrations. Still, installing doors correctly is one of the real pleasures of cabinetmaking. If everything isn't flat and square or if the hinges aren't installed properly, the doors won't work the way they should. For an overlay cabinet door, the process is more forgiving: The door simply closes against the cabinet or face frame. An inset door is another story. It has to be trimmed to fit the door opening exactly, with an even gap all around between the face frame and the door.

I like the appearance of inset doors because they don't look as clunky as overlay doors. When an inset door is fitted correctly with a narrow, even reveal, the cabinet has a line of detail that is otherwise missing. This more finished look is associated both with traditional designs, such as Shaker, and with more modern styles. A cabinet built with inset doors also says something about the cabinetmaker. Although making inset cabinet doors takes time, the results are worth it to me, and the process goes surprisingly quickly once you've honed the technique.

For this kitchen project, I built the carcases first, then added the face frames. Typically, I use butt hinges (more on that later), so I mark and cut the hinge mortises on the face frames before I attach them to the carcases. I like to cut the hinge mortises on the stiles before the face frames are even glued up. I just pop a piece in the vise, I cut the mortises, and I'm done.

The doors are next. I start by building a door to the same dimensions as the opening. It's tempting to make it slightly smaller so that there's less trimming involved, but that move can backfire. When gluing up the door, make every effort to keep it flat. You can compensate for a slight amount of twist (see "In a Perfect World, Doors Are Flat," on p. 95), but if the door is too badly skewed, you'll have to make another one. If the door or the opening is out of square,

TOOL TALK

THE LIE-NIELSEN® LOW-ANGLE JACK PLANE that I use has a thick plane iron that's set at 12°, which slices easily through difficult end grain. It's pricey, but it's the kind of tool that makes the work much easier. I'm always dragging it out onto my bench.

DECIDE ON THE SIZE OF THE REVEAL. On a tablesaw, cut a shim equal in thickness to the reveal (⅛ in. on a side is typical for paint-grade work), and trim it to length so that it can sit inside the bottom of the door opening.

BEGIN TO TRIM THE DOOR. Use a low-angle jack plane to flatten the bottom of the door. Because the stile's end grain is exposed at the door's top and bottom, work inward from each edge to avoid tearout. Another method is to use a crosscut sled on a tablesaw and, referencing the door's hinge side against the fence, to trim the bottom of the door.

fitting the door may result in a reveal that looks too big. Ideally, the door opening and the door itself will be square, but that's often not the case. Once the cabinet and the door are made, forget about square and deal with what's there.

I trim one edge of the door at a time and then work my way around, beginning with the bottom of the door and ending at the strike-side stile. It's possible to do all of this work with hand tools alone, but it's faster and sometimes more accurate to do at least some of the cutting on a tablesaw and, if you have access to one, a jointer. The tool choice is yours.

When I've fitted the door, I place it in the opening and mark the hinge locations. I like to use good-quality brass butt hinges. To me, butt hinges look best on traditional cabinets. I see that classic hinge barrel paired with an even reveal and think, "That looks right." While I appreciate that European hinges are easy to adjust to get a door to hang properly, I have never gotten past how big and bulky they look when you open the door. I've also used some European hinges that will not hold their adjustment. Surface-mounted hinges look fine on some styles of cabinets, but I never seem to build those styles. Piano hinges are great for heavy, specialty doors, but they're not an everyday item. Ditto for concealed hinges. If I were building cabinets that have really contemporary, minimalist styles, I think that my choices might be somewhat different.

HINGE SIDE IS NEXT TO BE FITTED.

BOTTOM SHIM CREATES A REFERENCE.

DON'T CARE ABOUT SQUARE. The idea is to fit the door in the opening, not make a square door. With the door in the opening atop the shim, press the hinge side against the stile. Ideally, there should be a consistently tight fit from top to bottom on that side. This gets a little awkward because the door won't go completely into the opening quite yet. (Just try not to drop the door, as the author did.)

ADJUST BY SHAVING. If necessary, use a jointer or similar plane to adjust the door's hinge side until it fits tightly against the face-frame stile while resting on the bottom shim.

USE A BOARD JACK

IT'S DIFFICULT TO SECURE A CABINET DOOR in a bench vise so that the work is well supported and at a convenient height. The author made this support (historically called a board jack) from plywood scraps. He attached an appropriately sized leg to a block screwed to the benchtop, then reinforced the leg with a plywood gusset. For this job, he made one jack for working vertically and another for working horizontally.

DON'T REMOVE TOO MUCH MATERIAL. The top is trimmed in two steps to minimize the risk of taking off too much of the door. Begin by placing the door on the bottom shim and marking both sides of the top of the door so that it will fit just inside the opening (top left and above). Trim off the excess on the tablesaw with a crosscut sled (bottom left). Remember to reference the hinge side against the fence. If the amount to be removed isn't a 90° cut, insert shims between the sled fence and the door edge to adjust the angle of the cut. Check the fit, and then mark the reveal at both sides so that it equals the reveal at the bottom. Trim the reveal to the marks with the crosscut sled, using the same shims if necessary.

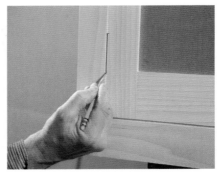

GO FOR THE TIGHT FIT FIRST. It's best to cut the hinge mortises on the face frame before it's assembled. If you haven't done so, though, now's the time. Mark and trim the strike edge of the door (above), either with a pass on the tablesaw or with a handplane. The door should squeeze into the opening so that there will be just enough space to install hinges. With the bottom of the door still resting on the shim, mark the hinge locations on the door.

TOOL TALK

ONE OF MY FAVORITE TOOLS in my shop is a simple knife made from a short length of an old file. The handle isn't fancy, but the blade is superb. My dad gave me the knife when I first started making furniture. Now that he's gone, it's pretty special. Because it has a double bevel, it's not good as a marking knife, but it has many other uses.

Possibly my most important tool for projects such as cabinet doors is my Lie-Nielsen low-angle block plane. A standard block plane's blade is mounted at a 20° angle to the sole. A low-angle's blade is mounted at 12°, which makes it possible to plane end grain and cross-grain without tearout. It's great for removing millmarks, adjusting the fit of a drawer or door, truing up mortise-and-tenon joints, and a hundred other things. Lie-Nielsen uses excellent steel that takes a good edge and stays sharp for a long time. The body is bronze and doesn't rust. I've had this plane for a long time and have dropped it on concrete floors more than once, so it's a little dinged. Still, it works beautifully. My son made the leather case for it.

CUT THE MORTISES. Move the door into a bench vise and mark the mortise locations with a chisel. With a carbide straight spiral bit chucked into a laminate trimmer, use the hinge plate as a gauge to set the depth of the bit and cut the mortises (above). A piece of ¾-in. scrap clamped to the back side of the door creates a more stable base for the trimmer (left).

KEEP YOUR OPTIONS OPEN. Remove the shim, hang the door with only one screw per hinge leaf, and check the fit. The strike side will probably need an adjustment or a back bevel. If not, and if the door closes evenly against the stop, put in the rest of the hinge screws.

The Correct Reveal Is Consistent and Not Too Thin

After you've built and installed a few doors, it's easy to see where the pitfalls lie. For the most part, it's all about the reveal. It's tempting to make a very narrow reveal (1/16 in. or less) because it looks so classy when it's done. Tolerances this small, though, lead to trouble. In the summer, even frame-and-panel doors swell slightly; at any time of year, the wood can twist or warp slightly, causing the doors to bind. This is much harder to judge on painted doors because you have to take into account the thickness of the paint when you fit them. Going back to refit a door that's painted is a nuisance.

Doors that are too loose look like the builder didn't care enough to get it right. An uneven reveal is worse because your eye instantly picks up on it. It's obviously out of level or plumb, like a crooked picture frame on a wall. I think the best compromise is to err a little on the loose side and make the reveal even.

IN A PERFECT WORLD, DOORS ARE FLAT

THEORETICALLY, ALL DOORS AND FACE FRAMES are square and flat; in reality, they're often not. A door that's slightly twisted might hit the strike with one corner before the other and not close properly (see the photos below).

There's no perfect solution to this problem, but you can try adjusting the position of the hinges on either the door or the cabinet to compensate. Take out the single screw you've used, move the hinge in or out, and insert a screw through another hole to fix the hinge in its new position. You can glue a sliver of wood into the first hole and redrill it later.

It may take more than one try and adjustments in both hinges before you find the best compromise. You want the door to close evenly on the stop; a tiny lip at one corner of the opening won't be noticeable.

If you can't get all the way there by adjusting the hinge positions, plane the back side of the door where it first strikes the stop. Reducing the thickness of the door by a few passes of a plane shouldn't be visible to the casual eye.

WHEN A DOOR GOES WRONG. A warped door won't land evenly on the strike side and may protrude beyond the face frame at the top or bottom.

SHIFT ONE HINGE. By moving the location of the hinge diagonally opposite the problem corner (left), it's possible to make the door land evenly on the strike. Mark the leaf location before moving it.

REDUCE THE DOOR. The alternative is to plane the back side of the door where it hits the strike (right) until the entire side hits evenly.

Upgrade to a Trash Drawer

BY REX ALEXANDER

After I've built and installed a custom kitchen, the feature that gets the most praise isn't the finish, the way I've carefully aligned the grain patterns, or the consistent reveals around the doors and drawers. It's always the pullout trash drawer, and for good reason. Not only does the trash drawer hide refuse and recyclables, but it also helps contain the odor that can come from an empty cat-food can or the grease from last night's dinner.

The best aspect of this design is that it can be an easy upgrade to integrate a drawer into an existing cabinet, preferably in or near the sink base. Once you've built the drawer, it's only a matter of removing the cabinet door and installing new drawer slides. Commercially produced versions are available, but why spend the money when you can do it yourself for a few bucks?

The materials are easy to find in any home center or lumberyard. I've found that a good size for the plastic wastebasket is about 10 in. wide, 14 in. deep, and 16 in. tall, which leaves enough room for a drawer above. For drawer slides, I use simple epoxy-coated, side-mount models from Blum (www.blum.com). They are inexpensive, but they're rated for 100 lb. If you choose a different type of slide, be sure to determine the necessary clearance before building the trash drawer.

Build the Drawer

Made from ½-in. birch plywood, the trash unit is essentially a drawer turned upside down, reinforced with an angled support, and attached to the cabinet door. Start by cutting the sides for the drawer and joining them with biscuits.

Make a cardboard template that fits snugly beneath the outside rim of the wastebasket; the templated hole is traced onto the top. After drilling a hole for blade access, cut out the basket hole with a jigsaw. Use a 4-in-1 rasp or sandpaper to clean up the edges for a final fit. Nail and glue the top into place flush with the top edges of the drawer.

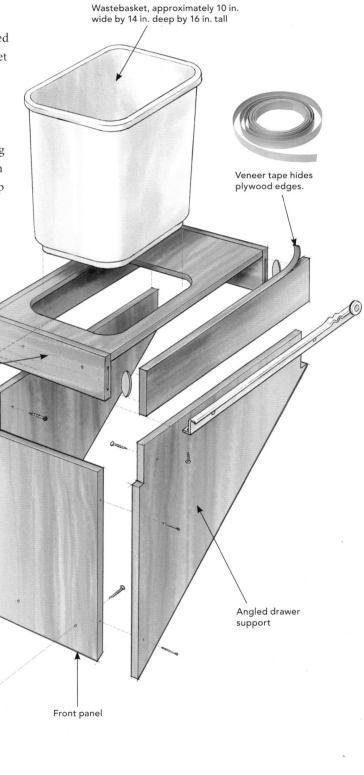

Wastebasket, approximately 10 in. wide by 14 in. deep by 16 in. tall

Veneer tape hides plywood edges.

Drawer

Existing cabinet door

Angled drawer support

Front panel

IN FACE-FRAME CABINETS, you can screw spacers to the cabinet sides, as the author is doing here, or you can use a slide hanger, as seen on the back of the slide in the drawing on p. 97.

USE TAPE AND SHIMS TO INSTALL THE DOOR. Along the bottom of the cabinet opening lay shims of the intended reveal thickness.

Support the Door

Notch the angled drawer supports on the front and back so they slide inside the drawer. Fasten them with 1-in. screws.

Cut the front panel, then glue and nail it between the angled supports. Drill four ¼-in. holes, two in the drawer front and two in the front panel for the screws that attach the drawer to the cabinet door.

Hang It in the Cabinet

Before you install drawer slides, make a jig from ¼-in. medium-density fiberboard (MDF) or plywood. Drill holes that correspond to those on the slides and attach the jig to a small block at one end. With the jig aligned to the slides' position, use an awl to start pilot holes for the mounting screws.

Use tape and shims to install the door. Drill ¼-in. holes in the drawer box's front face and near the bottom of the front panel. Attach heavy-duty double-stick carpet tape to the front of the unit. Lay shims of the intended reveal thickness (usually about ⅛ in.) along the bottom of the cabinet opening. Remove the backer on the tape, position the door on the shims, and push the door onto the tape. After checking the reveals on the sides, ease out the drawer, and screw the door to the unit from inside.

Countertops

Amazing Countertops

BY ROB YAGID

BAMBOO

PAPER

SOLID GLASS

RECYCLED GLASS

SCRAP METAL

Deep into a kitchen-remodeling project, I'm still undecided about what type of countertops to install. Few elements of a kitchen draw as much attention—or as much money—so I'm considering my options carefully. Like most people, I want countertops that are going to withstand years of abuse but that will still look beautiful when I'm ready to sell sometime down the road. I'm not prepared to settle on just any countertop material, though, and going against popular opinion, I'm steadfast in my aversion to granite.

Don't get me wrong. Granite and other natural stones are great countertop materials. Slabs are available nearly everywhere, they're durable, and they look great. But it seems as if everyone is putting stone counters, especially granite, in their homes these days. Granite is so prevalent that it has become, to a degree, boring. What was once a material used to achieve a distinctive, high-end style has now become expected. Solid-surface material and engineered stone don't offer much more excitement. Instead, I'm considering countertop materials that few people know about and that even fewer are using in their homes.

If you're looking for a countertop that will make a dramatic style statement instead of helping create a kitchen that feels common, consider products made of glass, paper, bamboo, or scrap metal. Besides being durable and beautiful, many of these products promote sustainable building practices by recycling unlikely materials. They might not be the most popular products on the market or the most classic ones, but that's a good thing.

Bamboo Is Renewable and Durable

It's hard not to be impressed by bamboo. The material is actually a type of grass, but it's 16% harder than maple. Bamboo reaches harvestable maturity in less than 5 years—as opposed to the 50-year to 70-year growing period of hardwoods—and continuously replenishes itself by sprouting new shoots from an extensive root system. With its warm natural appearance, and its ability to be easily cut and shaped with common tools, it's no wonder bamboo is being made into kitchen countertops.

Strips of bamboo are assembled into counters in end-grain, edge-grain, or flat-grain orientations in dimensions as large as 30 in. wide, 96 in. long, and 2 in. thick, though custom sizes are available. Bamboo can withstand a significant amount of abuse but should be treated like any wood counter. Trivets

TONES AND TEXTURES CAN VARY. Edge-grain bamboo counters tend to be slightly more monochromatic, while other grain orientations offer more visual texture. The darker color of bamboo is achieved by heating the material, which caramelizes its natural sugars.

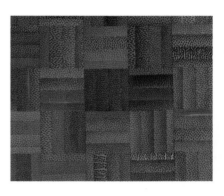

NOT YOUR ORDINARY BUTCHER BLOCK. End-grain bamboo countertops conjure up images of traditional maple butcher block. End-grain bamboo, often referred to as parquet, is significantly harder than maple, making it a more durable cutting surface.

SOURCES

BAMBOO REVOLUTION
www.bamboorevolution.com

ENDURAWOOD™
www.endurawood.com

SMITH & FONG
www.plyboo.com

TOTALLY BAMBOO
www.totallybamboo.com

prevent burns from hot pots and pans, and an application of penetrating sealer helps prevent staining. Water-based polyurethane sealers tend to leave bamboo looking dull, so manufacturers recommend the use of food-safe tung oil to seal all faces of the countertop, including the bottom.

Like wood, bamboo countertops are only marginally stable. Dimensional changes occur with seasonal fluctuations in temperature and humidity. Unlike wood, bamboo shouldn't be stained because achieving an even appearance is often difficult.

A major benefit of using a bamboo countertop is that the entire length of its surface can be used as a cutting board. Any scratches or knife marks can be left or sanded away. A yearly application of proper tung oil will help keep the countertop looking new.

Paper Counters Look and Feel Like Stone

Paper might not seem like a suitable raw material for countertop fabrication, but when saturated with resin, heated, and compressed, the result is surprisingly stonelike. This type of paper-based panel is durable and has been used for years in industrial and marine applications, while also being the surface of choice for skateboard parks. Several manufacturers make these counters, but different processes result in varying performance traits.

Panels made of postconsumer waste paper are typically sought for their green attributes. This recycled paper is less uniform than virgin material, however, and can result in a countertop that varies in thickness, which can lead to installation difficulties—

EASILY TOOLED, NOT EASILY DAMAGED. Paper countertops can be cut or routed to have crisp, defined edge profiles. However, manufacturers suggest that paper counters be finished with eased edges because the material can be sharp. Cutting and shaping ease are by no means a reflection of this countertop's surprisingly strong durability.

especially at butt joints. Virgin material, though less green, allows for tighter tolerances during fabrication.

The type of resin used to bind paper together also has an impact on the countertop. Phenolic resin, though extremely strong, is caramel in color, which limits the range of color choices. Also, UV-exposure causes phenolic resins to darken over time.

Klip Biotechnologies LLC has a paper-based countertop, EcoTop®, which is made with a different type of manufacturing process. Joel Klippert, the creator of EcoTop, describes the material as "a blend of bamboo fibers, which add dimensional stability to the counter; recycled demolition wood fibers; and recycled paper." These materials are bound together with a VOC-free water-based resin. The resin won't darken due to UV-exposure and is clear, which enables Klip Biotechnologies to make counters from white to black and many colors in between. Unlike other paper-based counters, EcoTop does not need to be installed by a certified technician.

All paper-based countertops can be cut and shaped with carbide-tipped blades and router bits, just like solid-surface material. Panels are available in sizes as large as 5 ft. wide, 12 ft. long, and 1¼ in. thick, depending on the manufacturer. These countertops are stain resistant but should still be properly finished. Some manufacturers provide their own finish product, which is a combination of natural oils and waxes that enrich the appearance of the top while protecting it from damage.

Damage that does occur, such as scratches and scorch marks, can be sanded out of the top. However, it's difficult to do without creating a blemish, so refinishing the entire top is recommended. A yearly application of mineral oil or an approved finish will help keep this top looking new.

Solid Glass Is Modern and Easy to Clean

Glass countertops bring a clean, modern look to a kitchen. Contrary to popular perception, they are durable and are extremely sanitary because glass is nonporous and easy to clean. Glass countertops can be installed in a variety of ways with edge treatments that range from polished to chiseled in appearance.

A glass top being fixed directly to a cabinet typically receives a coat of paint on its bottom surface before being secured with silicone caulk. The paint helps hide the contents of the cabinet and gives the counter a finished look. Glass can also be installed over an opaque substrate like melamine or suspended on piers so that it appears to be floating. Stainless-steel locating pins can also be used to keep these countertops in place.

Fabricators use three types of glass to create countertops. Float glass, the material found in modern-day windowpanes, can be used to make counters as large as roughly 6 ft. wide, 10 ft. long, and ¾ in. thick. Manufacturers often temper this glass to improve its strength and safety in the unlikely event that it breaks.

Slump glass is distinguished by its shapes and textures. Slump glass is simply float glass that is placed on top of a carved mold, then heated so that the glass relaxes and "slumps" into the contours of the mold.

Kiln-fired glass, also known as cast glass or art glass, is made of recycled glass fragments that have been placed in a kiln and heated until they bond back together. Kiln-fired glass is as strong as the other types of glass, if not stronger. Thick glass countertops are most often made of kiln-fired glass; they can be more than 2 in. thick. Kiln-fired tops

SOURCES

ECOTOP
www.kliptech.com

PAPERSTONE®
www.paperstoneproducts.com

RICHLITE®
www.richlite.com

SHETKASTONE
www.shetkastone.com

BEAUTY MEETS FUNCTION, AT A COST. Manufacturers can form glass into nearly any shape, texture, and color. This allows their tops to have great visual appeal while masking fingerprints and scratches. Similar to most other art, the more elaborate the piece (left), the higher the price tag.

can be made only as large as the kiln fabricators have access to, typically 6 ft. wide by 12 ft. long.

Glass-countertop fabricators are split in their recommendations for where their products can or should be used. "Glass counters shouldn't be used anywhere they'll receive a significant amount of abuse," says Jim Duncan of Duncan Glass. Along with some other manufacturers, Duncan thinks that glass tops should be reserved for nonutility areas in the kitchen, such as accent pieces or island tops. Others say that glass performs like natural stone and can be used safely as a work surface. Fabricators agree on one point, however: Glass scratches. Although scratches and fingerprints are less noticeable on a textured or colored top, repair or replacement of a glass counter can be expensive.

Glass tops have few maintenance requirements. Just clean them with a nonabrasive product like Windex®.

SOURCES

BROOKS CUSTOM
www.brookscustom.com

DUNCAN GLASS
www.jduncanglass.com

SMOKE AND MIRRORS
www.smokeandmirrorsllc.com

THINKGLASS™
www.thinkglass.com

ULTRAGLAS®
www.ultraglas.com

Recycled-Glass Counters Are Now Easier to Find

Although countertops made of cement and recycled glass have been around for more than a decade, production has been low, and manufacturers have been scarce. These days, more and more companies are salvaging glass fragments, which are available in countless colors and shapes, and mixing them with cement or epoxy resin to make countertops. Recycled glass is a major component of each mix, making up roughly 75% to 85% of the finished countertop, depending on the manufacturer.

Fabricators shape and install these countertops like natural stone, with a similar selection of edge profiles. Sizes as large as 9 ft. by 5 ft. are available. Leaving a hot pot on the surface won't result in burn marks on a recycled-glass countertop, but it could affect the top's sealer. For this reason, trivets are recommended.

Recycled-glass counters constructed with a cement binder are slightly different from those made with epoxy resin. The cement binder can be stained by acids in wine, vinegar, and citrus juices, so these countertops need to be sealed, maintained, and cleaned of spills with more diligence than counters made with resin. Resin, however, is not as hard as a cement-based surface and always requires the use of trivets and cutting boards.

Most cement-based counters come sealed but require resealing every couple of years with an impregnating sealer. Resin-based counters don't need sealing but should be polished with a paste wax to maintain their finish.

SOURCES

ENVIROGLAS
www.enviroglasproducts.com

ICESTONE®
www.icestone.biz

TIGER MOUNTAIN INNOVATIONS
www.trinityglassproducts.com

VETRAZZO
www.vetrazzo.com

FROM THE CURB TO THE KITCHEN. When bottles and windows are broken, windshields fractured, and traffic lights decommissioned, some of this glass is recycled, and a lot of it ends up in the landfill. More and more of it, however, is being used to make unique, durable countertops.

MAKING CONCRETE COUNTERS IS EASIER THAN EVER

BECAUSE THEY ARE CRAFTED BY HAND, no two concrete countertops are ever exactly alike, resulting in a top that evokes a true artisanal feel. While the number of concrete countertop specialists has continued to grow, so too have the resources for first-time fabricators.

Manufacturers like Cheng Design® and Buddy Rhodes now provide all the materials needed to design and fabricate concrete countertops. They sell specially blended concrete mixes, pigments, sealers, and sink molds. Instructional videos and books are also available. They even host instructional workshops around the country.

If you've been having trouble finding a durable countertop that has true custom appeal, there has never been a better time to build it yourself.

SOURCES

BUDDY RHODES
www.buddyrhodes.com

CHENG DESIGN
www.chengdesign.com

To locate other fabricators and suppliers:
Concrete Network: www.concretenetwork.com

Laminate Never Looked So Good

Created in 1914 for use as an electric insulator, plastic laminate has long proven itself as a highly durable material. It wasn't until many years after its creation, though, that people realized it would make an excellent countertop surface. Laminate is nonporous, stain resistant, and warm to the touch. It also absorbs impact (which leads to fewer broken glasses) and requires little maintenance. When laminate is bypassed as a countertop material, it's often because of a style threshold defined by shiny surfaces and poor imitations of stone and wood.

Modern laminates, though, are better than they have ever been, thanks to higher-quality decorative layers, newly developed textured surfaces, and refined edge details that eliminate the telltale seam that marks laminate transitions. Just about anyone with basic carpentry skills can fabricate laminate counters, and with today's products, they can create countertops that look anything but plastic.

UNIFORM EDGES ARE MORE CONVINCING. By eliminating the seam at a laminate top's edges, manufacturers like VT Industries can create counters that are more easily passed off as solid-slab material.

Scrap-Metal Countertops Save Resources

As the green-building trend continues to grow, products made from recycled materials are becoming more popular. Of the nearly 3 million tons of aluminum that are discarded every year in the United States, a small portion is being used to create countertops that can set your kitchen apart.

Available through dealers and fabricators nationwide, Alkemi countertops are made by mixing aluminum shavings with UV-stable polymeric resin. The countertop material contains at least 60% postindustrial scrap aluminum, which conventional recyclers don't use. Installed over a plywood substrate with silicone caulk, these counters are easily worked by carbide-tipped tools and are maintained like ordinary solid-surface materials.

Eleek Inc. of Portland, Ore., fabricates solid ¼-in.-thick countertops and tiles made of recycled aluminum that has been cast in reusable silicone molds. The products are an environmentally friendly alternative to metal countertops such as stainless steel, zinc, and pewter and still have an easy-to-maintain, industrial aesthetic. Each countertop is custom-built and available with an integrated rolled front edge and backsplash, so further on-site fabrication is not needed. Eleek's countertops and tiles are installed with mastic when placed over cement board or construction adhesive when applied to a plywood substrate. Eleek's products come with one caveat. They can't be cut on site without compromising the powder-coated finish. This places a much larger emphasis on precise templating and layouts before ordering.

SOURCES

FORMICA®
www.formica.com

PIONITE®
www.pionite.com

VT INDUSTRIES
www.vtindustries.com

WILSONART®
www.wilsonart.com

SOURCES

ALKEMI
www.renewedmaterials.com

ELEEK INC.
www.eleekinc.com

POLISHED OR HONED, BUT ALWAYS MADE WITH ALUMINUM. Alkemi uses only aluminum shavings in its countertops. The variety of colored shavings, like bronze or copper, is acquired by anodizing the shavings before mixing them with resin. Alkemi tops are available with either a smooth, honed surface (above left) or a textured surface (above right).

ARTISTIC FINISHES HELP CREATE NATURAL SURFACES. Eleek countertops and tiles can be powder coated in a variety of colors or given a natural-looking patina by an in-house artisan. Their patina finishes help convey truly custom work, and no two products look exactly the same.

Making Wood Countertops

BY DAN VOS

The most common thing I hear when people first see my wood countertops is, "Wow, that's beautiful. But are wood countertops durable enough for a kitchen?" My answer is, "Mine are."

Having made a career of building wood countertops, I've developed construction methods and finishing techniques that make them both durable and beautiful. Beauty comes from the nature of wood itself, from the way I orient its grain, and from the finish I apply to it. Durability comes from design and construction specifications appropriate for the use of the top. For instance, no matter how much you love the way that it looks, a face-grain pine top is not an appropriate chopping surface. Pine is soft, and face-grain construction is not durable enough to handle pressure from knives.

My shop is production oriented, with special tools and work surfaces that allow us to build large, complicated countertops efficiently. But as you'll see in the process of making the face-grain walnut island counter shown here, all you need to make a wood counter is a large work surface, a jointer, a planer, a router, a random-orbit sander, and a handful of bar clamps. Before you jump into a countertop project, though, it's a good idea to explore the aesthetics and durability of different wood species and three types of construction for wood counters. Then you can determine if a top like this one is right for you.

Expect Wood to Change Color and Move

I try to guide my clients toward a wood species and grain orientation that appeals to their aesthetics and also suits how they will use the countertop. Where nothing more than a tough chopping surface is what the client wants, I usually recommend an end-grain top of hard sugar maple (more on grain orientation later). When a homeowner wants visual interest, there are lots of wood species that make great face-grain or edge-grain tops. Among domestic hardwoods, cherry, walnut, beech, and oak are good choices; among tropical hardwoods, sipo, santos, African mahogany, and jatoba (Brazilian cherry) are all stable and are all easy to work with.

I don't get caught up with the hardness ratings of various wood species, but I avoid some that are either inordinately difficult to work or are better suited to outdoor use, such as cypress, cedar, and hemlock. Also, some of the superhard tropical woods, such as bloodwood and ipé, have problems with end-checking.

Bear in mind that wood can change color over time due to age, ambient conditions, or the type of finish you use. For example, the tung oil–based finishes I use bring out amber tones in lighter woods, and they deepen and enrich darker species.

FACE GRAIN. With the milled faces of each board oriented up, face-grain tops are typically the easiest to glue up. They are not the most durable or knife-friendly counters, but if wood grain and color are what you're after, this type of construction may be right for you. See this walnut top built on the following pages.

END GRAIN. End-grain, or butcher-block, counters like this teak top are the most functional. Not only can they handle repeated chopping but they're also self-healing. Maintenance is as simple as occasional applications of mineral oil. These busy-looking tops are the most challenging to build.

EDGE GRAIN. Ripping flatsawn stock into strips and gluing them up on edge creates a top that has less of the color and grain characteristics of a face-grain top but more durability. As seen in this mesquite island top, it takes a lot of 1-in. to 2-in. strips to make an edge-grain top, so the glue-up is a bit more challenging.

MILL THE STOCK. For a standard 1½-in.-thick countertop, I start with 2-in. roughsawn boards. I buy boards longer than I need and have enough material to make the blank wider than the finished top will be. Before choosing or arranging boards, I skip-plane each one (see the top board in the photo at left) to reveal its grain, color, and blemishes.

PREPARE THE SURFACES' MATING EDGES. Use a jointer or a router and guide to create one perfectly straight edge. If you use the latter technique, rip the board on a tablesaw, removing just enough material to create a parallel straightedge. Flatten the board on a jointer and plane it to within 1/32 in. of final thickness. The remaining 1/32 in. will be removed later when the blank is sanded.

Once you determine which species to use, make sure to buy kiln-dried stock to minimize the potential for movement. I test one or two boards from every order to be sure the moisture content is between 6% and 9%. Still, every board and every top will move, especially across the grain. You have to take that movement into account when you build and install a wood top.

To balance the stresses between boards, it is a good practice to alternate the growth-ring pattern in the glue-up. It is also a good idea to turn boards frequently during the planing and jointing process. Working both sides of the boards before glue-up can remove some of their internal stresses and reduce their propensity to go their own way. If you have time, you also should acclimate the wood to the site before gluing up the counter.

To accommodate wood movement when installing wood counters, I fasten them through slotted screw holes. For tops held tight to a wall, you can use a matching backsplash to hide seasonal gaps or slot only the screw holes nearest the overhanging areas. The top should transfer most of its stress toward the path of least resistance.

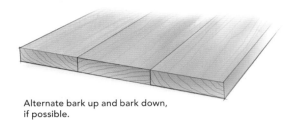

Alternate bark up and bark down, if possible.

LAY OUT FOR LOOKS FIRST. Pick the best face of each board, and lay the boards side by side. To help keep the top flat over time, try to arrange them so that they alternate bark up and bark down (see the drawing at right). But don't sacrifice a perfect face for a top that will be well fastened to the cabinets. Draw a triangle across all the boards to maintain the arrangement.

> **TIP**
>
> **IF THE BOARDS JOIN NICELY** at the center but the ends are open, you need to get the edges straighter. If the opposite is true and you're making a long top, you can rely on clamps to close a gap up to $\frac{1}{16}$ in. Springing the joint in this manner builds stress into the top that actually counters potential wood movement.

Build It for the Way You'll Use It

When homeowners say they want a "pretty" wood counter, I usually end up building a face-grain top like the one featured here. The wide face of a board is where color and grain come alive. However, the cost of the rift-sawn, quartersawn, and flitchsawn stock that I commonly choose for these tops can be significantly more than what you would pay for suitable edge- or end-grain materials. Face-grain tops have pros and cons when it comes to durability. A teak face-grain top, for example, is an excellent choice for sink areas because it likes water, but you'll cry wet tears on it the first time it's marked by a knife.

When I'm putting together a face-grain top, much more effort goes into the pre-glue-up layout than with other kinds of tops. I skip-plane both faces of the rough boards to reveal flaws, color, and grain

before choosing which to use. Then I carefully lay out the boards, keeping visual characteristics and internal-stress characteristics in mind until I'm satisfied with the balance of cosmetics and stability. Just before finishing, I spend extra time with face-grain tops, detailing small flaws with colored epoxy. Gluing up a face-grain top, however, is easier than gluing up edge- or end-grain counters because there are typically fewer boards to join.

Edge-grain tops offer the best combination of durability, beauty, and cost. When made from boards 1 in. to 2 in. wide, they can show a lot of color and a straight, elegant grain pattern, but when used for food prep and chopping, edge-grain tops scar and acquire a patina. The glue-up is more involved with edge-grain tops than with face-grain tops because there are more glue joints. Here, you can save money on lumber by starting with flatsawn boards that will be ripped and can be oriented to reveal a rift-sawn or quartersawn face.

GLUE UP THE BLANK. For most tops, I use Titebond II® (or Titebond II Extend for a few more minutes of open time). On oily tropical hardwoods, I use West System® epoxy (105 resin and 205 hardener). Glue joints are generally stronger than wood, so I don't biscuit the tops for strength. Sometimes I use them for alignment. For tops wider than 36 in. or that use more than five boards, consider gluing up the top in two halves and then gluing the halves together. Leave the top clamped for at least four hours, preferably overnight.

GLUE BOTH FACES LIBERALLY. Starting about 3 in. in from the ends, space clamps every 12 in. Top clamps will be placed between the bottom clamps after the glue is applied. Start with an outside board, tip it up, and run a glue-line down the middle. You can't put on too much glue, but you can use too little. Use a solder brush to spread glue.

ADD PRESSURE A LITTLE AT A TIME. Start by tightening the middle clamp just enough to hold the top together. Check the joints for alignment, and tighten the remaining clamps from the outside, bottom clamp first, then top, then bottom, and so on. Check the top with a straightedge between clamps. Cupping reveals uneven pressure. You'll need to loosen the clamps and start again. Scrape away glue squeeze-out with a putty knife.

End-grain counters are the last word in chopping. They are resistant to scarring, are self-healing, are easy on fine knife edges, and soak up finishes like nobody's business. But end grain is a busy look. There are lots of glue joints and lots of growth rings. Performance comes at a price, too. Not only are these the most expensive tops I make, but because of the laborious construction process, they're also the most difficult to manage in the shop, being fussy to put together and somewhat brittle until installed. It doesn't matter what type of stock you use for an end-grain top as long as it is all the same. In this way, the individual pieces expand and contract similarly.

Be Prepared to Work Quickly

I'm often asked what tools are absolutely essential, even for someone planning to build only one wood countertop. I think that a 10-in. tablesaw, a 6-in. jointer, and a portable planer are important to get the job done right. I assume that anyone planning to build a countertop has a router and a random-orbit sander. The number of bar clamps you need depends on the length of the top, but a general rule is one clamp per foot, plus one.

I started making wood tops as an amateur woodworker, and the biggest mistake I made back then was not sufficiently planning for handling and working large boards and slabs. Today, I've tweaked my production shop to the nth degree. I have plenty of handling clearance, but I keep machines close enough to make it easy to move materials around. You might not have the luxury of a space as large as mine, but with careful planning before you begin to build, you can spare yourself a lot of unnecessary frustration.

The first steps require milling long boards with a planer and jointer and ripping them on a tablesaw or with a circular saw and straightedge. Here, dust control is an important consideration. For the remainder of the work, you need a well-lit open space, preferably a workbench, though you can glue up a top on the floor. The space should be easy to keep clean, within reach of an outlet, and easy to maneuver around from all sides.

MAKE SHAPES AND CUTOUTS WITH A TEMPLATE. First, use the template to trace the shape on the top. Rough-cut the shape with a jigsaw; then use the template again to guide a router and pattern bit to shape the top. Use the same process for sink cutouts, but work with the top upside down. This way, you can screw the template to the top.

SHAPE AND SAND THE TOP. I make the blank approximately 2 in. longer and ¾ in. wider than needed so that the first step out of the clamps is to cut it to size. Start by ripping one edge and then using it as a reference to rip the top parallel and crosscut to square. Shaping and sanding require a series of sandpapers from 60 grit to 220 grit.

FILL KNOTS AND BLEMISHES WITH EPOXY. After scraping away any loose material, use five-minute epoxy with a coloring dye (www.homesteadfinishingproducts.com) to fill knots and other blemishes.

CUT TO LENGTH AND WIDTH, PARALLEL AND SQUARE. With a circular saw outfitted with a high-quality blade and edge guide, rip one of the long edges. Measure across for a parallel rip. Repeat this process to crosscut the ends if they're being cut square.

SAND, THEN SAND MORE. With 60-grit sandpaper on a random-orbit sander, correct any cosmetic defects, paying special attention to the joints. Use a straight-edge to make sure that the top is perfectly flat. Sand with 80-, 100-, 120-, and 180-grit sandpaper. Start sanding the edges once you've gotten to the 120-grit paper. Wet the top with mineral spirits to reveal remaining defects.

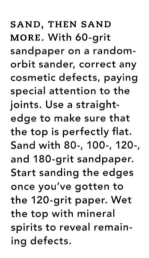

PROFILE THE EDGES. Use a bottom-mount, bearing-guided router bit. Depending on the profile, you might need to make multiple passes. Sand the profile with 120- to 180-grit sandpaper. Soften or ease all sharp edges. Finally, sand the entire top to 220 grit.

Once you begin the glue-up, you have to work quickly. You have only about eight minutes, so take the time to get the clamps spaced out and ready to use and have glue bottles, brushes, and cleanup supplies close at hand. It's also a good idea to have someone available to help because a lot needs to happen during those eight minutes.

When the clamps come off, you'll have to manage the large, heavy blank. Consider making a simple cart with heavy-duty casters. You also should make screw blocks (¾-in. plywood cut into 2-in. by 3-in. pieces, with a 1⅝-in. drywall screw flush-set through one side). The screw blocks are used to raise the top above the work surface to allow air to circulate, which helps prevent the top from warping and cupping, and to make it easier to apply finish to the edges.

INSTALL IT WITH MOVEMENT IN MIND

USE SLOTTED SCREW HOLES
Fastening the counter through elongated screw holes in the bracing at the top of the cabinet allows the counter to move freely as the boards expand and contract.

DON'T USE ADHESIVES UNLESS YOU HAVE TO
If you glue down the top, it won't be able to move and can crack. Bar tops set on pony walls or other narrow edges, however, may need adhesive to keep the top stable.

SUPPORT OVERHANGS
An overhang more than 4 in. on an edge should have support such as a corbel or a decorative or hidden bracket. Overhanging ends, on the other hand, need no extra support. In this direction, the wood countertop is inherently strong.

SITE MODIFICATIONS NEED TO BE SEALED
If you scribe the countertop to fit tightly to a wall or cabinet or make a penetration for a faucet or sink on site, be sure to reapply finish to the cut area.

KEEP WATER FROM GETTING TRAPPED
Standing water will eventually erode even the most durable materials. No matter what type of sink or faucet you install, make sure to apply a heavy bead of caulk between the sink or faucet and countertop.

Renewable Finishes for a Long-Lasting Countertop

Like choosing a wood species and construction technique, I choose the most appropriate finish based on how the top will be used. For tough, hard, built-up protection, I use Waterlox, which combines the amber tone of tung oil with hardeners to create a film on the surface of the counter. For tops that will be used for food preparation, I use a mix of tung oil and citrus solvent, which is food safe. This penetrating finish cures in the grain but doesn't build up on the surface. For smaller end-grain chopping blocks, regular applications of mineral oil are sufficient. These finishes are easy to repair and renew, which is the key to a long-lasting wood countertop, and both are water resistant.

Whichever finish I'm using, I work in a finishing room isolated from the dust and debris of the fabrication shop. If you don't have this luxury, make sure to clean the work area before finishing. And even though these finishes are safe, make sure you have adequate ventilation and wear gloves.

FINISH THE COUNTER. For most tops, I use one of two tung oil–based finishes: Waterlox or a 50/50 mix of pure tung oil and citrus solvent, shown here. No matter what finish I'm using, I coat all surfaces, including the bottom. While I work, the top rests on the tips of drywall screws driven through small plywood blocks placed atop the worktable.

FLOOD AND WIPE THE FIRST COATS. A wood counter lets you know how much finish it needs by the way it absorbs (or doesn't). Most wood species suck up the first two coats, so start by flooding the top with a foam brush. After a few minutes, wipe off the excess finish.

WET-SAND THE LAST COAT. When the counter stops absorbing the finish at a dramatic rate, likely by the third coat, apply the finish, and wet-sand it with fine foam sanding pads. Once you've sanded the entire top, wipe off the excess finish. Use a power buffer to bring the finished top to life.

Tiling a Backsplash

BY TOM MEEHAN

Saturday is estimate day at our store, Cape Cod Tileworks. Of the five or six estimates we do on Saturday mornings, at least a third of them are for kitchen backsplashes. Whether the room is new or old, a backsplash is a great opportunity to express a kitchen's qualities, including color, creativity, boldness, subtlety, and craftsmanship. If you haven't done a lot of tiling, a backsplash is a great way to get your feet wet.

Layout: A Road Map for the Backsplash

Once the tile has been selected, the next step is layout. For this project, my client chose tumbled-marble tile. Its coarse natural texture makes a particularly nice contrast to a smooth, shiny kitchen countertop, such as granite.

The layout for most of this backsplash is fairly simple: three courses of 4-in. by 4-in. tile topped off

by a narrow border; a filler course takes care of the space between the border and the wall cabinets. The challenging part is the patterned area behind the stove. Taller and more intricate than the rest of the backsplash, this area requires a layout that is dead-on accurate (see the photos below). My first step is measuring the exact dimensions of that space.

Over the years, I've found that doing the layout directly on the wall doesn't work well. Instead, I draw a full-size layout of the patterned area on a sheet of cardboard. Then I cut and arrange all the tiles as needed to fit the layout. I don't start to set tile on the wall until the test-fit is complete. This backsplash features small square dots at the intersections of the

diamonds. At this point, I mark and cut these types of elements as well.

If a backsplash is interrupted by a window, it looks best if the tiles on each side of the window are the same size, which often means using partial tiles elsewhere. I plan the size and location of these partial tiles to please the eye.

Electrical outlets have to be incorporated into most backsplashes. A symmetrical layout around an electrical box looks best and is the easiest to cut. In extreme cases, the box can be moved for a proper-looking layout.

TEST-FIT THE TILES ON A FLAT SURFACE. For the area above the stove, the author first measures the exact dimensions (top left photo). Decorative elements such as the border and the square accent tiles are cut and fit (bottom left photo). Then he transfers them to a sheet of cardboard, where all the tile is dry-fit (right photo).

TROWEL ON THE MASTIC. White mastic is the adhesive of choice for this project because a darker color might show through the light-colored tile. The entire backsplash is spread before any tile is set.

Install the Tile in the Right Order

Before mud and mastic start flying, it's critical to protect appliances, countertops, and other finished surfaces. For this installation, a rubber shower-pan liner and a piece of cardboard protect the countertop and floors. The rubber liner is great because it can take a little impact if something is dropped on it. It also stays put, unlike a plastic drop cloth.

When I'm ready to set tile, I spread all-purpose mastic on the wall using a trowel with ¼-in. by ¼-in. notches (see the photo above). Because the tumbled marble for this backsplash is a fairly light color, I used nonstaining white mastic, which prevents the tile from spotting or darkening.

I set the bottom course of tiles for the backsplash first, after putting spacers under the tiles to keep them ⅛ in. above the counter. If the counter has to be replaced in the future, this space provides enough

room to slip in the new countertop without disturbing the backsplash.

To install each tile, I press it tightly against the wall about ¼ in. from its final position, then slide it in place to ensure a tight bond. With the bottom course in place, I turn to the trickiest part of the job, the patterned area behind the stove. Border pieces go in first (see the photos on the facing page). To create visual interest, I like the border to stand slightly proud of surrounding tiles, a subtle strategy that's not difficult to do. Before installing each border piece, I butter the back with mastic. When the tile is pressed in place, the extra mastic makes the border stand out slightly from the rest of the tile. Setting a few of the regular backsplash tiles outside the border helps keep the border pieces straight.

As I place tiles, I make the grout joints roughly ¼ in. wide. Because these tiles are irregular, the joint

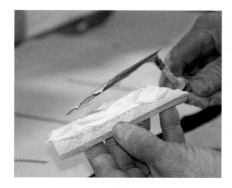

START AT THE BORDER. To make the border tiles stand slightly proud of the rest of the tile, the backs receive a coat of mastic first (top left photo). This will cause the tiles to stand out from the rest of the field when they're pressed into place (bottom left photo). To install a tile, press it against the wall and slide it about ¼ in. into position. Align diamond-shaped tiles along their long edges (right photo).

size varies somewhat. Instead of relying on spacers, I shift the tiles slightly as the different sizes require.

For the diamond pattern of the backsplash, I install the tiles in a diagonal sequence to keep them aligned along their longest straight edge. The tiny square accent pieces go in as I set the larger diamond tiles.

Once the stove backsplash is done, the rest of the job goes quickly. The main backsplash is only four courses high, and it's fairly easy to keep the grout lines level and straight.

As for the cut tiles that fit against the end walls and upper cabinets, I cut them for a tight fit with little or no grout joint. Grout is most likely to crack where different materials meet.

Seal the Tile before Grouting

I leave the tile overnight to let the mastic set up. The next day, I wipe down the backsplash with a good impregnator/sealer, which helps protect the marble and acts as a grout release. Grouting tumbled-marble tile is a little more difficult than grouting standard glazed tile. Grout tends to catch and collect along the irregular edges and on the surface of tumbled marble as well as in the relief of the border tiles.

I always use sanded grout with tumbled marble. Sand mixes with portland cement to add body and strength to the grout, making it superior at filling the wide joints between irregular tile edges. Border tiles such as the ones in this project also demand a stronger grout because they sit farther out than the rest of the tile.

WORKING AROUND AN ELECTRICAL OUTLET

SYMMETRICAL COVERAGE LOOKS BEST when tile meets an electrical box. Mark the edges of the box on surrounding tiles and cut them to fit (see the top photo below). Cut the tile so that the ears on the outlets and the switches overlap the edges of the tile. Before installing the tiles around the box, back out the screws that secure the outlets and switches. Longer screws may be necessary to make up for the added thickness of the tile (see the bottom photo below).

I mix a stiff but workable batch of grout that won't fall out of the joints as I float it on in a generous coat. When all the joints are filled, I let the grout sit until it is firm to the touch, usually 15 minutes or so. Then I wipe the tile with a grout sponge dampened with clean water. I make sure to wring out the sponge before wiping the tile; too much water can dissolve the cement and weaken the grout. When cleaning marble tiles, I pay extra attention to rough spots in the marble and to the patterned areas in the border tiles. These areas may need a little more effort to remove excess grout.

After washing it, I let the grout set up for another 15 minutes (less, if the room is warmer than normal). Then I use a clean terry-cloth towel to wipe the grout haze off the tile surface. At this point, I also use a putty knife to remove any grout stuck in corners or in other places where I want to see a clean, straight grout line.

The next day, I do a final cleaning with a good tile cleaner. Because some cleaners corrode or stain, I keep the countertop, stove, and sink protected. A day or two after cleaning, I finish the job by applying sealer to the tile and grout. If the tile is stone (as in this case) and I sealed the tile before grouting, an additional coat of sealer also protects the grout. I apply the sealer with a disposable foam brush and give the backsplash behind the stove a couple of extra coats to protect the tile and grout from grease.

SEAL. GROUT. SEAL AGAIN. Stone tile should be sealed before grouting to prevent the grout from sticking to it (above). After grout is applied (right) and becomes firm, remove the excess with a sponge and dry cloth.

WHEN THE GROUT HAS CURED FOR 48 HOURS, a final coat of sealer provides additional protection for the tile and the grout.

Storage

Secrets to an Uncluttered Kitchen

BY KATIE HUTCHISON

One of the highest compliments I've ever been paid came from my 6-year-old nephew after he walked through our living and dining rooms into the kitchen and asked, "Where's all your stuff?"

Believe me, it's there—just not in plain sight.

Our living quarters and kitchen are small, so squirreling things away is a necessity, but large, open kitchens can benefit from the same storage strategies as small ones. To preserve or create a sense of spaciousness, stuff needs to be discreetly gathered and stowed.

Because large, open kitchens and small kitchens have unique storage challenges, I'll explore examples of both types in detail. The best solutions offer efficient, unobtrusive, appealing storage options that enhance kitchen function, flow, and feel. And they don't have to cost a lot.

LARGE KITCHEN ELEVATION

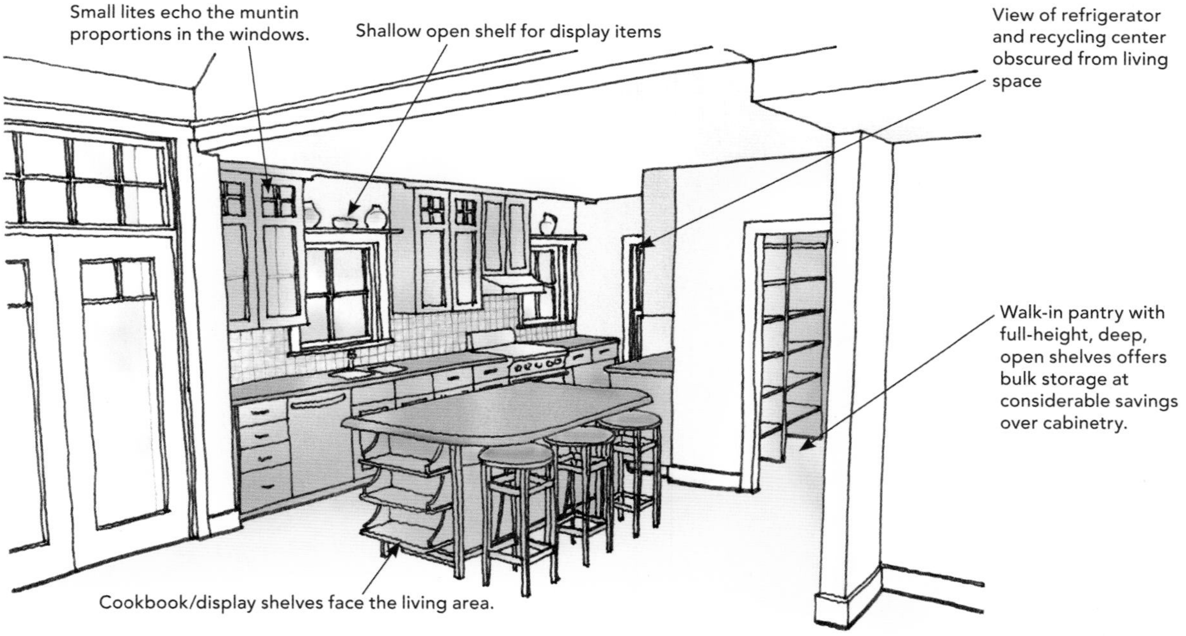

Small lites echo the muntin proportions in the windows.

Shallow open shelf for display items

View of refrigerator and recycling center obscured from living space

Walk-in pantry with full-height, deep, open shelves offers bulk storage at considerable savings over cabinetry.

Cookbook/display shelves face the living area.

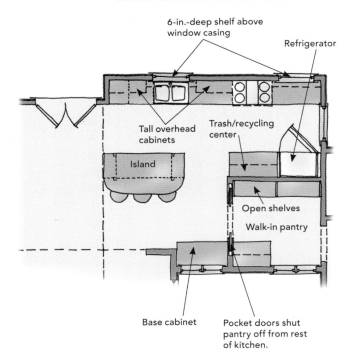

LARGE KITCHEN FLOOR PLAN

6-in.-deep shelf above window casing

Refrigerator

Tall overhead cabinets

Trash/recycling center

Island

Open shelves

Walk-in pantry

Base cabinet

Pocket doors shut pantry off from rest of kitchen.

If custom inset cabinets are out of reach, consider combining custom surrounds or dividers with stock, infill, overlay cabinets. Aligning the face of the surrounds or dividers with the face of the stiles and rails on the cabinet doors and drawers creates the illusion of inset cabinetry. Extending dividers for base cabinets to the floor creates "legs" between cabinets, enhancing the furniture-like look.

Limit Cabinets in Large, Open Kitchens

Some say that if you have a basement, no matter how big, you'll manage to fill it with your belongings. Large kitchens run the same risk. The trick is to keep a large kitchen, especially one that's part of an open plan, light and airy rather than filling it with cabinetry.

To reinforce an expansive feel, leave ample room for windows and minimize overhead cabinets. In the example shown at left and on p. 123, relegating much of the storage out of sight allows the island to float without overhead cabinets or a dividing storage wall between it and the living space.

SMALL KITCHEN ELEVATION: SINK WALL

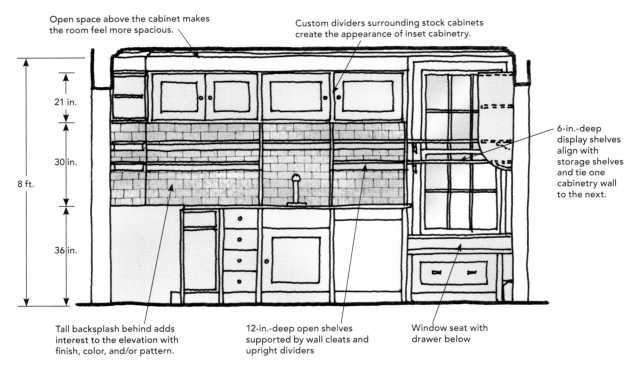

Open space above the cabinet makes the room feel more spacious.

Custom dividers surrounding stock cabinets create the appearance of inset cabinetry.

21 in.

30 in.

8 ft.

36 in.

6-in.-deep display shelves align with storage shelves and tie one cabinetry wall to the next.

Tall backsplash behind adds interest to the elevation with finish, color, and/or pattern.

12-in.-deep open shelves supported by wall cleats and upright dividers

Window seat with drawer below

SMALL KITCHEN FLOOR PLAN

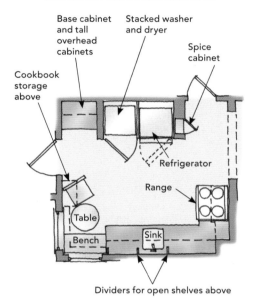

Base cabinet and tall overhead cabinets

Stacked washer and dryer

Spice cabinet

Cookbook storage above

Refrigerator

Range

Table

Bench

Sink

Dividers for open shelves above

SMALL KITCHEN ELEVATION: APPLIANCE WALL

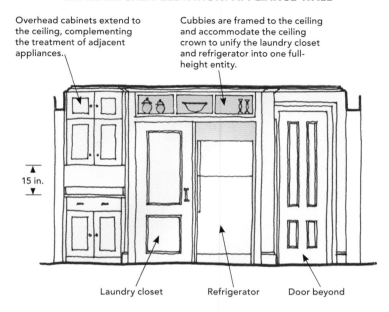

Overhead cabinets extend to the ceiling, complementing the treatment of adjacent appliances.

Cubbies are framed to the ceiling and accommodate the ceiling crown to unify the laundry closet and refrigerator into one full-height entity.

15 in.

Laundry closet

Refrigerator

Door beyond

Tuck bulk storage—including the refrigerator—and pantry space off the end of the kitchen that is most remote from open living spaces.

A tall pantry cabinet can abut the refrigerator, or as in this example, a base cabinet with tall overheads can serve a similar function. Because their contents are mostly out of view, the tall overheads don't need doors here. Large baskets or bins can be used without doors in this out-of-sight area as well, providing a welcome break from monolithic cabinetry.

Cabinets visible from the living space can be dressier. Glass-fronted overhead cabinets contribute to a more open look than opaque doors. Simple 6-in.-deep shelves above the windows provide display space.

Layers of Storage Work in a Small Kitchen

Storage in a small kitchen with a circulation path through the middle doesn't have to be inadequate or overbearing. With close attention to a functional layout and cabinet density and height, even a 138-sq.-ft. kitchen provides sufficient storage without feeling confined or cluttered.

On the sink wall (see the bottom drawing on the facing page), a combination of short overhead cabinets and open shelves meets a variety of storage needs. Holding the top of the cabinets 9 in. below the ceiling gives the room a greater sense of spaciousness than if the cabinets were extended to the ceiling. The opaque fronts on the overhead cabinets conceal food packaging and less attractive wares, while the open shelves offer easy access to everyday glassware and china unlikely to gather dust due to frequent use. The 12-in.-deep shelves below the upper cabinets are supported by upright dividers that taper to 4 in. deep at the counter. The uprights continue the vertical lines of the base cabinet uprights, neatly organizing the sink wall. The shelves add a custom touch and a location to display attractive kitchenware at a fraction of the cost of cabinetry. The width of the uprights between the cabinets can account for differences between the length of a wall and stock-cabinet dimensions.

Shown above is the opposite wall, where the largest appliances are placed farthest from view. This wall bundles together the refrigerator and stackable washer and dryer, the tallest and deepest appliances. Cubbies above them take advantage of storage potential while keeping a more open feel than closed overhead cabinets would.

Off-the-Shelf Kitchen Storage Solutions

BY DEBRA JUDGE SILBER

HINGED HELPER. The front baskets of Häfele's Magic Corner II pull out and swivel to open at 90°. To take advantage of the storage space in the blind corner recess, the back baskets move into the cabinet opening; just pull them forward to find what you need. The unit is used with a hinged door and mounts on two walls of the cabinet.

f I could've squeezed just one more cabinet into my kitchen when we remodeled, believe me, I would've done it. But a kitchen isn't terribly useful if you don't leave enough room between countertops to enter and exit, and not terribly pleasant if you obstruct every view with a plywood box, no matter how important it is to have every saucepan at your fingertips.

Fortunately, it's not the number of cabinets but what they hold that counts. That's good news not just for me and for my small kitchen, but also for anyone who needs to wring the most functionality out of a kitchen whose storage capacity is about equal to that of the average linen closet.

Unless you're a carpenter with time to spare (or someone who knows a carpenter with time to spare), maximizing kitchen storage space usually comes down to buying the right manufactured solution. In a perfect world, that's done when the cabinets are installed. But what if you're dealing with a previous homeowner's cabinet configuration? Or if you've tapped out both your budget and your creativity just getting your own new cabinets into your kitchen? In cases like these, you're likely to start exploring the world of aftermarket storage options.

Manufactured storage solutions can be found in home centers (order the better ones through the kitchen department) and, to a greater extent, through online dealers. The choices are so wide, in fact, that finding the right solution may seem as hopeless as rummaging for a lost lid in the dark recesses of a blind corner. For this chapter, I set out to find the most sensible off-the-shelf solutions for what I consider primary kitchen-storage challenges. In terms of space, that means blind corners, high shelves, and undersink cabinets. In terms of specific items that defy convenient storage solutions, that would be food, small appliances, trash and recycling bins, and (my own nemesis) cookware.

In my search, not only did I exploit my own battles with kitchen chaos, but I also consulted designers and architects to find what solutions they rely on and recommend to their clients. Their choices were notably consistent, particularly in regard to the two biggest players in the storage game: Häfele® and Rev-A-Shelf®. Both brands not only supply cabinet-makers with internal storage features but also offer many of the same solutions to be installed after the fact. But beware: You will pay for quality. In some cases, the storage components you add will cost as much as the cabinet itself. Also, prices vary widely—especially online. It pays to shop around.

Coping with Corner Cabinets

Austin designer J. Patrick Sutton hates kitchen corners so much that he goes out of his way to design floor plans that don't have them. But that's little consolation if the kitchen you're cooking in has one or more. Storage options for corners are dictated by the cabinets used to create the corner. Open corner cabinets are dominated by lazy-Susan arrangements, most of which must be installed before the counter-top goes in, though some can be retrofitted (see the top photos on p. 128). A blind corner, created when one base cabinet is installed against a wall with another abutting it at a 90º angle, offers deep space, but that space is tricky to access. That may be why there has been such a parade of inventions to mine the storage potential of the blind corner.

PETAL PULLOUT. Häfele's LeMans corner pullout shelves are shaped like wavy flower petals. The shelves slide and then swing out of the blind corner opening. They have a nonslip surface and can hold up to 65 lb.

CURVING AROUND A CORNER. Rev-A-Shelf's Half Moon shelves pivot and pull out of a blind corner. The ⅝-in.-thick multi-ply wood trays come sized for door openings as small as 12 in. and can be used in framed or frameless cabinets.

NOT-SO-LAZY SUSAN. Open corner cabinets are typically equipped with lazy Susans, which are difficult if not impossible to install after the fact. The Lazy Susan Drawer System from Knape and Vogt®, however, can be retrofitted into an existing cabinet (although the manufacturer suggests you get a professional to do it). It features two slide-out center shelves to simplify access and is available as a full-round for an angled door or kidney-shaped for a 90° double-hinged door.

Smart Solutions for Problem Spaces

Undersink storage solutions are designed to maneuver around plumbing and to help you corral the clutter of cleaning supplies. Spills are inevitable in this area, so baskets that unhinge and remove easily, allowing access to the floor of the cabinet for cleaning (and retrieval of small items), are a plus.

One of the most challenging storage spaces in our kitchens is of our own making. The banishment of kitchen soffits has yielded lots of useful space—most of it completely out of reach. "We've gone up, but

SPACE FOR SPONGES. Forgotten space in front of the sink bowl can be used with a tilt-down sink tray attached to the front plate. Rev-A-Shelf's trays are made of extruded polymer and can be trimmed to fit cabinets up to 36 in. wide.

RIGHT FOR A TIGHT SPACE. There are many variations of sliding baskets for undersink storage. One is Whitney Design's Glidez Sink Sliding Organizer (C26512). The commercial-grade chrome organizer comes with full-extension ball-bearing slides already attached; the offset second tier can be mounted to either side of the 12-in.-wide bottom shelf so that it can adapt to either side of the cabinet.

THE NEXT STEP. Only 4 in. by 18 in. when folded, this step stool by Häfele fits under a toe kick or inside a cabinet door. It gives you an additional 18 in. in height to reach upper cabinets. Consider the cost of a carpenter if you want a neat installation under the toe kick.

the average height of the consumer hasn't changed," says Alan Zielinski, a second-generation designer and owner of Better Kitchens in Niles, Ill. Zielinski is one of a slew of designers whose first choice in dealing with out-of-reach areas is not to bring high cabinet shelves down to the cook, but to bring the cook up to them—specifically, with a tiny folding step stool made by Häfele. Pull-down or motorized shelves are another option, but they take up so much room that designers recommend you think hard before installing them.

Trade Doors for Drawers

Base cabinets aren't usually considered hard-to-reach storage areas. But by maximizing storage capacity and accessibility in whatever base cabinets you have, you can reserve out-of-the-way shelves for rarely used or decorative items.

Citing "one-motion" accessibility, designers have been arguing for some time that cabinets outfitted with drawers are more functional than those with shelves behind doors. "I almost never put doors on base

COME ON DOWN. Rev-A-Shelf's 5PD series chrome wall-shelf system brings the contents of 24-in. and 36-in. wall shelves 10 in. closer. The system uses a gas-assisted lowering mechanism and mounts to the side or bottom of the cabinet.

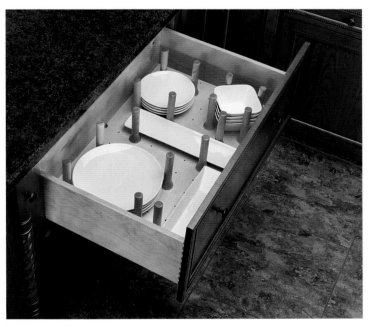

WOODEN POSTS HOLD PLATES IN PLACE. Rev-A-Shelf's Large Drawer Peg System consists of a 39-in. by 21-in. board and 16 pegs.

MADE-TO-ORDER DRAWERS AND INSERTS. CCF Industries markets a double-decker wine drawer (right) and combination spice and knife drawers (left) that are made-to-order.

ROLLING REPLACEMENT. Replace stationary shelves with a pullout, and you gain single-motion access to the entire cabinet. Rev-A-Shelf's 448 series base-cabinet organizers have adjustable shelves and are designed to be fitted into existing cabinets.

SLIDING SHELVES. Preassembled pullouts from Shelves That Slide are made of Baltic birch and feature Blum slides. They can be made in dimensions to fit almost any cabinet.

cabinets anymore," designer J. Patrick Sutton says. Part of the credit goes to improved hardware: Heavy-duty, full-extension slides make it possible to fill a drawer with heavy items, such as plates, and access them from the top with the drawer pulled out. Soft-close mechanisms minimize the jarring that might topple contents.

With drawers' popularity has come a plethora of inserts—dividers, trays, and pegboards—made of wood or plastic that can be trimmed to fit any drawer and secure a variety of contents. With pegboards, once the base is fitted to the drawer, the dividers or posts can be adjusted at will. "It's much more practicable than what I had done 10 years ago, which is design highly customized systems," Sutton says.

Sensible Storage for What You Use Every Day

Once upon a time—before command centers and conversation stations—kitchens revolved around food. Even today, every kitchen still needs someplace to store the potatoes.

The multijointed swinging and folding pantries introduced a few years ago may still turn heads, but they're not necessarily the only way to serve up the

HEAVY-DUTY PULLOUT. Häfele's frame-and-basket pullout is available in sizes that fit cabinets from 12 in. to 16 in. wide.

TWO TO GO. Omega National Products's KitchenMate™ dual waste pullout has ball-bearing slides and fits 18-in. cabinets.

THREE-BIN RECYCLING CENTER. The 5349 series from Rev-A-Shelf includes three 25-qt. containers and an 18-qt. canvas bag.

EASY LIFT. Rev-A-Shelf's appliance lift (right) uses spring tension and shock dampers to lift and hold up to 60 lb., while the lift from Knape and Vogt (above) operates with a gas cylinder.

LIDS ON TOP. Rev-A-Shelf's 2 Tier Cookware Organizer (5CW2 series) has independently operating shelves that hold up to seven lids and a variety of sizes of cookware. The shelves also can be mounted to the door.

soup cans. Designer Alan Zielinski, for example, steers his clients to simpler pantry units that pull straight out. He points to more access, more light, and less wasted space (all that swinging can eat up as much as 20% of a pantry's capacity). When choosing a pullout unit, check the weight limitations, and look for adjustable shelves.

Trash and recycling bins can be tricky to locate in a kitchen because of their size and because they're most useful where they can be easily accessed. While the number of bins you'll need depends on local regulations (and your own diligence), most kitchen designers advise a minimum of two. Look for sturdy construction; David Alderman, president of Dave's Cabinet Inc. of Chesapeake, Va., recommends pullout bins that attach to the cabinet sides and door rather than the cabinet bottom. "When you're pulling at the top and it's attached at the bottom, it's almost like you're prying it open," he says.

Aftermarket storage solutions for small appliances are fairly limited, with the possible exception of countertop garages (some updated with lift-type doors instead of problematic tambour doors) and rolling shelves outfitted with heavy-duty, full-extension, soft-closing hardware that allows full access and stable operation. Mention appliance lifts, and homeowners and designers fall into two camps: those who love them and those who feel they waste space and money. (They take up all or most of a 36-in.-high cabinet.) Nonetheless, all the major cabinet outfitters offer them.

Pots and pans wouldn't be nearly as problematic to store if they had no handles, had no lids, and weren't necessary virtually every time you fire up the stove. With all these requirements, good, functional cookware storage can be a challenge.

In the end, good kitchen storage is not about fancy gadgets; it's about finding the simplest tools for keeping just what you need right where you need it. And there's no shortage of products on the market to do just that.

SOURCES

MANUFACTURERS

ACCURIDE®
www.accuride.com
Drawer slides

BLUM
www.blum.com
Hardware, slides

CCF INDUSTRIES
www.ccfdrawers.com
Custom drawers and drawer inserts

HÄFELE
www.hafele.com/us
Cabinet organization, hardware, accessories

KNAPE & VOGT
www.knapeandvogt.com
Storage solutions, drawer slides

OMEGA NATIONAL PRODUCTS
www.omeganationalproducts.com
Wood cabinet accessories

REV-A-SHELF
www.rev-a-shelf.com
Kitchen, bath, closet storage

SHELVES THAT SLIDE
www.shelvesthatslide.com
Sliding shelves (made-to-order)

ONLINE RETAILERS

CABINET PARTS
www.cabinetparts.com
Cabinet hardware, accessories

KITCHENSOURCE.COM
www.kitchensource.com
All varieties of kitchen-organization products

OVIS®
www.ovisonline.com
Cabinet organizers, hardware, accessories

ROCKLER®
www.rockler.com
Hardware, storage, organization products

WOODWORKER'S HARDWARE
www.wwhardware.com
Hardware, kitchen and bath storage, lazy Susans

Design the Perfect Pantry

BY PAUL DEGROOT

Ask your neighbors what they dislike about their pantries, and you'll likely get an earful: "It's too small" or "I can't find anything in it." I hear these complaints on cue from clients. Clearly, the way we store our soup and cereal warrants careful planning.

Whether you are building a new kitchen or remodeling what you have, you need to consider what makes a pantry work and which kind is best for your situation. Here I'll describe the three main types of pantries: cabinets, reach-ins, and walk-ins. I'll also offer a suggestion for a hybrid pantry/ mudroom that the homeowners walk through as they enter the house. The drawings are meant to illustrate the basics; the photos show some of my actual projects.

Just keep two things in mind as you read and when you plan your pantry: Good design means keeping things simple, and the right location often trumps size. Sometimes, a hardworking cabinet is all you need for convenient access to all your kitchen goods.

The Basics: Location and Lighting

Convenience and visibility are the essential attributes of a great pantry. Regardless of size, the pantry should be in a handy location, positioned in the kitchen or immediately next to it. A modest pantry cabinet placed within the kitchen footprint will be more convenient for regular use than an oversize walk-in down the hall. Plus, every pantry's utility will be improved with counter space for sorting and unloading groceries.

Pantries also must have proper lighting so that you can see the contents well. Ceiling-mounted linear fluorescents work well for walk-in pantries. Install the fixtures parallel to the longest shelving runs for best light. Due to the extra cost, most of the cabinet pantries I design don't have internal lighting, so I make sure that there is adequate kitchen lighting directly outside the cabinet. Often, this means that I will locate one or two recessed fixtures about 16 in. from the face of the cabinet. A reach-in closet pantry will benefit from a low-profile fluorescent light mounted inside, especially when a tall header blocks ambient light from the high shelves. I specify slim, no-frills fluorescents with rounded acrylic diffusers for these above-door applications.

Electrical codes are strict about the types and the locations of lights installed in closets. Treat pantry lighting with similar caution. If you must use incandescent fixtures, be sure to place them well away from any open shelves that might be packed with paper goods and combustibles.

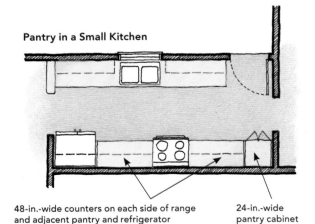

Pantry in a Small Kitchen

48-in.-wide counters on each side of range and adjacent pantry and refrigerator

24-in.-wide pantry cabinet

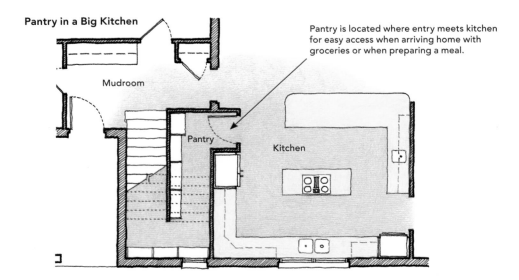

Pantry in a Big Kitchen

Mudroom

Pantry

Kitchen

Pantry is located where entry meets kitchen for easy access when arriving home with groceries or when preparing a meal.

A Better Pantry May Not Be Bigger

Cabinet pantries are space efficient, typically occupying just 4 sq. ft. to 8 sq. ft. of floor area. For big families and others who buy in bulk, I sometimes supplement the in-kitchen pantry cabinet with a larger pantry elsewhere.

Reach-in closet pantries range in size from 6 sq. ft. to 12 sq. ft., assuming a 24-in. depth and a width from 3 ft. to 6 ft. There are occasions where a 24-in. depth is not possible. In these cases, a 12-in. depth is the minimum, but 16 in. or more would allow some storage flexibility. It's difficult to see and access items at the extreme sides of a wide reach-in

closet pantry with a narrow doorway. Except on the smallest of reach-ins, I use pairs of doors with the sidewalls of the closet no more than 6 in. from each door jamb.

Surrounded by 2×4 stud walls, pantry closets waste a fair amount of volume with studs and drywall. A simple remodeling strategy is to substitute a tall cabinet pantry in the same location as an old closet. Trading a 4½-in. thick wall for a ¾-in. plywood end panel nets inches of extra shelf width. The result is a user-friendly pantry in a compact package that can match the rest of the kitchen cabinets.

A compact walk-in can be made with an interior footprint of about 4 ft. by 4 ft. and an L-shaped

CABINET PANTRY

This type of pantry requires the smallest footprint, but it can still pack a lot of storage. Cabinet pantries can be stock items ordered from national cabinet shops or they can be custom-built from designers' plans. The author prefers the arrangement shown here: A full-height, cabinet-depth pantry with fully extending drawers below a series of pullouts and stationary shelves. Depending on the width of the pantry, it may have a single door or a pair of doors no wider than 18 in. each.

Plan View

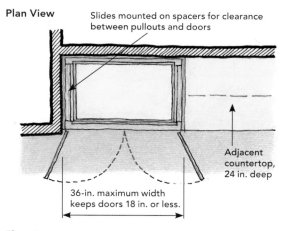

Slides mounted on spacers for clearance between pullouts and doors

Adjacent countertop, 24 in. deep

36-in. maximum width keeps doors 18 in. or less.

Elevation

15-in. (approximately) upper cabinet for large items and/or vertical dividers

12-in.-deep adjustable upper shelves

18-in.-deep middle shelves

Cereal boxes are among the tallest items and need 11 in. to 12 in. of clearance.

4-in. pullouts for taller items

2-in. pullout for cans and spices laid flat

Two large drawers on full-extension slides anchor the pantry.

BLOCKING FOR CLEARANCE. The drawback of sliding shelves behind doors is that the inside of the doors tends to get scratched. The farther you can fur out the shelves from the inside of the cabinet, the better the chance of keeping the doors in good shape.

HARDWORKING DOORS. Using the back side of a cabinet-pantry door for storage takes away from the potential depth of shelves, but it offers an area where commonly used goods won't get lost in the clutter.

LIGHT YOU DON'T HAVE TO THINK ABOUT. Good lighting allows you to see clearly. A fixture should be placed inside the pantry or on the ceiling directly outside it. A door-operated switch means you don't have to turn the light on manually or remember to turn it off.

arrangement of shelves on two walls. While the length of the room is variable, the width depends on the shelving arrangement and the walking aisle. I consider 44 in. to be a minimum width, affording a 28-in. aisle and 16-in. shelves on one wall only. A long, narrow room like this will still feel tight. Widening such a pantry allows for more comfortable browsing space, wider shelves, and/or shelves on two parallel walls. Note that a room wider than 8 ft. will likely have wasted floor space in the middle. A typical walk-in pantry might take up 30 sq. ft., at 6 ft. wide by 5 ft. deep. A large walk-in could easily double that area, especially if a client wants room for a counter, a step stool, and a spare refrigerator.

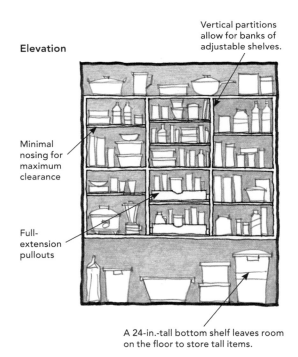

REACH-IN PANTRY

Enclosed by stud walls, this pantry is a small closet. Reach-in closet pantries tend to be affordable and easy to build. Some have pairs of doors concealing 4 ft. to 7 ft. of shelving across the back wall. Better reach-ins have the widest doors possible for good visibility of the contents. Considering that wide doors take up substantial wall space, this pantry is best located just off the kitchen proper so the kitchen walls can be loaded with cabinets, appliances, windows, and other essentials.

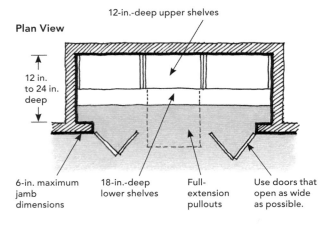

Plan View

12-in.-deep upper shelves

12 in. to 24 in. deep

6-in. maximum jamb dimensions

18-in.-deep lower shelves

Full-extension pullouts

Use doors that open as wide as possible.

Elevation

Vertical partitions allow for banks of adjustable shelves.

Minimal nosing for maximum clearance

Full-extension pullouts

A 24-in.-tall bottom shelf leaves room on the floor to store tall items.

REACH IN, ONCE IN A WHILE. Commonly used goods are stored in the cabinet pantry inside the kitchen. Nearby, a secondary reach-in pantry holds the bulk and is used for restocking.

It's All about Storage

While deep shelves can hold more stuff, it's a frustrated cook who can't find the rice hidden behind a train wreck of juice boxes and pasta. For better visibility, I like to stagger the depth of shelves.

A simple pantry with fixed wooden shelving is quick and easy to build. If your budget dictates this approach, consider mounting 16-in.-deep to 18-in.-deep shelves starting about 24 in. above the floor so that you can keep taller items on the floor below. At eye level, switch to 12-in.-deep shelves. Bulkier items on the lower shelves may be taller than 12 in., a common vertical shelf spacing, so allow extra height there—if not all the way across a wall then at least across a portion of it. However, it is common to experience a trial-and-error fitting when first loading a new pantry, so adjustable shelves rate highly on the convenience meter. They also readily accommodate an additional shelf.

For full-height cabinet pantries, I position two big full-extension drawers nearest the floor, enabling items stored in the back to be found easily. Above these drawers, I usually spec a pair of tall doors concealing a combination of pullouts and fixed shelves. This way, users can see the entire pantry at once. I sometimes add a second pair of shorter doors at the top of the cabinet. This space is good for oversize items that are used infrequently. It also can be outfitted with vertical dividers for cookie sheets and the like.

User preferences and heights dictate modifications to my basic cabinet-pantry template. Tall folks may want an additional pullout inside the main compartment. Some like spice racks or small shelves mounted on the inside of the cabinet doors.

Narrow spaces in a base-cabinet arrangement also can be used for pullout pantry units, where the entire assembly extends out from the cabinet frame. Either custom-built or ordered from a catalog, these units have front panels hiding multiple shelves behind, with access gained from both sides when the units slide out. Häfele, Rev-A-Shelf, and others sell cabinet-pantry hardware narrow enough to squeeze into a 4-in.-wide space.

WALK IN TO CONVENIENCE. For a family that buys in bulk, a large walk-in pantry not only hides groceries but also offers a place for a second fridge and freezer as well as a beverage cooler (see the drawing on p. 140).

WALK-IN PANTRY

Usually the biggest of the lot, a walk-in pantry is ideal for those who buy in bulk and/or live far from the grocery store. Roomy walk-ins are large enough to use three or four walls for storing items such as dry goods, paper towels, pet food, appliances, and brooms. Smaller walk-ins usually have just two walls of shelving. A popular and affordable option for a small walk-in pantry is to put it in a corner of the kitchen, with the door set on a 45° angle between adjoining counters. For those wanting fewer cabinets and an open, minimalistic look in their kitchen, a walk-in pantry just outside the room can be a solution that doesn't compromise the kitchen aesthetics.

Plan View

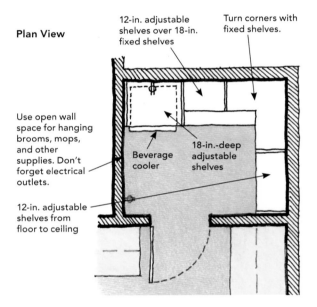

12-in. adjustable shelves over 18-in. fixed shelves

Turn corners with fixed shelves.

Use open wall space for hanging brooms, mops, and other supplies. Don't forget electrical outlets.

Beverage cooler

18-in.-deep adjustable shelves

12-in. adjustable shelves from floor to ceiling

Elevation

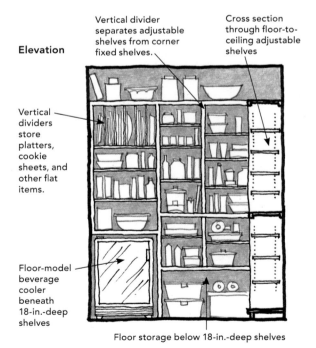

Vertical divider separates adjustable shelves from corner fixed shelves.

Cross section through floor-to-ceiling adjustable shelves

Vertical dividers store platters, cookie sheets, and other flat items.

Floor-model beverage cooler beneath 18-in.-deep shelves

Floor storage below 18-in.-deep shelves

Don't forget that wall space inside a walk-in pantry is useful for hanging a mop and brooms, so don't put shelves everywhere.

Give some thought to keeping small appliances in the pantry, plugged in and ready to use. A deep pantry shelf or counter is a possible location for a seldom-used microwave oven. I have a client who keeps a toaster and coffeemaker in her walk-in pantry to reduce the clutter on her counters. Built-in beverage centers take up valuable kitchen real estate. I saved money by putting a freestanding model in our pantry below the staircase.

Doors Shouldn't Get in the Way

While I almost always use standard 24-in.-deep units for cabinet pantries, the width depends on the design specifics of the kitchen. Maintaining a width of 36 in. or less allows me a pair of cabinet doors, each less than 18 in. across. Wider doors can be heavy and unwieldy to open. When I have more than 36 in. of width for a built-in pantry, I place two separate cabinets side by side, with three or four doors across the front.

Have you ever had a closet with cheap bifold doors? Used daily, the light-duty hardware gives out; the doors stop gliding and eventually derail. It doesn't have to be so. Outfitted with commercial-grade hardware, bifold door panels are good options for wider reach-in pantry closets. The beauty of these doors is their ability to provide wide openings while being unobtrusive when open. I like to use a pocket door when it is likely to remain open quite a bit or when a swinging door is going to be in the way.

For a single door to a walk-in pantry, I never use less than a 24 in. width, but most folks will appreciate the extra passage of a 30-in. door. You will need a 32-in.-wide door if a big appliance has to get through it, but don't forget that swinging doors take up space. A wide pantry door that opens against a counter will block access. With outswing pantry doors, I keep the doorknob nearest the counter for best functionality. When an outswinger won't work,

PUT IT AWAY ON THE WAY IN. A hybrid pantry/mudroom located between the garage and the kitchen is convenient when you arrive home with groceries and when you are preparing dinner. Counter space near the pantry is always a good idea.

I fit a pocket door into the blueprint or arrange an inswinger to park against an unused interior wall.

Finally, an automatic light switch that is activated by the door is a nice touch for a pantry because you're likely to be coming or going with your hands full.

WALK-THROUGH PANTRY

Sometimes the pantry is part of a mudroom or utility room next to the kitchen. It's often a walk-through room instead of a walk-in. A good example is a pantry/mudroom you pass through from the garage or back porch to the kitchen. This arrangement provides a handy place to wipe your feet and put away items. Storage can be out of view behind doors or it can be open shelving and bins lining the walls. As a mudroom, it needs space for stowing backpacks, feeding the dog, charging a smartphone, or washing dirty hands. Some might allocate space for an extra freezer or refrigerator.

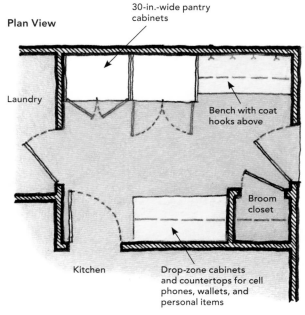

Plan View

30-in.-wide pantry cabinets

Laundry

Bench with coat hooks above

Broom closet

Kitchen

Drop-zone cabinets and countertops for cell phones, wallets, and personal items

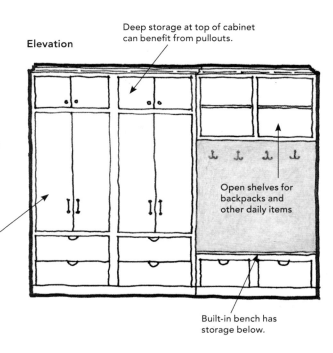

Elevation

Deep storage at top of cabinet can benefit from pullouts.

Open shelves for backpacks and other daily items

30-in. side-by-side pantry cabinets nearest kitchen

Built-in bench has storage below.

A Clever Kitchen Built-In

BY NANCY R. HILLER

Modern kitchens are made for storage, but it never seems to be sufficient. Recently, my company built a cabinet to provide generous storage on a shallow section of wall in our clients' kitchen. It was space that normally would have gone to waste because it was too shallow for stock cabinets.

The inspiration for this custom-made cabinet came from a traditional piece of British furniture known as a Welsh dresser. In use since the seventeenth century, the dresser originally provided the main storage in a kitchen; built-in cabinets did not become the norm until the early twentieth century. More commonly known in the United States by the less-elegant term *hutch*, the dresser typically has a shallow, open upper section that sits on a partially enclosed base. The dresser described here also exemplifies the sort of planning, production, and installation essential for genuinely custom built-in cabinets.

A Strategy for Storage that Doesn't Waste Space

The kitchen had a section of unused wall about 11 ft. long, which I thought could be used for storage and display space without impeding traffic flow. Although 1 ft. of depth is shallow for a base cabinet, it is enough

to hold a surprising variety of kitchen wares: cookbooks, decorative china, coffee mugs, small mixing bowls, jars of beans or pasta. Knowing that one of my clients had grown up in England and would be familiar with Welsh dressers, I suggested a similar cabinet with more-contemporary lines, customized for her family's budget and for the available space.

The upper sections would have open shelves, but the base cabinets would be enclosed with doors and drawers to keep their contents free of the dust and debris that collect at a kitchen's edges. Enclosing the lower sections also would give a nice visual weight to the wall without making it appear too heavy. The break between base and upper cabinets would be at 32 in., not the typical kitchen-counter height of 36 in., because I wanted this piece to look more like furniture than a regular kitchen cabinet.

Building Smaller Components Makes the Project Easier

The six-piece unit is divided into three uppers and three bases for ease of production, delivery, and installation (see the drawing on the facing page). To make the six plywood cases and the solid-maple counter resemble a single piece of cabinetry, I used a complete maple face frame on the center section

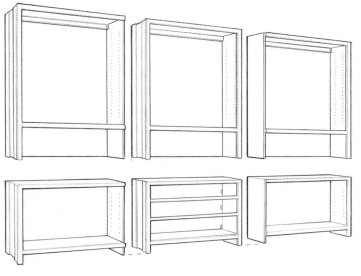

MORE PARTS MAKE CONSTRUCTION EFFICIENT. This type of modular cabinet construction allows a majority of the assembly work to be done in the shop. Consequently, I get more control over the processes and their costs.

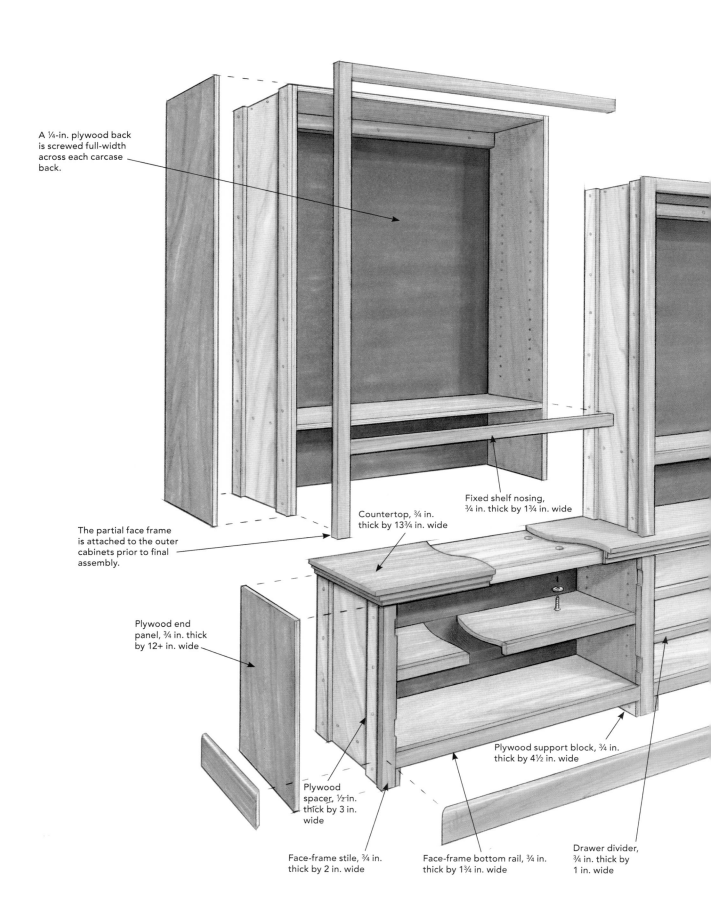

A ¼-in. plywood back is screwed full-width across each carcase back.

The partial face frame is attached to the outer cabinets prior to final assembly.

Fixed shelf nosing, ¾ in. thick by 1¾ in. wide

Countertop, ¾ in. thick by 13¾ in. wide

Plywood end panel, ¾ in. thick by 12+ in. wide

Plywood support block, ¾ in. thick by 4½ in. wide

Plywood spacer, ½ in. thick by 3 in. wide

Face-frame stile, ¾ in. thick by 2 in. wide

Face-frame bottom rail, ¾ in. thick by 1¾ in. wide

Drawer divider, ¾ in. thick by 1 in. wide

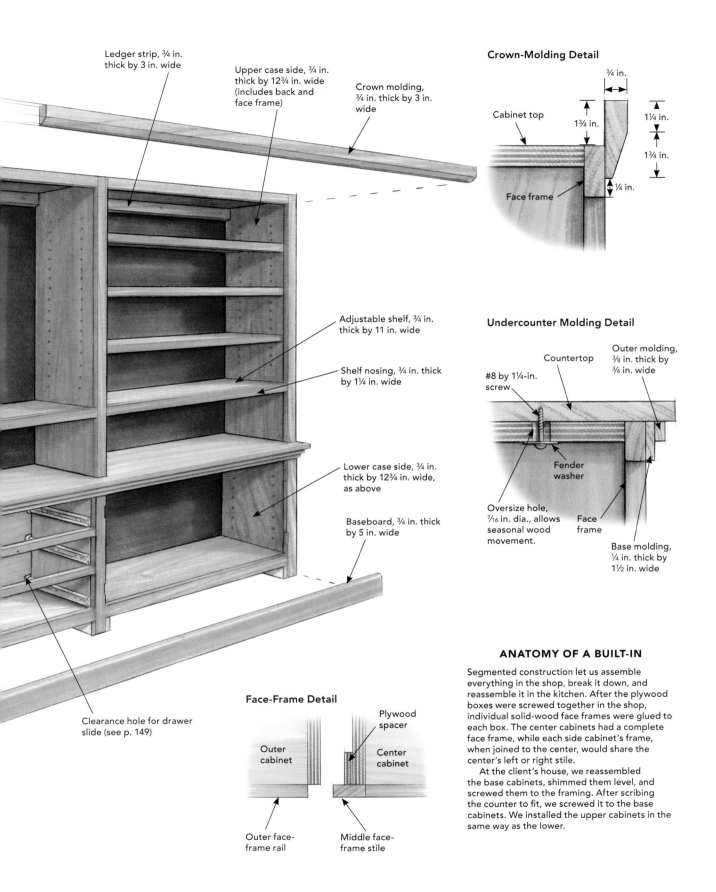

Ledger strip, ¾ in. thick by 3 in. wide

Upper case side, ¾ in. thick by 12¾ in. wide (includes back and face frame)

Crown molding, ¾ in. thick by 3 in. wide

Adjustable shelf, ¾ in. thick by 11 in. wide

Shelf nosing, ¾ in. thick by 1¼ in. wide

Lower case side, ¾ in. thick by 12¾ in. wide, as above

Baseboard, ¾ in. thick by 5 in. wide

Clearance hole for drawer slide (see p. 149)

Crown-Molding Detail

¾ in.

Cabinet top

1¾ in.

1¼ in.

1¾ in.

¼ in.

Face frame

Undercounter Molding Detail

Countertop

Outer molding, ⅜ in. thick by ¾ in. wide

#8 by 1¼-in. screw

Fender washer

Oversize hole, ⁷⁄₁₆ in. dia., allows seasonal wood movement.

Face frame

Base molding, ¼ in. thick by 1½ in. wide

ANATOMY OF A BUILT-IN

Segmented construction let us assemble everything in the shop, break it down, and reassemble it in the kitchen. After the plywood boxes were screwed together in the shop, individual solid-wood face frames were glued to each box. The center cabinets had a complete face frame, while each side cabinet's frame, when joined to the center, would share the center's left or right stile.

At the client's house, we reassembled the base cabinets, shimmed them level, and screwed them to the framing. After scribing the counter to fit, we screwed it to the base cabinets. We installed the upper cabinets in the same way as the lower.

Face-Frame Detail

Plywood spacer

Outer cabinet

Center cabinet

Outer face-frame rail

Middle face-frame stile

of the upper and lower casework and a partial face frame on each end. The end cases would butt tightly against the center unit and share its face-frame stiles to make the unit appear as one piece (see the drawing on pp. 144–145).

Although 10-in. slides are available for many purposes and would have been ideal for this job, they are rated for drawers only up to approximately 2 ft. wide. For smooth operation, I needed hardware designed for oversize openings. Given the location of the adjacent door casing, which limited the cabinet's depth to a maximum of 12¾ in., and a design that called for inset drawer faces, we needed to create ¼ in. of additional depth to accommodate the 12-in. slides by routing out the plywood cabinet back in those locations.

For ease of production, I typically use a full-width applied back on built-in cabinets rather than rabbeting the cabinet sides to accept the back. Scribed on site, a finished end covers the seam between the cabinet and the ¼-in. back. After cutting biscuit slots to join the case sides to the tops, I used cleats fastened with glue and brads or screws to support the case bottoms. The biscuit- and cleat-supported butt joints were reinforced with 1½-in. screws once the casework was put together.

As we assembled the cases, I checked for square and twist. I also cleaned off squeezed-out glue before it dried.

Solid-Wood Parts Need Special Consideration

Depending on the finish, I use either mortise-and-tenon joinery or pocket screws to assemble face frames before gluing them to carcases. Although pocket screws are quick and simple, I don't think the joint is as immobile as a glued mortise and tenon. Although a hairline gap isn't as noticeable in natural wood, I've learned the hard way not to use pocket screws for painted work that needs to look seamless. For this project, once the face frames were pocket-screwed, we glued and clamped them to the carcases.

The solid-maple counter was made by edge-joining two or three full-length boards. To increase the glue surface and to keep the boards even during clamping, I used biscuit joints about every 18 in. along the

DRAWER SIZE AND WEIGHT DETERMINE DRAWER SLIDE HARDWARE

A DRAWER THAT'S 40 IN. WIDE REQUIRES SPECIAL SLIDES to withstand the stresses placed on it when it's fully extended. However, the full-extension, heavy-duty 12-in. drawer slides from Accuride (model 3640; www.accuride.com) that I chose turned out to be ¼ in. longer than the inside of the base cabinets. Fortunately, cutting a hole in the cabinet's back (see the photo at right) made just enough space.

To install the drawers, we hang the drawer box first and apply the face later (see the photo on p. 149). Typically, we hang the box with special low-profile screws that can be purchased with the drawer hardware. The box should be hung initially about ⅛ in. behind its final position. In this instance, we were working with ¾-in.-thick applied drawer faces, so the box was set back ⅞ in.

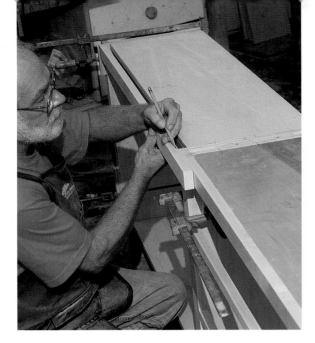

FIRST ASSEMBLY IS DONE IN THE SHOP FOR A BETTER FINAL FIT. After Jerry Nees glued the center face frame to the center cabinet, he clamped the base cabinets together in the shop. The left and right portions of the face frame then can be scribed to fit and glued to their respective cabinets. The process is repeated for the upper cabinets.

SOLID DETAILS FOR LONG-LASTING DOORS

For most cabinet doors, I make stiles and rails from stock that's slightly thicker than ¾ in. I prefer to use mortise-and-tenon joinery (see the drawing at right), but cope-and-stick is also a viable option (see the drawing below). I cut the grooves and tenons on the tablesaw, using a dado blade and (for the tenons) a sliding miter gauge. I use a ⁵⁄₁₆-in.-wide mortise-and-tenon joint; I have found that my mortising machine's ⁵⁄₁₆-in.-dia. auger bit and hollow chisel are less likely to break from overheating than are ¼-in. tools. My door panels are typically solid wood. If the groove is ½ in. deep, I make the panel ⅛ in. less all around to allow for some expansion. In summer, when the relative humidity is high here in Indiana, I make the panels extend closer to ⁷⁄₁₆ in. into a ½-in.-deep groove.

Cope-and-Stick Option

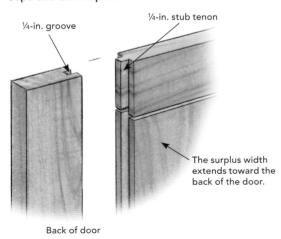

¼-in. groove

¼-in. stub tenon

The surplus width extends toward the back of the door.

Back of door

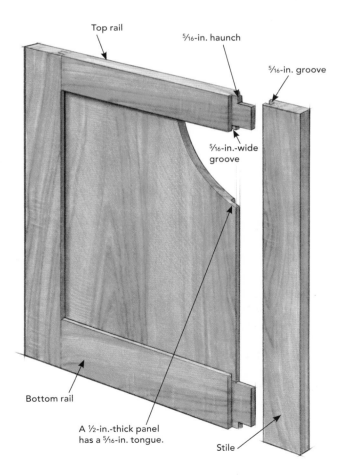

Top rail

⁵⁄₁₆-in. haunch

⁵⁄₁₆-in. groove

⁵⁄₁₆-in.-wide groove

Bottom rail

A ½-in.-thick panel has a ⁵⁄₁₆-in. tongue.

Stile

length. I determined the approximate location of the finished end so that I could avoid the nightmare of exposing a biscuit when I made the final cut. I sand and finish counters in the shop before I scribe and install them.

When I make cabinet doors, I keep the stock as thick as possible, at least ¾ in. and ideally ⅞ in. I flatten door stock on the jointer, then run it through the thickness planer to ensure that it is flat, square-edged, and uniform thickness. Using bar clamps rather than pipe clamps can help keep doors flat. I lay the door directly on the clamp-bar surface so I can detect any deflection and clamp the door to the bar using smaller clamps if necessary. I check for square by comparing diagonal measurements and hold a straightedge across the top and bottom of the frame to ensure that the rail and stile joints are glued up flat, not bowed. I also check for twist, either by sighting across the bare surface of the door or with the aid of winding sticks. Finally, I check the back of the door to make sure the panel is centered in the frame, and I adjust it if necessary by applying pressure with a wide chisel.

When the doors are dry, I rough-fit them to the cabinet openings using a handplane or a tablesaw. Then I rout and chisel mortises for the butt hinges on the cabinets' face frames; the mortises in the doors will come later.

Next, I install the case backs and the solid ledgers. These hanging strips are screwed not just through the ¼-in. plywood cabinet back, but directly through the top, the sides, or both. If the strips go only through the back and the back should somehow detach from the case, the entire assembly could fall forward, causing damage and possibly injury.

Installation Starts at the Highest Point of the Floor

Because this design called for an applied base molding, I could shim the casework up to level and count on the baseboard to hide the shims. I began from the high point on the floor and shimmed the cases up to level as necessary. The sections also were clamped

together, so I could treat the three cabinets as a single unit if the wall behind them wasn't flat.

I use solid wood for counters because it generally holds up better than plywood and looks better with wear. When a solid counter is attached to a plywood case, the wood has to be able to move with changes in relative humidity. I set the counter in place and scribe as necessary, then attach it with screws in oversize holes that allow for wood movement.

As with the bases, I scribe the right face-frame stile to conform to irregularities in the wall, then screw together the upper units to form a single assembly before attaching it to the rear wall. No shimming is necessary because these upper cases are placed on a surface that should be level. I scribe the finished ends as needed and glue them in place. I also sand the face-frame edges flush if necessary.

Hang the Doors and Drawers after the Casework Is Locked In

After applying the baseboard and crown molding, we work on the doors. For inset applications, I like to plane doors and drawer faces to size after installing the casework. Although this technique is unconventional, I find it more efficient. Once in their final position, cabinets don't always sit quite the way they did in the ideal conditions of the shop, so postponing this final fitting until the installation is complete means the work is done only once.

After shimming the doors in place with the proper margins (about 3/32 in. for stain grade, more for painted work), I mark the positions of the hinge mortises on the door stiles. Once marked, the door is clamped in a vise or on sawhorses, where I rout the mortises and mount the hinges. Once the door is rehung, I do a final fitting with a handplane.

Setting the drawers is the final stage. After finalizing the fit, I use a pair of screws and fender washers to hold the drawer face in position. Once I'm satisfied with the fit, I drive in four additional screws to lock the face to the drawer box.

DRAWER CONSTRUCTION AND INSTALLATION:
HANG THE BOX, THEN ATTACH THE FACE

I usually make drawers from ½-in. solid stock and dovetail the corners; it's a joinery option that my customers expect. (For less-expensive projects, I use biscuits or a rabbeted joint, as shown in the detail drawings below.) I groove the inside faces of the front and sides to accept the drawer bottom (I use ⅜-in.- or ½-in.-thick plywood for the bottoms of extra-wide drawers to prevent them from sagging). I also rip the back even with the top face of the drawer bottom so that I can slide in the bottom once the drawer sides are glued. Securing the bottom with small screws (but no glue) provides the option of a removable drawer bottom.

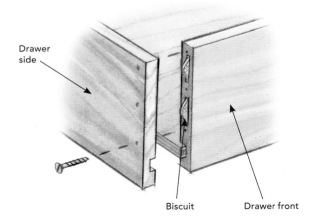

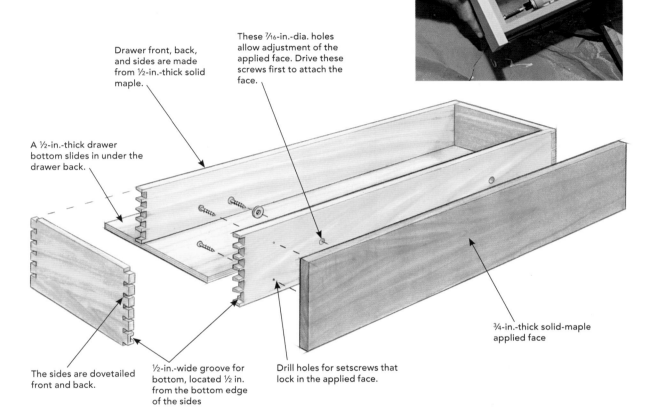

Drawer front, back, and sides are made from ½-in.-thick solid maple.

These ⁷⁄₁₆-in.-dia. holes allow adjustment of the applied face. Drive these screws first to attach the face.

A ½-in.-thick drawer bottom slides in under the drawer back.

¾-in.-thick solid-maple applied face

The sides are dovetailed front and back.

½-in.-wide groove for bottom, located ½ in. from the bottom edge of the sides

Drill holes for setscrews that lock in the applied face.

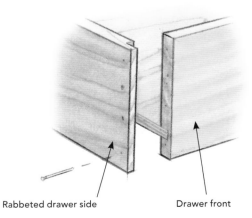

Rabbet-Joint Option

Rabbeted drawer side

Drawer front

Biscuit-Joint Option

Drawer side

Biscuit

Drawer front

Maximize
Pantry Storage

BY REX ALEXANDER

The minute I walked into Judy and Carl Rawski's home, I could tell they were tidy people. Not a thing was out of place. They both talked about how they had revamped many of their kitchen-cabinet interiors to make them more efficient but were stumped when it came to a closet they had designed at the end of a cabinet run. Frustrated with the usual wire shelving or boards resting on cleats, they were looking for lots of storage that was accessible, easy to clean, and attractive.

I like simplicity when designing a pantry, so I came up with the idea of building a closet-size cabinet to eliminate wasted space. Shallow drawers installed at various heights inside the cabinet would span the opening and make stored items easy to reach.

Prepare the Closet for the Cabinet

I wanted to use all the available space in the closet but still have the pullout shelving slide past the butt-hinged doors, even if they were opened only 90°. This meant the cabinet sides would need to be about 1½ in. inside the existing door jambs (see the drawing on p. 152). To inset the cabinet, I used 2×2 blocking at the front and 2×4 blocking at the back of the closet, which left enough room for a 32-in.-wide carcase.

I also installed blocking against the door's head jamb so that the cabinet's head casing would match the sides. On the closet floor, I attached ¾-in. by 1½-in. screw blocks perpendicular to the front edge, followed by two 4¼-in.-tall base supports. Smaller blocks serve as nailers for the side casings.

Cut the Parts, Finish, Then Assemble

The Rawskis' kitchen cabinets have maple interiors, so I used maple plywood for the pantry closet. After I cut the parts, I put a dado head in my tablesaw and cut the tongue-and-rabbet joints for the carcase.

I finished all the parts before assembly. After taping off the areas to be glued, I lightly sanded all the surfaces with 220-grit sandpaper, then applied a satin polyurethane with a fine-nap roller. Two coats adequately protect the wood and give the surface a nice sheen. The finish levels out perfectly, and roller marks disappear. After removing the tape from the joints, I applied glue, clamped together the pieces, and nailed the joints for insurance. Squaring up the carcase was easy once the ¼-in. plywood back was fastened in place.

REPLACE SHELVES with shallow drawers and you can stop diving deep to find the soup.

Install and Trim the Unit

I mounted all the drawers with Blum 550mm epoxy-coated drawer slides (www.blum.com). They handle up to 100 lb., are easy to install, and operate smoothly.

The carcase slid into place along the base supports and between the blocking. I screwed the carcase to the blocking at the front and back of the closet. Then I nailed quartersawn oak trim flush with the inside edge of the cabinet; the trim floats on the outside edge for expansion and contraction. Finally, I filled the nail holes in the trim and installed the drawers onto the slides.

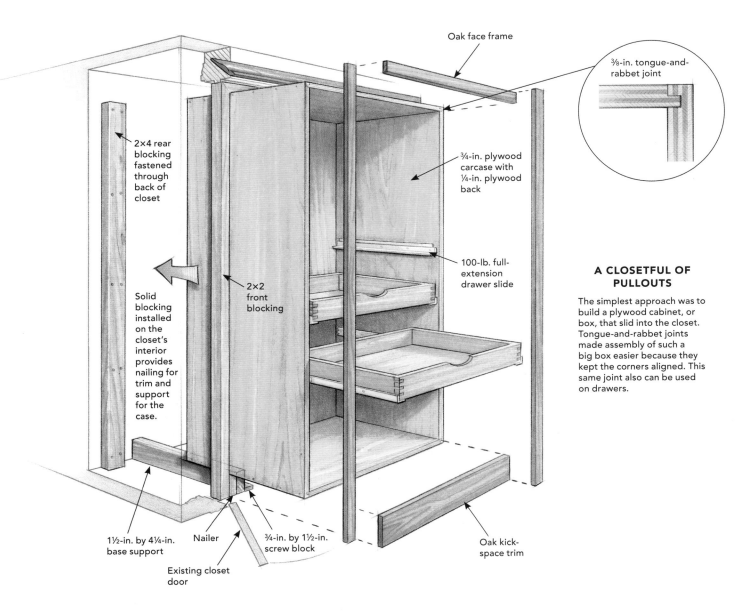

Oak face frame

⅜-in. tongue-and-rabbet joint

2×4 rear blocking fastened through back of closet

¾-in. plywood carcase with ¼-in. plywood back

100-lb. full-extension drawer slide

Solid blocking installed on the closet's interior provides nailing for trim and support for the case.

2×2 front blocking

A CLOSETFUL OF PULLOUTS

The simplest approach was to build a plywood cabinet, or box, that slid into the closet. Tongue-and-rabbet joints made assembly of such a big box easier because they kept the corners aligned. This same joint also can be used on drawers.

1½-in. by 4¼-in. base support

Nailer

¾-in. by 1½-in. screw block

Existing closet door

Oak kick-space trim

THREE DRAWER VARIATIONS

Dovetails

The drawers shown in the photo on p. 151 were built of solid maple with hand-cut dovetail joints, which are almost as labor-intensive as they are good looking. The scooped fronts were cut with a bandsaw and sanded smooth. The drawer bottoms were made of ½-in. plywood glued into a ⅜-in. by ½-in. rabbet.

Wider bottom pin hides drawer bottom

Tongue and Rabbet

I've used this joint on drawers made from ½-in. Baltic-birch plywood. It's easily cut with a dado cutter in a tablesaw. Rout the rabbet for the bottom after assembling the drawer sides, front, and back.

Biscuits

The third variation is also made from ½-in. Baltic-birch plywood, but has mitered corners that are joined with 0-size biscuits. The biscuit joiner must be kept square to the stock when cutting, or the miter will be offset.

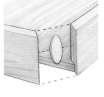

A Built-In Corner Seating Nook

BY JOSEPH LANZA

My friends Debbie and Tom decided to make better use of a small room next to their kitchen. They wanted a built-in seat that could serve as an informal dining area and a place for board games or homework. After measuring the space and designing the seat in cross section, I made a SketchUp® model of a seat with enough room for four people, storage drawers below, and a cabinet in the back of the corner seat. Tom and Debbie liked the design, but before I started building, I made a 24-in.-wide plywood mockup to make sure they would be comfortable sitting in it. We agreed that the mock-up was more comfortable with a ¾-in. plywood block under the front edge. I gave the seat an additional 5° tilt, then made a new SketchUp model of the base of the seat.

Because I would be working alone, building the seat in the shop and installing it as a complete unit were out of the question. Even if I had the strength to do so, the house was built in the eighteenth century, so plumb, level, and square had long since vanished. Because there was sure to be lots of scribing and fitting before the seat was in place, it made sense to break down the job into manageable parts. I decided to start with a level plinth, then to install the base as four separate boxes. Next, I would install the seat and the corner-cabinet unit, and then finish up with all of the solid-wood parts (the seat back, nosings, and moldings). I could make all the parts in the shop, then assemble everything together at the house.

Build Boxes to Form the Seat

For the boxes below the seat, I used dimensions from the SketchUp model to cut parts from ¾-in. birch plywood. Because the seat has a 10° pitch, the joint between the cabinets at the top is a compound miter. To cut the joints, I used a circular saw with the blade set to a 3.81° bevel and a shooting board. The bevel angle came from a chart I found online (www.wood-shoptips.com/tips/012003/012003.pdf). I cut the corner cabinet to the dimensions on the SketchUp model, but I made the two adjoining cabinets 1 in. longer so that I would have room to scribe and fit the joints in place.

Next, using a dado and rabbet joint that was glued and nailed, I made drawers from ½-in. Baltic-birch plywood. I delayed making the applied drawer fronts until the boxes and the face frames were in place and I could get an accurate measurement.

While in the shop, I ripped ¾-in. pine plywood to 16 in. for the seats. The back just overlaps the back edge of the seat. I also milled other parts, such as the solid-pine roundover nosing for the seat, the pine grooved paneling, the face frame, and the cap stock.

THE CRITICAL ANGLES

Unlike a built-in or a set of stairs, a bench might look fine on paper, but the real test is whether it feels comfortable. A short mockup built of plywood gives both the designer and the client a good sense of the bench's ergonomics.

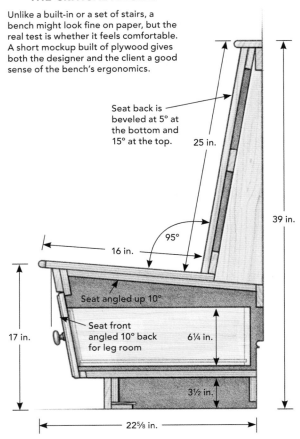

Seat back is beveled at 5° at the bottom and 15° at the top.

25 in.

39 in.

95°

16 in.

Seat angled up 10°

Seat front angled 10° back for leg room

6¼ in.

17 in.

3½ in.

22⅝ in.

Playing by Old-House Rules

Once on-site, my first task was to install the plinth, which is essentially a plywood box 3½ in. high that is analogous to a cabinet's toe kick. Starting at the high point, I leveled each side across, shimming with blocks and screwing the base to the baseboard. I hid the plywood and the gaps with a 1× pine kick board that I scribed to the floor.

The corner base unit was next. I marked left and right reference points an equal distance from the inside corner, then centered the corner base between the two points and screwed it to the plinth. Next, I scribed each of the flanking base units to the corner, checked the fit, and pocket-screwed the top edges together. I also screwed them together at the sides and into the walls.

The next part of the puzzle was the corner seat back. Built in the shop, the unit doubles as a storage

JOIN BASE UNITS WITH A COMPOUND ANGLE

Begin with a level framework of plinth boxes. The plywood seat bases sit atop the plinth boxes and will eventually house drawers. Because the seat is angled back, the corner boxes are joined with a 22.5° angle and an approximately 4° bevel.

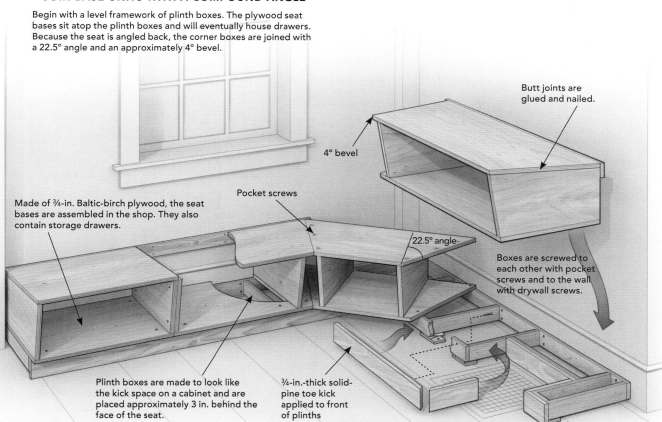

Butt joints are glued and nailed.

4° bevel

Made of ¾-in. Baltic-birch plywood, the seat bases are assembled in the shop. They also contain storage drawers.

Pocket screws

22.5° angle

Boxes are screwed to each other with pocket screws and to the wall with drywall screws.

Plinth boxes are made to look like the kick space on a cabinet and are placed approximately 3 in. behind the face of the seat.

¾-in.-thick solid-pine toe kick applied to front of plinths

A SCRIBE MAY BE NECESSARY. Position the opposite side base and check the fit. Use a set of scribes to mark the cut.

A SAW GUIDE IS A MUST. When trimming scribed cuts, a site-built saw guide is a fast way to make an accurate cut.

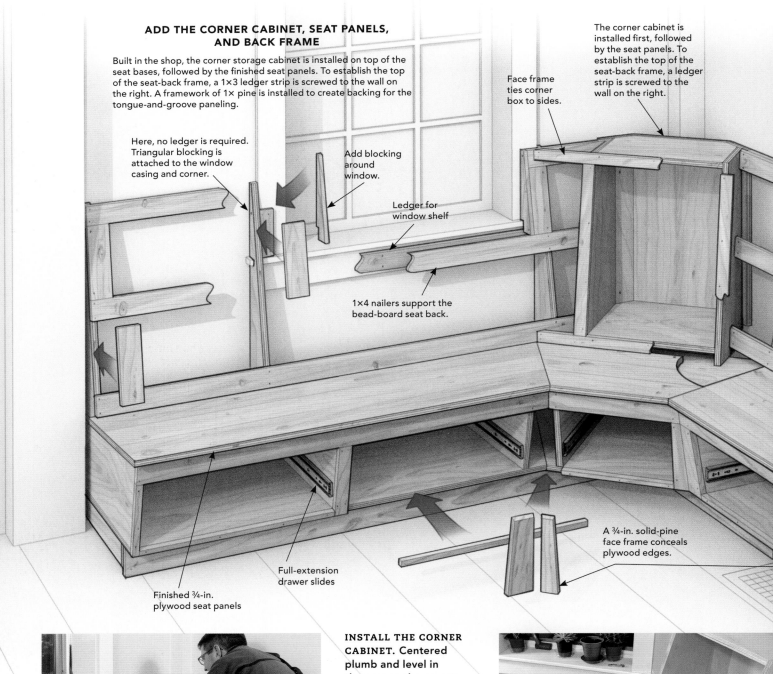

ADD THE CORNER CABINET, SEAT PANELS, AND BACK FRAME

Built in the shop, the corner storage cabinet is installed on top of the seat bases, followed by the finished seat panels. To establish the top of the seat-back frame, a 1×3 ledger strip is screwed to the wall on the right. A framework of 1× pine is installed to create backing for the tongue-and-groove paneling.

Here, no ledger is required. Triangular blocking is attached to the window casing and corner.

Add blocking around window.

The corner cabinet is installed first, followed by the seat panels. To establish the top of the seat-back frame, a ledger strip is screwed to the wall on the right.

Face frame ties corner box to sides.

Ledger for window shelf

1×4 nailers support the bead-board seat back.

Finished ¾-in. plywood seat panels

Full-extension drawer slides

A ¾-in. solid-pine face frame conceals plywood edges.

INSTALL THE CORNER CABINET. Centered plumb and level in the corner, the corner cabinet in part anchors the framing for the seat back and establishes the width of the seat.

Triangular blocking for the seat back is notched around the ledger.

1×3 ledger

ASSEMBLE ELEMENTS OF THE BACK FRAME. On the right side, a 1×3 ledger screwed to the wall establishes the height of the back. Triangular pieces of plywood blocking are plumbed up and nailed to the base. Horizontal nailers then are attached across the top, middle, and bottom.

A LEDGER FOR THE WINDOW SHELF IS NAILED TO THE WINDOW APRON. On the left, the triangular blocking is attached to the window casing and corner post; no ledger is needed.

FIT THE PLYWOOD SEAT PANELS. Start by locating the corner piece, which determines the location of the adjacent panels. After being scribed to fit, the panels are clamped in place and attached with screws driven from below.

TIE BOTH SIDES TOGETHER. The corner storage unit's face frame is extended across to the sides to provide blocking for the seat-back transition.

cabinet. The idea was to use the storage unit as a reference when it came time to frame the rest of the seat back. I positioned the corner unit so that it was parallel to the front and level, then toe-screwed it to the seat and to the wall.

I opted to fit and install the plywood seat panels first, then have the seat back land on the seat. Otherwise, I'd have to scribe the seat to the back, leaving a visible joint. Beveled to the same angles as the seat base, the panels were ripped at 16 in. wide and cut to length to form an equal overhang at the front and sides. I attached the panels with screws driven up through the base.

The Seat-Back Frame Is a Custom Fit

Because the walls were not flat or plumb, I began making the seat-back frame with a series of triangular plywood panels connected by 1×4s. Notched over a ledger, the triangles' bases were screwed to the seat bases. Next, I attached horizontal 1×4s across the top, middle, and bottom as nailers for the beadboard seat back. After both sides were complete, I covered the corner unit with a face frame.

Once these parts were fit and nailed up, I filled in the rest of the seat back, choosing the appropriate widths to fit the space. The right side went quickly, but the left was complicated by a window. There, I had to notch the first piece and lower a few more to make room for a small shelf below the windowsill.

When the back was complete, I glued and nailed the nosing to the front and side edges of the seat. Below the seat, I covered the veneer edges of the plywood with 1× solid stock, then filled in the face frames in the corners and above the drawers. After mounting the drawers on full-extension slides, I cut and fit the drawer fronts. Then I finished the beadboard paneling on the ends of the unit and added the final face-frame piece.

To cap it off, I started with a piece of ¾-in. pine plywood, which I fit into the corner by ticksticking. I then scribed solid cap pieces to the wall along each side, butting them to the side of the plywood

CAP THINGS OFF WITH SOLID PINE

The seat back and sides are covered with ¾-in. solid-pine bead board milled in the shop. The area on each side of the window casing is filled in with the same stock. The plywood cap is scribed in place on the corner cabinet and butted to the solid-pine cap stock that runs along the back. Solid-pine nosings hide plywood edges.

Scribe caps to wall for a consistent overhang.

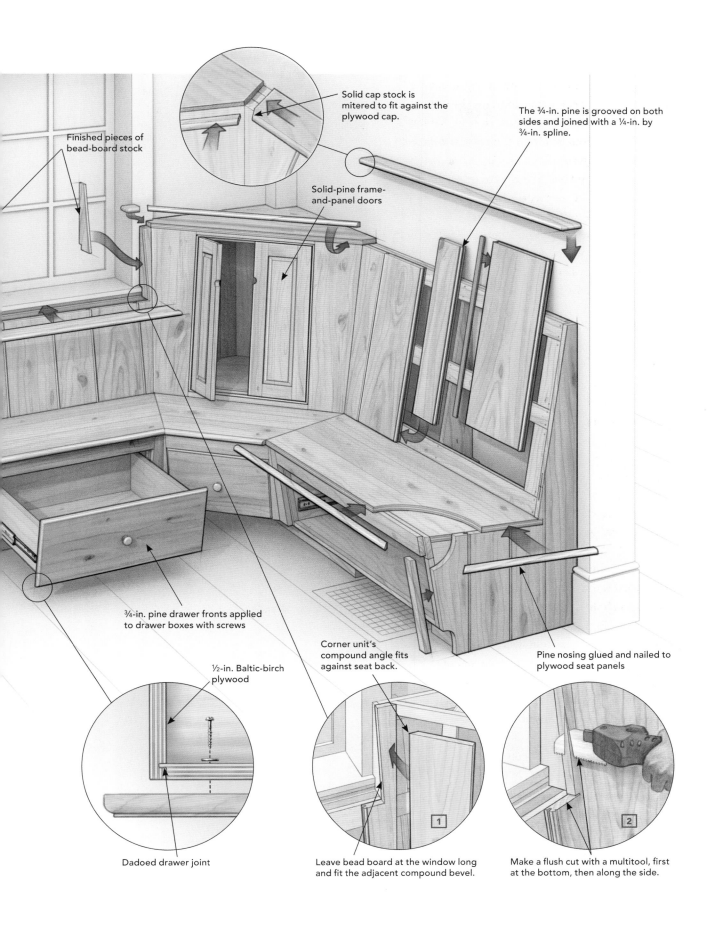

Solid cap stock is mitered to fit against the plywood cap.

The ¾-in. pine is grooved on both sides and joined with a ¼-in. by ¾-in. spline.

Finished pieces of bead-board stock

Solid-pine frame-and-panel doors

¾-in. pine drawer fronts applied to drawer boxes with screws

½-in. Baltic-birch plywood

Corner unit's compound angle fits against seat back.

Pine nosing glued and nailed to plywood seat panels

Dadoed drawer joint

Leave bead board at the window long and fit the adjacent compound bevel.

1

Make a flush cut with a multitool, first at the bottom, then along the side.

2

and mitering them where they met the nosing on the front edge. I hung the doors on the corner unit with full-overlay cup hinges and fit a quirked bead against the face frame around them. Finally, I cleaned up my pencil marks and finish-sanded the unit. After I left, the painter came in and applied oil-based stain, sealed it with a coat of shellac, and brushed on two coats of polyurethane.

FIND THE ANGLE. The corner unit's bead board intersects at a compound angle. From the edge of the face frame, measure top and bottom.

INSTALL THE BEAD BOARD FROM THE CORNER OUT. Starting to the right of the bottom of the corner unit, nail the first board on a plumb line.

FIT THE BOARD. After cutting the compound angle with a saw guide, nail it against the first board. After repeating the process on the other side of the corner unit, fill in the rest of the boards out to the ends.

Flooring

Flooring Options for the Kitchen

BY MATTHEW TEAGUE

MAKE NEW FLOORS OUT OF OLD TIMBERS. More and more companies, including Carlisle Wide Plank Floors (which made this walnut floor), use carefully managed old-growth trees, salvaged logs, and recycled beams to make new floorboards that offer rich character and antique charm.

As the most highly trafficked space in the house, a kitchen's floor has to withstand everything from spills to stilettos. The kitchen is the social heart of the home, playing host to dinner-party guests, friends, and family on a regular basis. The floor needs to look good, be comfortable to walk on, and wear well over time.

Sorting through the array of flooring materials can be a downright dizzying process, and finding the right balance between style and function is often the most difficult task. Each type of flooring has strengths and weaknesses, which greatly affect how it'll live in your kitchen. Whether you're looking for the charm of hand-scraped hardwood, the comfort of cork, the durability of concrete, or the "greenness" of palm, I'll pinpoint the benefits of each product and highlight its flaws. Before you dive in, remember: No single type of flooring material is best. The right kitchen-flooring choice is a reflection of your overall taste, the needs of your home, and your budget.

Wood Maintains a Tradition of Durability and Comfort

Aside from rock and dirt, wood floors probably have the longest history of any flooring type. While traditional, unfinished solid-plank flooring continues to be installed in kitchens across the country, there are two other wood-floor options available that just might outperform it. Engineered and prefinished wood flooring can be installed more quickly than unfinished solid-wood boards without abandoning their look, comfort, or durability. A wood floor's longevity, however, depends largely on the way it is finished and maintained. For years, oil-based urethanes were the finish of choice, but modern water-based finishes are just as durable and can be applied faster and with less odor. Sweeping regularly helps prevent dirt from wearing away the finish.

SOLID WOOD

Solid-oak floors have made up the bulk of the wood-flooring industry for years, but that doesn't mean that wood floors have limited style. Solid-wood flooring can be made out of everything from ash to zebrawood and milled to most any width you'd like. In the kitchen, hardwoods perform best. Although softwoods like pine look good and are readily available, they're not as tough as hardwood species and wear quickly under heavy use. Some hardwoods are harder than others, but all are rugged enough to handle everyday abuse in a kitchen. Solid hardwoods will last as long as your house, and they're also comfortable underfoot. Wood flexes just enough to ease the tension on your feet, legs, and back.

If your tastes lean toward traditional hardwood and you're in the market for an environmentally friendly floor, take a look at flooring made from recycled lumber or from the old-growth timbers now being hauled up from some lake bottoms.

ENGINEERED WOOD

Engineered floorboards are more dimensionally stable than solid-wood flooring, meaning they're less likely to expand or contract due to humidity fluctuations. This stability makes them a great choice for flooring installed over a radiant-heating system. They're also just as comfortable as solid wood. The floorboards are made of multiple layers of wood stacked in a cross-grain pattern and glued up under pressure, much like plywood. The top layer features

SIMILARITIES GO ONLY SO DEEP

SOLID-WOOD FLOORING'S THICKNESS allows it to be refinished time and again over its life span. Engineered flooring's thin top layer of wood is only 1/16 in. to 1/8 in. deep, making it difficult to refinish without causing damage to the veneer. Both types of flooring can be ordered prefinished, eliminating the on-site finishing process while providing a finish of higher quality in terms of durability.

SOLID-WOOD FLOORING

ENGINEERED-WOOD FLOORING

PROS

Easy on your feet; warm underfoot; durable; wide range of species, stains, and prices; solid wood can be refinished multiple times; engineered wood installs quickly; prefinished floors can be used immediately.

CONS

Can be expensive; susceptible to water damage; softer species dent easily; refinishing is an involved process; solid wood expands/contracts with humidity; prefinished floors offer limited stain options; limited refinishing options with engineered flooring.

HARDWOOD FLOORING THE EASY WAY. Some engineered floors, like these made by Bruce® Hardwood Flooring, come prefinished and are installed simply by locking each board together with a specially designed tongue-and-groove joint.

Laminate Performs and Looks Better Than You Think

As much as some laminate flooring looks like solid wood, it is anything but. Laminate flooring is composed of four different layers of material and can be made to look like anything from marble to distressed oak. The top layer of a laminate board, called the wear layer, is usually a clear resin-based melamine that is incredibly durable and scratch resistant. Beneath the wear layer is a photo layer, which is a paper image of the specific material that you see on the face of the board. These layers are bound to a core made of high-density fiberboard (HDF) and a backing, usually made of melamine, that lends stability and moisture resistance. Because of the relatively inexpensive materials that go into laminate flooring, it is one of the most economical options available.

One of the major benefits of laminate flooring is the speed with which it can be installed. Laminate floors are floating, meaning they don't need to be fastened to a subfloor. While laminate floors of old had to be glued together, most new laminates snap together using an interlocking tongue-and-groove arrangement. This joint not only makes installation quick and easy, but it also pulls the boards tightly together, which helps prevent liquids from penetrating the seams, a nice quality in a kitchen floor.

While the durability of laminate has always been high, the flooring tended to look fake. Newer laminate flooring is more convincing than ever. In addition to laminate's durability and low cost, the product offers plenty of deflection, making it comfortable underfoot. Caring for a laminate floor is easy and requires only occasional damp-mopping.

a veneer of the best-looking wood, while the layers underneath can be made of less expensive wood.

Engineered wood floors usually come prefinished. Manufacturers claim that their applied finishes are much more durable than any finish that can be applied on site. That said, kitchen activity can be ruthless, and even the most durable wood floors may need to be refinished at some point. Although some manufacturers boast that you can sand an engineered wood floor to refinish it, the top layer of wood is only $\frac{1}{16}$ in. to $\frac{1}{8}$ in. thick, making it difficult to sand without exposing the layers underneath.

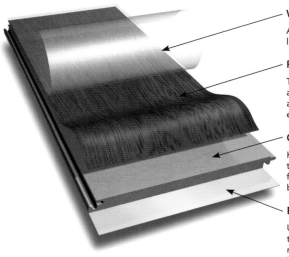

Wear Layer

A hard-wearing film gives laminate flooring its durability.

Photo Layer

The photographic image allows laminate to mimic anything from marble to exotic hardwood.

Core

Known as the carrier board, this piece of high-density fiberboard is considered the backbone of each plank.

Backing

Usually made of melamine, this sheet provides extra moisture resistance to the bottom of each board.

MUCH MORE THAN A REPRODUCTION OF WOOD. Laminate comes in a number of shapes, colors, and textures to fit whatever aesthetic theme your kitchen may have. These tiles are made by ABET Laminati®.

DISTRESSING

KNOTS

SAWMARKS

NOT THE LAMINATE YOU REMEMBER. Thanks to advanced manufacturing processes at companies like Mannington and Quick-Step®, laminate can be adorned with qualities found only on true wood floors.

LAMINATE

PROS
Durable; easy on your feet; low maintenance; can be installed over old flooring; quiet; easy installation; low to moderate cost; scratch resistant; damaged planks can be replaced; built-in vapor barrier reduces moisture absorption.

CONS
Cannot be refinished; some are expensive; limited style choices; not hypoallergenic; wet environments may cause fiberboard core to swell.

SOURCES

LAMINATE

ABET LAMINATI
www.abetlaminati.com

FORMICA
www.formica.com

LUMBER LIQUIDATORS
www.lumberliquidators.com

MANNINGTON
www.mannington.com

PERGO®
www.pergo.com

QUICK-STEP
www.quick-step.com

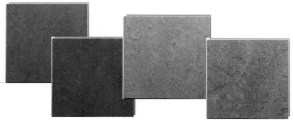

Linoleum Is Low Impact and Biodegradable

After falling out of vogue when vinyl became the kitchen floor of choice in the 1960s, linoleum has under gone a revival in recent years due to its standing as an environmentally friendly flooring option. Linoleum takes less energy to manufacture than most flooring, and it is made primarily from natural materials: linseed oil, wood flour, limestone, tree resins, and natural jute. Linoleum also can be installed using a solvent-free adhesive. When made of all-natural products, linoleum is 100% biodegradable and has no VOC emissions. Forbo, the company that introduced Marmoleum®, even recycles all of its postproduction waste.

Available in sheets and tiles of varying sizes and in more than 150 colors and patterns, Forbo's Marmoleum and Armstrong's Marmorette are highly versatile from a design standpoint. Linoleum also wears well and actually gets better with age: Exposure to air causes linoleum to harden, but it remains resilient, comfortable, and quiet underfoot. It's also hypoallergenic.

LINOLEUM

PROS
Biodegradable; antistatic; resilient; comfortable underfoot; many colors available; hypoallergenic; homogeneous throughout; durable; easy installation.

CONS
Difficult to repair; difficult to find installer; seams may be visible and intrusive.

SOURCES

LINOLEUM

ARMSTRONG WORLD INDUSTRIES
www.armstrong.com

FORBO FLOORING SYSTEMS
www.forbo-flooring.us

Vinyl Is Low Maintenance

Vinyl has been vastly improved—in both design and quality—since its no-wax heyday in the 1960s. Sheet vinyl is available in widths ranging from 6 ft. to 12 ft., while vinyl tiles are usually sold in 12-in. squares. Vinyl even comes in plank form to mimic hardwood. Each type is available in an almost endless array of colors and designs.

Vinyl is generally composed of four layers. A clear wear coat, usually made of urethane, helps prevent scratches and eases cleanup. A layer of clear vinyl provides durability. The printed layer, similar to laminate flooring, creates the look of the floor, while a backing of either felt or fiberglass adds rigidity. Vinyl with a felt backing must be glued to a subfloor. Fiberglass-backed floors are more comfortable and generally don't require any adhesive because they are far less likely to curl up at the edges.

Some manufacturers produce inlaid vinyl flooring in which granules of color are embedded to lend a richer appearance. Inlaid patterns wear better than vinyl with only a printed photographic image, but they typically cost a bit more. Many manufacturers also add texture to create a more realistic, 3-D effect that closely mimics the surfaces they intend to replicate.

VINYL

PROS
Resilient; durable; inexpensive; easy on your feet; quiet; low maintenance; water resistant; wide sheets hide seams in small rooms; easy to install; wide variety available; easy maintenance.

CONS
Seams visible in wide rooms; seams susceptible to water damage; gloss finishes are slippery when wet; can fade or yellow; pattern can wear off; seams may lift.

SOURCES

VINYL

AMTICO® INTERNATIONAL INC.
www.amtico.com

ARMSTRONG WORLD INDUSTRIES
www.armstrong.com

CONGOLEUM®
www.congoleum.com

MANNINGTON
www.mannington.com

Tile and Stone Are at Home in the Kitchen

Tile is often the first material that comes to mind when people think of a kitchen floor, and it has probably been that way for a while. Archaeologists have discovered thin slabs of fired clay dating back to about 4700 B.C.E. Today's tile isn't much different. Modern tile consists of clay and minerals that are shaped, pressed, and fired at high temperatures to create a hard surface. Tile is available in a variety of colors and shapes and in sizes that range from 1-in. circles to 6-in. arabesques to 2-ft. squares. With so many options, the patterns possible with tile approach infinite.

Ceramic tiles are available in nonporcelain and porcelain versions. The current market, however, is seeing a surge in the use of porcelain in the kitchen. Porcelain tiles are made from ingredients similar to those found in fine dinnerware and are fired at higher temperatures than nonporcelain tiles. The end product is incredibly dense, with a water-absorption rate that's much lower than nonporcelain tile, which makes it frost resistant and an excellent choice for indoor or outdoor kitchens. Porcelain is also homogenous throughout, meaning that if you drop a cast-iron pan and chip the tile, the material below is the same color as the surface. Nonporcelain tiles achieve their color from an applied glaze, and damage is more noticeable.

When shopping for tile, remember that all tiles can be used on walls, but not all tiles can be used on floors. Floor tiles must be rated as such, and for durability, kitchen tiles must be at least a category III (out of a I to IV rating). What's a strength to some might be a weakness to others: Tile's density, hardness, and rigidity make it durable, but that also can translate into sore legs for cooks who stand in the kitchen for a long time.

Spills are inevitable in the kitchen, so look for tile that has good slip resistance. Unglazed tiles offer better traction than glazed tiles. However, unglazed tiles and grout lines must be sealed, and textured floors are more difficult to clean.

TRIED AND TRUE. Beyond its durability and ease of maintenance, tile offers the largest variety of colors, shapes, and sizes, which makes a one-of-a-kind kitchen much more attainable.

CONSISTENCY IS KEY. Most porcelain tile maintains the same color throughout its depth, so damage to the surface won't be so apparent.

TILE AND STONE

PROS
Countless sizes, shapes, and colors; low maintenance; can be stain resistant; colors won't fade; works well with radiant-floor heat; can create very natural look (stone); inexpensive (some tile).

CONS
Cold underfoot; susceptible to cracking or chipping; grout may stain or crack; grout requires maintenance; gloss finishes can be slippery when wet; hard on your feet; noisy; dropped items likely to break; must be sealed regularly (stone); can be very expensive.

LIMESTONE

TRAVERTINE

GRANITE

MARBLE

GRANITE

GRANITE

STONE DOESN'T HAVE TO BE SO RUGGED. Stone can be cut into smooth, uniform tiles to create a more reserved yet equally durable kitchen floor.

SOURCES

TILE AND STONE

CERAMIC TILES OF ITALY
www.italytile.com

CROSSVILLE® INC.
www.crossvilleinc.com

DALTILE® CORP.
www.daltile.com

GREEN MOUNTAIN SOAPSTONE® CORP.
www.greenmountainsoapstone.com

MARBLE GRANITE DEPOT
www.marblegranitedepot.com

THE MOSAIC TILE CO.
www.mosaictileco.com

TILE COUNCIL OF NORTH AMERICA
www.tcnatile.com

*For stone tile, look for tile dealers rather than stone dealers.

STONE

Stone flooring can bring the rustic feel of the outdoors into your kitchen, or it can be configured in sleek, uniform, tilelike orientations to create a more refined-looking floor. Uniform layouts demand precut stones, which increase costs substantially. For more money, stones can be cut into specific shapes to fit into the layout of your choosing.

Except for soapstone, all stone should be sealed to increase its stain resistance. To care for a stone floor, you'll need either a damp mop or a stone cleaner; consult your stone or floor specialist to determine the best cleaning practices for the type of stone you install. As with tile, the grout between stones must be sealed occasionally; the frequency varies from one type of grout to another.

One-of-a-kind designs are possible with stone floors. There are numerous types of stone to choose from: marble, granite, limestone, soapstone, travertine, and flagstone among them. An excellent conductor of heat, stone flooring works well with radiant-floor heating systems. Although some stone wears better than others, the average stone floor is incredibly durable. However, with this durability comes hardness, which can be unforgiving to your feet and to dropped dishware.

Fringe Flooring

Concrete, brick, and stainless steel are less likely residential-flooring options, but they perform exceptionally well when placed in the kitchen, where durable, stylish materials are a must.

CONCRETE

Concrete can be stamped to simulate a tile, brick, or stone floor; finished in a variety of textures; and stained an almost endless spectrum of colors. Concrete can even be made into tiles.

Although concrete can be cold underfoot, it works well in conjunction with radiant-floor heat, it is easy to maintain, and it is arguably the most durable flooring material you can place in the kitchen. On the downside, concrete is extremely hard and does not deflect whatsoever when walked on or when a glass is dropped on it. It's also susceptible to staining if not sealed properly. Concrete is a low-cost product, but prices can soar when a professional finisher is called in to tackle the job.

BRICK

Forgotten for many years and likely inspired by the urban-chic look of factories converted for loft living, the charm of brick flooring is once again popular. More often than not, today's clay-brick

SOURCES

CONCRETE

CONCRETE NETWORK
www.concretenetwork.com

CONCRETE TILE MANUFACTURERS ASSOCIATION
www.concretetile.hypermart.net

SONOMA CAST STONE
www.sonomastone.com

BRICK

BRICK VENEER INC.
www.thin-brick-veneer.com

VINTAGE BRICK SALVAGE
www.bricksalvage.com

STAINLESS STEEL

PLANIUM
www.planium.it

*Contact tile dealers to find concrete tile

NEW BRICK VENEER

RECLAIMED BRICK VENEER

floors are composed of brick veneers ranging in thickness from $\frac{1}{2}$ in. to $\frac{15}{16}$ in. New veneers offer a smooth, consistent look, whereas veneers made from old reclaimed bricks tend to have a bit more character. Both types are installed just like unglazed ceramic tile. The slip resistance of brick and its durability make it a great choice for the kitchen. However, like natural stone, brick can be unforgiving on your feet, dishware, and wallet.

SOURCES

CORK

AMCORK
www.amcork.com

LUMBER LIQUIDATORS
www.lumberliquidators.com

SMITH & FONG PLYBOO®
www.plyboo.com

USFLOORS®
www.naturalcork.com

STAINLESS STEEL

There's nothing subtle about a stainless-steel floor, but if it's a clean, modern look you're after, it might be the best option. These metal tiles, which come as large as 24 in. by 24 in., are screwed in place over a thin rubber underlayment. There is no need for adhesive, and the installation is quick and dust free. While smooth steel can be slippery when wet, metal flooring is often embossed to increase slip resistance and add style. Stainless steel may be durable, but it's very expensive.

CORK

PROS
Easy on your feet; warm; unique texture; environmentally friendly; fire-retardant; hypoallergenic.

CONS
Edges of prefinished floors must be sealed; not the most durable flooring option.

Cork

Cork is harvested from live cork oak trees without cutting down the actual tree or corrupting the habitat in which it grows. The cork, which is similar to the outer layer of bark on a tree, regrows and is ready to harvest every 9 to 14 years. Multiple manufacturers now offer both unfinished and prefinished cork flooring in both tiles and glueless tongue-and-groove planks. Warm and comfortable to walk on, cork floors are also resilient. The flooring compresses underfoot, or under the impact of a dropped plate, and rebounds to its full volume. This resilience does have limits: If large appliances or furniture sits in the same spot for long lengths of time, the underlying cork can become permanently deformed.

Cork contains elements that repel bugs, mold, and mildew, so it's considered hypoallergenic. It also acts as an insulator to reduce noise transmission between rooms. You can buy cork floors that are natural in color or stained a variety of shades. You can even find cork floors with swirl patterns reminiscent of burl wood.

Rubber

Designed to withstand the trials of commercial kitchens, machine shops, and automotive centers, rubber flooring has no trouble standing up to the rigors of a residential kitchen. Available in a variety of colors and patterns, rubber floors don't have to look as industrial as you might think. The various raised patterns on rubber floors are designed to improve traction, but they also lend a decorative, contemporary look to a kitchen. Rubber flooring is available in both sheets and tiles and is generally installed with a solvent-free adhesive. While a few rubber floors are marketed for residential use, you also might consider buying a commercial rubber floor through a flooring dealer.

SOURCES

RUBBER

EXPANKO
www.expanko.com

QUALITY FLOORING 4 LESS
www.qualityflooring4less.com

RUBBER

PROS
Comfortable underfoot; contemporary look; durable; easy maintenance; can be custom colored; resilient.

CONS
Can be difficult to find; few experienced installers; expensive; some products can be damaged by spills.

If you're looking for the performance traits of rubber in an environmentally responsible product, look to the manufacturer Expanko® and its residential product, Reztec. This flooring is made of a combination of postindustrial-waste rubber, virgin rubber, and recycled tires. Reztec is available in 48-in.-wide rolls and three different tile sizes.

Bamboo

As hard as maple and as durable as oak, bamboo is marketed as an environmentally friendly choice. Although the term *sustainable* has different meanings to different people, it's difficult to argue against the sustainability of bamboo. Tonkin and moso—the varieties of bamboo used to manufacture most flooring—grow to full height in about six months and naturally replenish themselves once harvested. A lot of manufacturers, however, allow bamboo to

PUTTING OLD TIRES TO GOOD USE. This rubber flooring from Expanko is vibrantly colored, comfortable, and durable, and is made of rubber that would otherwise be tossed in the trash.

continue growing for four years to six years. This late growth lends significant strength to the bamboo. Most of today's bamboo is harvested in Asia and South America, but a number of manufacturers are experimenting with bamboo stands in some southern states.

There are four main styles of bamboo flooring on the market: flat grain, vertical grain, end grain, and strand woven. Each has a different price point, aesthetic, and level of durability. Flat-grain bamboo is considered the most economical because it's the least expensive type of bamboo flooring.

Bamboo is naturally pale yellow but is often put through a heating process, which caramelizes its natural sugars and gives it an amber tone. Bamboo flooring is available in a variety of other colors too, to complement any design theme.

FLAT GRAIN

VERTICAL GRAIN

END GRAIN

STRAND WOVEN

WHICH IS THE MOST DURABLE? All bamboo is tough enough for the kitchen, but end-grain and strand-woven bamboo are the hardest.

BAMBOO

PROS
Warm underfoot; durable; some give underfoot; available prefinished; available as an easy-to-install engineered product.

CONS
Limited color options; limited products on the market; prefinished planks leave seams unsealed.

⅝-in.-thick solid bamboo

⅛-in.-thick bamboo mounted to engineered planking

DIMENSIONALLY DIFFERENT. Bamboo flooring can be purchased as a solid product in ⅝-in.-thick tongue-and-groove strips or mounted on an engineered plank. Either type can be finished on site or purchased prefinished.

SOURCES

BAMBOO

CALI BAMBOO®
www.calibamboo.com

SMITH AND FONG PLYBOO
www.plyboo.com

TERAGREN®
www.teragren.com

US FLOORS
www.naturalcork.com

STAINED IRISH MOSS

JACOBEAN

COGNAC

PECAN

A BROAD COLOR PALETTE. Bamboo is difficult to stain evenly, but factory-applied colorants give this flooring an even, enriched look.

Palm

Palm, a relative newcomer to the flooring market, is made from the hard, dark wood of plantation-grown coconut palm trees that no longer produce coconuts. After about 100 years, coconut palms grow so large that nutrients from the soil no longer reach the nuts, so the trees stop producing and have to be cut down. The lumber, which often went unused, is sliced, dried, and laminated together—much like plywood—using nontoxic adhesives.

Sold in $\frac{5}{8}$-in.-thick, 72-in.-long tongue-and-groove strips, palm flooring installs much like traditional hardwood flooring. The end product is about 25% harder than red oak, so it performs relatively well in the kitchen. Palm wears and reacts with water in very similar ways to traditional hardwood floors. The finishing and maintenance requirements are similar as well.

Palm flooring is available in both edge-grain or flat-grain orientations and can be purchased unfinished or prefinished with natural, walnut, or ebony stains.

PALM

PROS
Warm and comfortable underfoot; durable; available prefinished; made of products that would otherwise go to waste.

CONS
Limited color options; limited products on the market; prefinished planks leave seams unsealed.

SOURCES

PALM

SMITH AND FONG PLYBOO
www.plyboo.com

For Great Tile Floors, Layout Is Everything

BY DAVID HART

Have you ever noticed the hallmarks of a bad tile layout? Slivers of tile at doorways or a line of tile that's not parallel to a long wall? I certainly have. A great tile installation doesn't start with the mortar, the wet saw, or even the grout. It starts with a proper layout. Not only will a well-planned tile floor or wall look great but it also can save money by reducing waste.

I spend up to a day laying out a tile job before I do anything else. Essentially, I create a grid on the floor that tells me where the tiles will land. By determining a layout and shifting it as necessary, I can reduce cutting and eliminate the most difficult cuts, such as those around vents, outlets, and plumbing fixtures. Of course, I'll still have to cut around those obstacles, but with careful planning, I can make sure they don't fall inside a single tile, which can take far longer than making a couple of straight or U-shaped cuts in adjoining tiles. The whole idea is to streamline the process for the installer, which almost always yields a better tile job.

Establish a Reference

To create a layout grid, you need to know the size of the tiles. This determines the size of the grid squares. From there, you can establish horizontal and vertical reference lines, and superimpose the grid on the floor.

A GRID REVEALS THE LAYOUT BEFORE INSTALLATION

FIND THE UNIT OF MEASURE FIRST

Arrange several tiles into a square block that will form the basis of the grid. The ideal block dimensions range from 24 in. to 32 in. sq. Include space for grout lines on two adjoining sides of each tile in the measurement. In this example, four tiles create a 24-in.-sq. block.

CREATE REFERENCE LINES ON THE FLOOR

Once the block size is known, measure and snap a chalkline along the axis of the room's length. Ideally, the line should be parallel to both walls. Next, pick the widest area of the room and, using a Pythagorean principle (that of the 3-4-5 triangle), establish a perpendicular line to the first. The larger the triangle, the more accurate the perpendicular line.

CHECK THE MEASUREMENTS AND ADJUST

Using the block as a unit of measurement, check the distances from the reference lines to the focal points. The ideal is to end with a half tile or more. Adjust the line (and grid layout) if the partial tile is less than half. When the layout is adjusted, snap a grid of chalklines that define each block or a multiple of blocks.

ORIENT TILES FROM THE SAME POINT

When tiles are installed within the grid, they all must be aligned to the same corner of each square. For instance, if the top and left sides are placed directly on the chalkline, space for a grout line will be included in the measurement at the bottom and right of the tile so they integrate with the adjacent tile block. This way, installers can start in different parts of a room, and when they meet, their work will match.

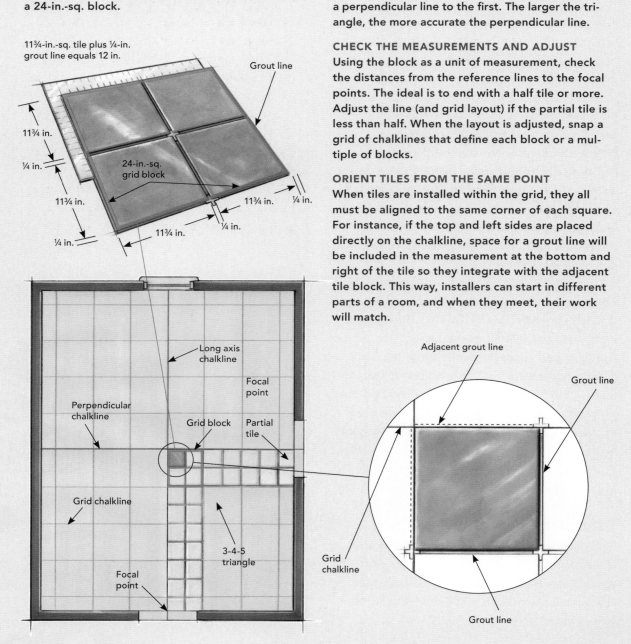

11¾-in.-sq. tile plus ¼-in. grout line equals 12 in.

Grout line

11¾ in.

¼ in.

24-in.-sq. grid block

11¾ in.

11¾ in.

¼ in.

11¾ in.

¼ in.

¼ in.

Long axis chalkline

Focal point

Perpendicular chalkline

Grid block

Partial tile

Grid chalkline

3-4-5 triangle

Focal point

Adjacent grout line

Grout line

Grid chalkline

Grout line

I start by laying a few tiles side by side along a straightedge, each separated by the width of the grout joint I plan to use, and then measuring the length of the group plus a line of grout on one outside edge. I'm aiming for a unit of measure that's between 24 in. and 36 in., a distance I can comfortably reach on a typical floor installation.

Once I determine the unit measurement, I snap a reference chalkline parallel to the longest straight wall in the room. That reference line can be any distance from any wall, including a centerline between two main walls, or the reference line can be the cumulative measurement of tiles and grout joints from a single wall.

Next, I measure from that line to various stops, such as walls, entryways, and cabinet bases, to determine the cuts I'll have. I always plan for at least half a tile at the most obvious places—doorways and long, visible walls, for example. In some cases, it's impossible to have large pieces everywhere, so I place narrow pieces in closets, under cabinet toe kicks, or behind toilets.

If my first reference line doesn't give me a layout that works, I erase the line with a damp sponge, adjust the location, and snap a new one. Then I snap lines at the unit-measure increments parallel to my reference line. It's critical to make sure the measurements are precise; a ¼-in. or even ⅛-in. error can throw off the entire layout.

Transfer the Grid to the Floor

Before I snap final lines, I review where the cuts will fall and then determine the best starting point. I choose an arbitrary point on my primary reference line and then measure in unit-measure increments to determine the locations of the cut tiles so that the largest pieces are in the most visible areas.

Once I determine my reference point on the vertical lines, I make a right triangle using the simple 3-4-5 rule governing right triangles. I use the longest combination of numbers, which will give me a longer perpendicular line. This serves as my primary horizontal line. I then snap lines at unit-measure increments, creating a grid of equal blocks on the

A SIMPLE GALLEY KITCHEN

In this example, 12-in. tiles in a 24-in. grid are laid over a long narrow plan. The focal points are at the sink, the cabinet kick spaces, and the doorways. The potential complicating factor here is the hexagonal eating nook.

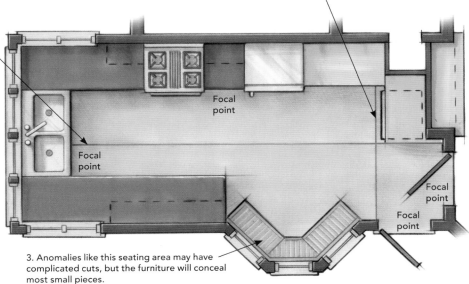

2. Establish a perpendicular line at the widest point, then adjust for focal points.

1. Start the first vertical line by measuring from the cabinet wall. The longest, straightest wall should always be the reference. Measure across to make sure the opposite wall is parallel to the line, and adjust if it isn't parallel.

Focal point

Focal point

Focal point

Focal point

3. Anomalies like this seating area may have complicated cuts, but the furniture will conceal most small pieces.

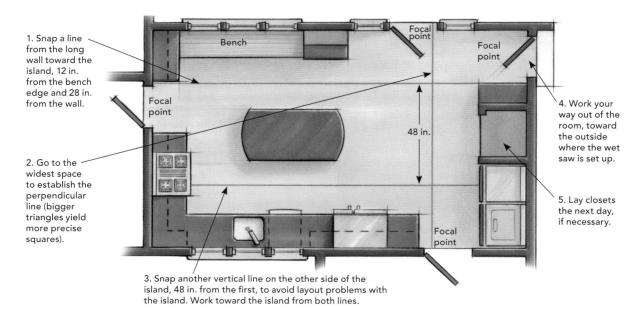

A LARGER KITCHEN WITH OBSTRUCTIONS

In kitchens, independent structures like islands can cause problems. Again, 12-in. tiles are used to form a 24-sq.-in. grid. The focal points are determined by sight lines from entrances and at the doorways themselves.

1. Snap a line from the long wall toward the island, 12 in. from the bench edge and 28 in. from the wall.

2. Go to the widest space to establish the perpendicular line (bigger triangles yield more precise squares).

3. Snap another vertical line on the other side of the island, 48 in. from the first, to avoid layout problems with the island. Work toward the island from both lines.

4. Work your way out of the room, toward the outside where the wet saw is set up.

5. Lay closets the next day, if necessary.

Bench

Focal point

Focal point

Focal point

Focal point

Focal point

48 in.

entire floor. With that grid, I can start anywhere on the floor, as long as I remember that the tiles in each square must be started in the same corner. That allows me to fill in places that I might not be able to reach if I work in a continuous path—inside small closets, under appliances, and in tight corners.

Diagonal Grids Start the Same

Floors installed on a diagonal take a little more time to lay out, but the steps are basically the same. To start, I mark a centerline down the longest portion of the room and then snap a perpendicular line. Next, I measure an equal distance down one side of the horizontal line from the center point and one side of the vertical line, and snap a chalkline through those marks. That gives me a diagonal reference line to determine cuts throughout the room. After I snap a series of lines, I can then go back and put down more lines to create a grid, following the same steps I use for tiles laid parallel to the room. Determining cuts on a diagonal can be much more time-consuming, and I often spend far more time working on the initial layout.

A Word about Choosing Tile

Many people say larger tiles make a smaller room look larger. I don't buy that theory, but then again, I'm just a tile installer. To me, a room doesn't look larger or smaller based on the size of the tile. I'm not a big fan of diagonal installations, either. The lines just get too overwhelming. Maybe that's just me, because plenty of people like a diagonal layout. The fact is, tile size, patterns, and layout are really a matter of personal taste. When dealing with a client, I do a dry run and lay a bunch of tiles on the floor both ways (straight and diagonal), then let the client decide between them.

My personal preference is for larger tiles. I think they look better, especially in larger rooms, but I've also done some installations with 18-in. by 18-in. tiles in smaller bathrooms and kitchens that looked great. Smaller tiles in big rooms, however, just look too busy; there are too many grout lines. Ultimately, what's really important is for the floor to look as though it had been there forever.

Save Time with a Prefinished Wood Floor

BY CHARLES PETERSON

When working with prefinished flooring, it's important to keep in mind that the finish is permanent. While that may sound a bit obvious, many contractors who are used to installing unfinished wood flooring sometimes find it difficult to transition to prefinished products. They're used to working atop floorboards that will receive aggressive sanding before the job is done—a safety net of sorts. However, the margin for error when installing prefinished floorboards is small. The most minor mistake or oversight—a dropped hammer, a rock stuck in the sole of a boot, an exposed fitting on an air hose—can have costly consequences. From job-site setup to the layout to the actual installation, getting every detail right is imperative.

I recently installed solid, ¾-in.-thick, prefinished, quartersawn white oak of various widths in my house. The installation process is similar regardless of the type of prefinished flooring you choose. Many of the important lessons that you'll learn here can even be applied to the installation of prefinished engineered flooring.

FACTORY-FINISHED PRODUCTS mean less work on site, but they demand a more careful installation.

THE SUBFLOOR MUST BE FLAT

The subfloor should be dead flat before a vapor retarder is installed. Raised plywood seams and other flaws can telegraph to the floor's surface. Adjust for flatness by sanding high spots or gluing down shims in low spots. The floor should be flat within 1/8 in. over 6 ft. Here, a layer of plywood was installed over the vapor retarder because the plank flooring will be glued down.

THE LAYOUT IS PARAMOUNT

Figure out where to start the floor installation by finding the focal point of the room and working out from there. The focal point may be a window, a doorway, or in this case, a fireplace. Your eye is drawn to the focal point in the room, so you want maximum control over the length of boards in this area and the way they break. Notched, ripped, or tapered boards should be left for more inconspicuous areas.

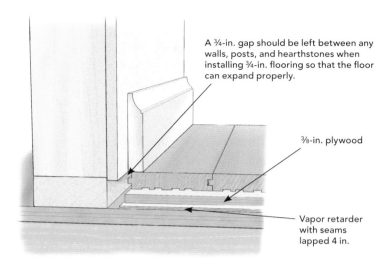

A 3/4-in. gap should be left between any walls, posts, and hearthstones when installing 3/4-in. flooring so that the floor can expand properly.

3/8-in. plywood

Vapor retarder with seams lapped 4 in.

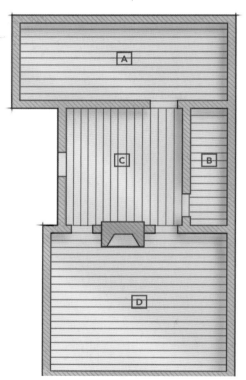

DIRECTIONAL DIFFERENCES

The direction in which the flooring runs has a profound impact on how a room looks and feels. Floorboards that run parallel to the longest wall in a room make the space feel longer and narrower (A), while boards running parallel to the shortest wall in a room make the space feel short and wide (B). Square rooms are simple because you can run the flooring in nearly any direction and it will look good (C, D).

RACK IT OUT. Lay out as much flooring as possible, but be sure to retain enough space for your flooring nailer. Racking gives you a preview of what the floor will look like. You'll notice boards with harsh, contrasting color tones or grain patterns right away, and you can refine how the boards break. Joints should be spaced at least three times the width of the flooring.

Get a Superior Finish

Many builders are opting for prefinished wood floors for reasons of speed. Depending on the scope of the project, in as little as a single day you can install a beautiful new floor that the homeowners are able to use immediately without having to go through the inconvenience of a long and messy sanding and finishing process. Moreover, the finishes, which are applied in a factory, tend to be better from a consistency standpoint than anything applied on site. (For more on factory-applied finishes, see "You Get What You Pay For," on p. 185).

Prefinished flooring is more sensitive to moisture changes due to its hard finish, which can be damaged if the floor is installed too dry. Acclimate the floor to the middle range of the expected interior moisture content of the house.

As good as prefinished floors can be, read the fine print of the manufacturer warranties carefully before ordering. A 50-year warranty may include clauses that make it impossible to collect on a claim. For instance, some manufacturers allow 5% to 10% of the boards to have defects. They leave it up to you not to install them. Also, wear is not considered a defect, no matter how quickly it occurs. Warranties typically cover only flooring whose finish has been completely worn off to expose bare wood; they don't cover the floor's cosmetic appearance. Maintenance is crucial. Variations in grain, color, or tone are also not considered defects, so carefully select the boards you will use in the racking process.

The Right Tools for a Flawless Floor

I recommend that you rethink every detail, from the type of boots you're going to wear—I wear non-marring white-soled work boots—to the placement of your tools when not in use. I place all my tools on a work mat to prevent accidental scratches. While a refined method of work is important, you'll never achieve a quality installation if you don't have the right tools on hand, and there are only a few to consider.

CUT THE FLOORING CAUTIOUSLY. Cutting prefinished floorboards to length should not be met with trepidation. If done properly, the finished edges will retain their perfect sheen. As with any milling or cutting task, always be sure the blade or bit comes to a complete stop before moving the stock. Failing to do so is an easy way to chip finished edges.

TIP

CROSSCUT BLADES with high tooth counts cut prefinished flooring best. Even so, a layer of painter's tape helps reduce tearout.

CREATE A FACTORY END. With a slot-cutting bit in a router, restore the tongue or groove on the end of the board. To restore the factory bevel, make a few passes on the edge of the board with a palm sander.

FINISH CUT ENDS. After restoring the factory bevel, wipe a bit of polyurethane finish on the exposed edge. Mohawk clear-finish markers (www.mohawk-finishing.com) are available in different sheens and make this task a breeze.

BUTT JOINTS DON'T CUT IT. Restoring cut boards to their factory-milling tolerance not only makes each individual board look better but also locks the boards together at the same height so that the floor is even across its surface.

HIDE FASTENERS AND FLAWS

NAILING OFF THE FLOORING is the easy part. After all, you already have your layout determined. Now it's simply a matter of pulling the pieces of the puzzle into alignment. Whether nailing with a finish nailer or a flooring nailer, be sure your compressor is set to the proper air pressure. Start with the air pressure at 70 psi to 75 psi, and adjust accordingly until the fasteners are set properly.

While you can get away with blind-nailing strip flooring, plank flooring needs extra hold-down power to keep it from moving radically. Before setting a board in place, apply a bead of urethane adhesive on the subfloor. Then nail the flooring every 6 in. to 8 in.

TOP-NAIL, BUT SPARINGLY. Whether you're installing the first or last row of flooring, you'll need to top-nail the boards. Glue the board down before tacking it with an 18-gauge finish nailer.

Almost all manufacturers of flooring nailers use a poppet-type valve system. The harder you hit the gun, the more the valve opens, which lets more air in to drive the piston. It's difficult to control the penetration of the fastener this way, however, because if you don't hit the gun hard enough, you'll sink the fastener insufficiently. On the other hand, if you hit the gun too hard, the piston can come into contact with the wood and crack the tongue.

On this job, I used a Primatech P250 (www.primatech.ca). Primatech guns have a valve assembly that controls nailing impact independently from the mallet strike. Tap the striking surface, and the pneumatic reciprocal action of the valve drives the piston and fastener with a constant, regulated, and uniform push. I typically run this gun with my compressor set no higher than 90 psi. Excessive air pressure can create too much force on the edge of prefinished products, causing edge crushing, unsightly finish cracks, splinters, burnished areas, or broken tongues.

Manufacturers make adapters that fit on the base of flooring nailers to prevent damage to the board's edge. These essential adapters transfer the force of the gun to the flooring tongue instead of to the delicate surface edge. It's important to adjust an adapter for the thickness and contour of the flooring being installed. My gun is outfitted with a fully adjustable base, also made by Primatech, that has bearing-mounted rollers.

With fasteners, I always opt for cleats on prefinished flooring. Staples tend to fracture the flooring tongue and damage the board.

Other tools you'll want to have on site are a miter saw fitted with a sharp crosscut blade (the higher the tooth count, the better), a palm sander for beveling end cuts, and a router with male and female bits for milling the tongue and groove on cut boards. I like the carbide-tipped bits made by Amana Tool® (www.amanatool.com) the best.

Finally, an 18-gauge finish nailer helps fasten boards the flooring nailer can't reach, like the first and last row of floorboards parallel to walls, or boards held tight to a hearth.

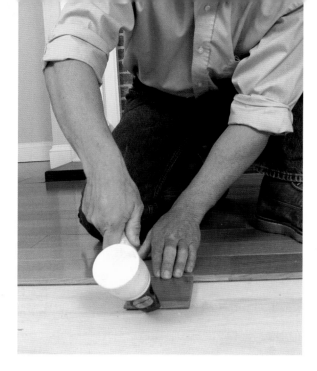

TIP FROM A PRO. Use a bash block made of scrap flooring to knock stubborn boards into place. The matching profile ensures that you won't damage the delicate edges of the floorboards.

Keep a Good Floor Looking Great

My greatest nightmare begins happily enough. I've just completed a prefinished floor with meticulous attention to detail, careful not to place a single scratch in a single board. Then the owners come home. They open the door, and in sprints the dog, digging in his nails as he fights for grip on the slick floor. Next come the kids from baseball practice, dropping bats, mitts, and dirt as they make their way to the kitchen in cleats, only to be followed by the parents, who grind that dirt into the floor with each step.

Wood floors and prefinishes are durable, but they still demand a little respect and proper maintenance. To help prevent damage, place mats and rugs in the areas that are used the most. Regularly sweep the floors with a soft-bristle broom or a vacuum with a soft-floor attachment, but never with a rug-beater attachment. Do not use wax or oil-based detergents or other household-cleaning agents on your floors; these products may dull or damage the finish. They also can leave a greasy film that makes floors impossible to recoat without sanding to bare wood. Most

COVER YOUR TRACKS

WHETHER YOU'RE SPOT-FILLING nail holes or covering up a mistake, these products can help you touch up prefinished floors.

MOHAWK® FIL-O-WOOD™
www.mohawk-finishing.com
This paste filler, tinted a variety of colors, can complement almost any wood species.

TIMBERMATE® WAXSTIX
www.timbermate.com.au
These wax sticks can be melted by a butane torch to fill deep or shallow scratches. Waxes can be custom-blended to meet the demands of almost any flooring tone.

MOHAWK MARKERS
www.mohawk-finishing.com
These permanent markers, available in a range of colors from blond to black, help hide shallow scratches in prefinished floors.

manufacturers make a no-wax wood-floor cleaner for their products.

If you have dogs or cats, make sure their claws are trimmed regularly because they can scratch the finish and even crush wood fibers. Also, all furniture should have a protective pad under each foot to prevent scratching or denting.

Even after all this care, there will come a time when the flooring needs to be refinished. Many of the new prefinishes have some form of mineral suspended in the finish. These minerals make the finish wear longer, but they are often the same aluminum-oxide minerals used in sanding abrasives. Abrading these finishes for a recoat can be a challenge. The

buffer tends to leave scratch or swirl marks as some of the particles tear away from the finish and grind into the floor. For this reason, most prefinished-flooring manufacturers recommend chemical-bonding systems instead.

Chemical systems either etch the surface or prime it to create a surface for the new finish to bond to. Two such systems are Basic® Coating's TyKote® system (www.basiccoatings.com) and Bona®'s Prep™ system (www.bona.com).

Finally, extra floorboards should always be stowed in a safe place in case a board needs to be replaced. Matching the finish and sheen of a single board can be a nightmare if you don't have a stockpile of spares.

BE PREPARED TO NAVIGATE TRANSITIONS. Reducer strips and T-molding are often used to join one floor surface to another, usually at doorways. You won't be able to make these products on site, so be sure to order them along with the flooring if you don't opt for alternatives.

CORK REPLACES REDUCERS AT THE HEARTH. It's important to install the flooring a full ¾ in. from any walls and hearthstones. Instead of covering this gap with reducer stock, you can fill it with cork. This cork was cut into rolls on the miter saw to match the thickness of the flooring and then fit snugly into the gap before the floorboard was nailed off.

UNINTERRUPTED DOORWAYS. Instead of using a reducer or T-molding to join wood floors at doorways, you can simply use a piece of flooring. This doorway's casing needed a bit of trimming so the piece within the door and the flooring butting up to the door would fit properly. Use a scrap of flooring as a guide and either a handsaw or a multitool to trim the casing and the doorstops to the right height.

YOU GET WHAT YOU PAY FOR

NOT ALL PREFINISHED FLOORING is created the same or costs the same. Expect to pay roughly $2.50 to $10.50 per square foot for basic prefinished flooring, and up to $20 or more per square foot for custom flooring, such as wide-plank hand-scraped, oiled products. Don't skimp on cost, though. Inferior products can be a pain to install. They also may wear faster than pricier products. Here are a few things you'll want to consider when shopping for your next floor.

1. **BEFORE YOU PURCHASE FLOORING,** put some of the floorboards together. Cheap flooring is hard to assemble, and you'll likely damage the boards. Also, their widths may be off by as much as ⅛ in.

2. **FIND OUT WHAT THE SHORTEST, LONGEST,** and average-size boards will be. Many prefinished boards come in very short lengths that make your floor look like a butcher block. Quarter-Sawn Flooring (www.quarter-sawnflooring.com), the manufacturer I used on this project, produces boards with an average length of 5 ft., although some boards are as long as 12 ft.

3. **DETERMINE THE MANUFACTURER'S** over-wood tolerance, which is the difference in height from one board to another when installed. I prefer over wood to be less than 0.012 in. Poor products will have tolerances of more than twice this amount and have large bevels on their edges to hide the difference.

4. **PAY ATTENTION TO THE THICKNESS OF THE FINISH,** not the number of finish coats. Some flooring with 10 coats may have 0.0017 in. of finish, whereas other flooring with only three coats will have 0.0024 in. of finish.

5. **SCRATCH THE FLOORING IN THE SHOWROOM.** Some finishes, but not all, leave behind noticeable white streaks when scratched. Scratching the floor before making a purchase gives you an idea of how it will look as it wears over time.

*Please note that prices were current in 2010.

Lighting & Mechanical

Kitchen Lighting Design

BY MATTHEW TEAGUE

With open floor plans, personalized storage and appliance options, designated workstations and social areas, even offices and kid zones, the kitchen has evolved. As such, a single, surface-mount light fixture centered in the kitchen ceiling is no longer sufficient. The truth is, it never was.

Fortunately, there has been progress in kitchen lighting as well, in both fixtures and design. Since no one fixture can provide the light necessary to create a kitchen that is both functional and comfortable, designers opt instead for a variety of light sources—some direct, some indirect—that work together to create layers and balance.

TASK

When it comes to workstations, the best spot for light is somewhere between your eyes and what you're looking at—the vegetables you're chopping or the bills you're paying. At a minimum, you'll want task lights shining on countertops, over the range, and above the sink. Depending on the kitchen, you may also need to light a dining table, an island, or a small desk. Many different types of fixtures can provide task lighting. The most common—and useful— are undercabinet lights, but pendants as well as track systems can also be used to provide task lighting. In general, you want a bright, white light.

DECORATIVE

Decorative, or architectural, lighting provides a focus for the room. Whereas decorative fixtures may also provide task, ambient, and accent lighting, what makes it decorative is the presence of the fixture itself. Chandeliers over a dining table are a common use of decorative lighting. Keep in mind, however, that a fixed chandelier hanging over a dining table makes rearranging difficult. Also, any light above a reflective surface has the potential to cause glare. Pendants paired with a track system allow for flexible decorative lighting; wall sconces can be used to define a space and set an elegant mood.

ACCENT

Accent lighting, also called feature lighting or highlighting, is intended to draw your attention to a particular detail. You can wash a plastered or textured wall with soft light from a sconce, or highlight a painting or a fireplace with focused recessed lights or track lights aimed at the object. If you have a green thumb, consider lighting a favorite houseplant.

KINETIC

Although it's the exception rather than the norm, some kitchens also have kinetic lighting, or a flame. Fireplaces and gas-lit sconces are the most common ways to lend kinetic light to a kitchen. Pizza ovens work too.

From Function to Flicker: Five Ways to Light a Kitchen

AMBIENT

Ambient light, often referred to as "fill" light, is the general lighting in the room. It is used to soften shadows and create a warm feeling. The goal is to use well-diffused light that illuminates the room throughout the day. Because natural light changes often, all ambient lighting should be dimmable. Chandeliers, recessed lights, and track and monorail systems all can be used to create ambient light. But you shouldn't rely on a single overhead fixture, which can produce objectionable shadows on walls and ceilings. Instead, choose properly spaced recessed lights, track or monorail fixtures with multiple bulbs, or a combination of ambient-light sources.

Recessed Lights Are Versatile

Recessed lights can serve as ambient, task, or accent lighting. For ambient light, set recessed cans about 30 in. from the wall and 4 ft. to 6 ft. apart, depending on the can diameter and the ceiling height (light should overlap). For task lighting, cans need to be located directly above the work surface. Choose a trim kit that allows you to focus the light in a specific direction to showcase a detail and create accent lighting. There are a variety of trim and baffle styles available (see examples of offerings from Halo® at right). The color and style of the baffle affect the color quality of the light produced.

BLACK TRIM AND DIRECTIONAL BLACK BAFFLE

SQUARE ANTIQUE COPPER TRIM WITH BLACK BAFFLE

SATIN NICKEL TRIM WITH PINHOLE BLACK BAFFLE

REMODEL HOUSING

NEW-CONSTRUCTION HOUSING

RETROFIT OPTIONS. In a kitchen remodel, you can install recessed cans without tearing out the ceiling. Unlike new-construction housings that nail between joists, special remodel housings slip through a hole in the ceiling and clip to the drywall. Halo 6-in. housings are shown here (www.haloltg.com).

THE SINK DESERVES ITS OWN SOURCE OF LIGHT. To keep this fundamental workstation well lit, you need to place a light as close to directly above the sink as possible. A recessed light works well. If your cabinet design includes a fascia that bridges the open space between the tops of wall cabinets, consider hiding an undercabinet fixture there.

Invisible Fixtures for Countertop Tasks

If you're considering undercabinet task lighting, first make sure the face frames of the upper cabinets hang down low enough to conceal the fixtures and to prevent glare. For the same reason, and because it's closer to where you work, undercabinet fixtures should be installed toward the front of the cabinets. Although undercabinet fixtures come in a variety of configurations, there are four common lamp types to choose from, each with its own set of pros and cons.

FLUORESCENT. Low-cost, long-lasting, and energy-efficient, fluorescents cast light that is bright and even; but unfortunately, most cannot be dimmed. Choose quieter fixtures with electronic ballasts.

XENON. These bulbs run cooler and last much longer than halogen bulbs. Some models offer high and low switching, eliminating the need for a dimmer. However, xenon fixtures may require installing a remote transformer, and light quality might diminish when the bulb is dimmed.

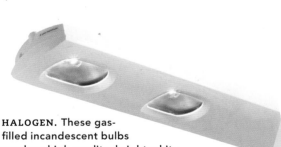

HALOGEN. These gas-filled incandescent bulbs produce high-quality, bright-white light and a lot of heat. So while they offer excellent task lighting, they might melt the chocolate in the cabinet above. Their life span is longer than that of only regular incandescents.

LED. Light-emitting diodes are the most expensive, but they use very little energy and likely will outlast your kitchen. Also, some models let you adjust the color of the light produced, from warm gold to cool white.

Pendants Hang Out in Style

Easy to install, pendants can provide ambient, task, and decorative lighting while lending style to the kitchen. The most popular application for pendants in today's kitchens is over an island. Allow at least 30 in. of clearance between pendants and a work surface or table. Pendants can be as decorative or as subtle as you wish. Some come with flashy glass globes that grab your attention immediately. The smallest are quite inconspicuous, only 2 in. to 3 in. in diameter, and hang on nearly invisible cords.

PICK A PENDANT. These days, it seems like a trio of pendant lights is an integral part of island design. However, there are many uses for pendants, and even more styles of this popular lamp. A blue glass globe from Bruck® lighting (www.bruck lightingsystems.com) is a sure attention grabber.

A SINGLE PENDANT from Rejuvenation® (www.rejuve-nation.com) has three lamps to provide enough light for a dining table.

HUBBARDTON FORGE® PENDANTS (www.vtforge.com) were used by project designer Leslie Sager as the primary light source to enhance the Japanese aesthetic in this kitchen.

Define the Dining Area with a Chandelier

Whether it's an ornate antique or a sleek, modern fixture, a chandelier is a decorative light source that can quickly establish your kitchen's style. Most commonly, chandeliers are used above a table to define the dining area. Although it is possible to use a chandelier as a kitchen's main source of ambient light, in most cases you'll need supplemental fixtures to reduce shadows and dark areas. A chandelier can also be used for task lighting, if a table doubles as a work surface, for example. Allow at least 30 in. of space between the table and the fixture.

A PERIOD FIXTURE MAKES AN EXCLAMATION POINT. Designer Lori Erenberg used fixtures from Fortuny Lighting (www.lightology.com) to boost the authenticity of this Craftsman-style home. The ornate chandelier defines the dining room with decorative and ambient light. Above, a chandelier from Kichler® (www.kichler.com).

WAVES OF LIGHT. A sleek track system from Sea Gull Lighting® includes fixtures that aim and swivel to provide a range of ambient, task, and accent lighting.

PENDANTS CAN HANG ON A TRACK TOO, as shown in the arcing fixture (Prima; www.primalighting.com) Amy Duerr-Day used above a similarly shaped island.

Flexible Fixtures Are on Track

Track-lighting systems allow you to change the direction of the light and even cast it a good distance away. You can point lights down at a kitchen island for task lighting while you're preparing a meal, and then aim them to accent a detail while you're eating dinner. These systems come in both high- and low-voltage options. Although these fixtures tend to look modern, they're available in a wide array of styles, sizes, and bulb types. Tracks can be straight or serpentine; some models allow you to hang pendants at varying heights, while others allow you to mix shapes and bulbs on a single track.

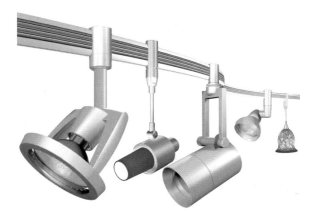

HALO'S FLEXIBLE TRACK SYSTEM can be shaped as you see fit and takes a variety of different fixtures.

A DOUBLE-LAMP SCONCE from Lithonia Lighting® (www.lithonia.com).

Wall Sconces Are an Elegant Accent

Hanging wall sconces alongside kitchen exits (to other areas of the house or to outdoor living spaces) helps establish separate living areas in an open floor plan. If your dining area is open to the kitchen, sconces on the wall behind the dining table lend a dramatic look that helps establish the mood and style of the room. Adding wall sconces in the dining area also helps cut down on tabletop glare caused by overhead fixtures. Sconces can provide a certain amount of ambient light, but they're more often used as decorative and accent lighting.

SCONCES UP AND DOWN. Architects Steven and Judy Selin used sconces from Conant Custom Brass (www.conantcustombrass.com) for task, ambient, and accent lighting in this kitchen. Some point down to illuminate the countertop; others point up to highlight the ceiling. Sconces are made to suit just about any task and are a great way to define your kitchen's style.

ARTISAN LIGHTS from Hubbardton Forge (photos left and center).

A GLASS GLOBE from Bruck.

CFLS: A SPECTRUM OF ENERGY-EFFICIENT LIGHTING

ACCORDING TO THE U.S. GREEN BUILDING COUNCIL, outfitting your home's five most frequently used light fixtures with compact fluorescent lightbulbs (CFLs) can cut your electric bill by as much as $100. That's because CFLs are four times more efficient than incandescents. In terms of watts, a 13-watt CFL produces as much light as a 60-watt incandescent bulb, and a 25-watt CFL is equal to a 100-watt incandescent. In an attempt to make shopping less confusing, most fluorescents are marked with their incandescent equal.

If these savings don't seem worth the cost of humming fixtures and poor-quality light, it's time to check out the newest products. Many new CFLs have electronic ballasts that regulate the current going into the bulb, cutting out the noise that many of us associate with fluorescent lighting. Electronic ballasts also eliminate flickering. There have been improvements in the quality of light produced by CFLs as well. In fact, the bulbs are now sold in multiple shades, including "soft white" for a warm tone; "cool white" for brighter, whiter light; and "daylight" for clear blue light. Other manufacturers market their products with such labels as "warm" and "neutral." If you want to dim CFLs, make sure you pair a dimming ballast with a dimmer designed to work with it. It's slightly more expensive, but the energy savings are guaranteed.

Layers Are the Secret to Effective Kitchen Lighting

Like the single fixture that lit your grandmother's kitchen, the most common mistake today is to rely on recessed lights alone. Every designer has his or her own approach to lighting, but most agree that it takes layers to light a kitchen effectively.

At a minimum, you should have ambient and task lighting. In a simple kitchen plan, dimmable recessed fixtures may provide both. Aimed at art or an architectural fixture, a recessed light can even qualify as accent lighting. But it is the addition of decorative and hidden fixtures that make the difference between a functional space and a well-lit kitchen. To achieve this goal, you'll need to mix direct and indirect lighting. Sconces, pendants, and chandeliers are examples of direct lighting: The fixture is visible. Undercabinet and cove lights cast a glow without a visible fixture to create indirect lighting.

According to Joseph A. Rey-Barreau, AIA, director of education for the American Lighting Association, "The key to kitchen lighting is to start with the sink." The sink is a kitchen's most fundamental workstation, so Rey-Barreau likes to install a dedicated light for cleanup tasks. He often incorporates undercabinet fixtures and recessed lights next. With undercabinet lights illuminating the countertops and recessed fixtures around the kitchen's perimeter (about 30 in. from the walls, not the cabinet fronts), he covers task and ambient lighting for most of the kitchen. Finally, he chooses an overhead light for the center of the room. It may be track lights or a trio of pendants over an island, for example. With this fixture, Rey-Barreau adds decorative lighting to the equation.

Dimmers Control the Mood

In some areas, like the kitchen table, you may want soft ambient light while eating meals and brighter task lighting while helping your kids with their homework. You may also want bright undercabinet lighting while you're chopping vegetables, but a softer glow on the backsplash while entertaining or for a night-light. All it takes is a dimmable fixture. Dimming not only makes the room more functional but also adds dimension to the space. "If there are no dimmed zones, you're left with no accents and no contrast," says Doug Stewart, a certified lighting designer at Hermitage Lighting Gallery in Nashville, Tenn. "The kitchen will appear flat and less dimensional."

As you can see, one fixture used effectively can cover multiple types of lighting. Aesthetically, the fixtures you choose should mesh seamlessly with the room. Pewter, satin nickel, bronze, and wrought iron are popular finishes today, as are glass pendants and globes, but it is important to make sure the fixtures and finishes you choose match the style and finish of the hardware in your kitchen. It's smart to bring material samples and to talk to professionals when shopping for light fixtures.

You Don't Have to Spend a Lot to Get a Lot

Whether you're designing a new kitchen, remodeling an old one, or simply replacing lights in an existing kitchen, you should do some legwork before talking to a designer or shopping for fixtures.

Study the kitchen's floor plan and identify workstations, social areas, and appliances that need to be well lit. Is there a detail that you'd like to highlight? Measure the ceiling and cabinet height. If you're remodeling, note where outlet and junction boxes are currently located. You can take along photos of your cabinets and countertops, samples of hardware, or an existing fixture for inspiration. Even paint samples can be helpful when choosing fixtures.

Just as important, have a firm idea of what you can afford to spend. "In the whole scheme of things," says Lynn Grubbs, an interior designer and owner of Lynn Grubbs Interiors in Nashville, "lighting is one of the more affordable ways to make a dramatic impact." For new kitchens (including major remodels) lighting is typically only 2% to 3% of the total cost.

"Prices have gone down dramatically in the last five years because of imports. You can now get the expensive look for the middle price," says Grubbs. Of course, you can spend as much or as little as you want. A recessed can with a basic white trim costs less than $30 at most home centers, while one chandelier at a lighting showroom may cost thousands.

Finally, don't underestimate the need for a lighting designer. At the very least, do your homework at a quality lighting center with knowledgeable associates. There is a wide range of products available. A good lighting consultant can even save you money, pointing you toward less expensive fixtures that achieve the same goals as top-of-the-line models. And don't hesitate to ask if your lighting consultant makes house calls. You'll thank yourself for taking the time to get the light right in the hardest-working room in your house.

Choose the Right Kitchen Sink

BY CLAIR URBAIN

Whether you're just fantasizing about your dream kitchen or are ready to roll up your sleeves to replace that chipped, stained, clumsy sink that's been there far too long, there are many options to consider when choosing this crucial kitchen fixture. What do you like and dislike about the sink you have? Is it too deep, too shallow, too big, or too small? What look are you trying to achieve, and what type of countertops do you have? You also need to consider how you use the sink, because an avid chef will have entirely different needs from a microwave master who serves quick-and-easy meals. To help navigate the countless options, break the decision into three areas: layout, material, and installation type.

LAYOUT

MATERIAL

INSTALLATION

FOLLOW THESE THREE STEPS to take your sink from a dingy dumping ground to a functional focal point.

Choose a Layout

Sink manufacturers continue to develop the look and configuration of sinks so that they better match the needs of today's users. A wide variety of bowl configurations allows you to match sink type to the type of cooking, cleaning, and other chores you do. The type of faucet you choose and other accessories you may want to add, such as soap or hot-water dispensers, also affect your sink decision.

BOWL SHAPE AND ORIENTATION

Bowls with straighter sides and tighter corner radii have more capacity. D-shaped bowls ⬜1 with a curved back provide more room for maneuvering large pans but may require moving the faucet to the countertop behind the sink.

In corners or in tight locations, L-shaped sinks ⬜2 or a sink placed on the diagonal may make better use of space.

⬜1

BLANCO® 440250

⬜2

FRANKE®

NUMBER OF BOWLS

Decide how many bowls you need based on the size of your kitchen and your typical activities in it. A large, single-bowl sink can be the best choice if you have a small kitchen or if you plan to wash most of your dishes in a dishwasher. Double bowls of equal size work well with multiple cooks in the kitchen, but if one cook focuses on prep work, a double-bowl design that includes a half-size or three-quarter-size bowl may be a better solution. Offset or shallow/deep double bowls and triple bowls 3 are becoming more common and may be better matches for your style of cooking and living. With a triple-bowl sink, one bowl can be used for dirty dishes, another can accept food scraps for the garbage disposal, and the third can be available for soaking or handwashing. This luxury often means installing nonstandard cabinetry to accommodate a larger sink footprint.

BOWL DEPTH

Because the standard sink-bowl depth is only about 8 in., dumping large pans or spraying down the sink can cause splashing. If you plan on washing large pans regularly, consider a sink with a 9-in.-or 10-in.-deep bowl. Some models have a lowered lip between the two bowls so that large pans can straddle both bowls comfortably and catch splashes during cleanup.

Think about how bowl depth will be experienced by users of different heights. If the bowl is too deep, it may be hard for a shorter person to reach to the bottom and may make a taller person stoop too much.

CONSIDER ACCESSORIES

First and foremost, make sure that the sink you choose can accommodate the faucet you want to mount to it. Does the sink have enough holes 4 for accessories, such as a sprayer and dispensers for soap and hot water? Do you need a dishwasher drain vent?

If you have your heart set on a certain sink but find that it has too many holes, you can attractively hide the holes you don't need with hole covers or extended baseplates.

Select the Sink Material

The decision process begins with a spectrum of materials ranging from steel to stone. With such a wide selection of mainstream and niche manufacturers, it's not hard to find examples of traditional or modern styling within each material category.

COMPOSITE

Composite sinks, best known by brand names such as Silgranit™, Americast, and Swanstone®, are made with a mixture of materials—usually quartz or granite—and a bonding agent. This combination produces a good-looking, resilient natural surface that can resist temperatures up to 500°F. Composite surfaces are also less vulnerable to dents and chips from dropped silverware or pans.

From a cost standpoint, composite sinks are an economical alternative to natural-stone sinks. Expect to pay more for undermount sinks and multibowl models.

3

PREMIER COPPER PRODUCTS

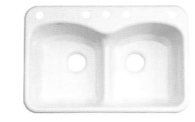

4

KOHLER® K-6626-5-0

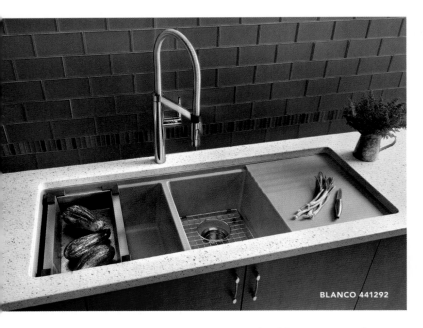

COMPOSITES. Pros: Very durable; resistant to heat; can be a convincing alternative to granite and other natural stones. **Con:** Moderately expensive.

FIRECLAY. Pros: Hygienic; strong; more durable than enameled sinks. **Cons:** More brittle; may not be compatible with garbage disposals.

FIRECLAY

Fireclay sinks not only are strong and beautiful but are also resistant to contamination and food-bacteria buildup. Unlike on enameled sinks, the glaze on fireclay is an inseparable part of the sink, rather than a coating. This means that fireclay generally can withstand much more abuse than porcelain-enameled cast iron. While strong, the fireclay surface can scratch, chip, and show burns. Also, fireclay sinks are comparatively brittle and may be incompatible with garbage disposals.

Fireclay can be cleaned with regular cleaners. Many fireclay sinks can even handle mildly abrasive cleaners, although nonabrasive varieties are recommended for everyday cleaning.

STAINLESS STEEL

Stainless steel is a popular material because it cleans easily, resists staining, withstands a wide range of temperatures, and is a fairly good value. It's also a natural complement to the stainless-steel appliances popular in today's kitchens.

The thickness of stainless steel is measured by gauge—the higher the gauge number, the thinner the steel. Typically, commercial-grade sinks are made with 16-gauge steel, and the cheapest residential sinks are made with 23-gauge steel, which is noticeably thin, especially when saddled with a vibrating garbage disposal. Models with sound-absorbing undercoatings can muffle some of the noise from dish clatter and garbage-disposal use; this also helps insulate the sink to reduce heat conduction from hot dish water.

Because stainless steel is such a popular sink material, there is a wide variety of styles, and price closely follows steel gauge and complexity of bowl design. Typically, undermount stainless-steel sinks are slightly to substantially more expensive than drop-in models.

Most stainless-steel sinks have a brushed-satin finish, but higher-end and designer sinks may be highly polished. The satin finish does a better job of hiding minor scratches.

Stainless steel cleans up well with only soap and water and a quick towel dry, which helps the surface

STAINLESS STEEL. Pros: Stain- and heat-resistant; easy to clean; a fairly good value; available in many shapes and sizes. Cons: Light-gauge models can be flimsy and noisy; highly polished sinks can show scratches.

form a strong, highly protective chrome-oxide film. Stubborn stains can be scoured lightly with a mild abrasive rubbed in the direction of the grain and then rinsed. Don't use steel wool on stainless-steel sinks because small particles can become embedded in the stainless steel and then rust.

Be sure to check that the model you choose is made from high-quality 304 stainless steel and that it meets ASME A112.19.3-2000 criteria for stainless-steel plumbing fixtures. Both pieces of information should be noted in the sink's specifications.

ENAMELED

Enamel-on-cast-iron or enamel-on-steel sinks are available in a wide variety of colors and are easy to clean. They can take the shock of a hot pan or pot being placed in them, but their rigid enamel coating can chip and crack if heavy items are dropped on them. A crack in the enamel will expose the cast iron or steel to water and air, which encourages rusting.

Enamel sinks can be dulled by aggressive cleaning, which can lead to more dirt accumulation and staining. Enamel-on-steel sinks tend to be the least expensive sinks.

ENAMELED. Pros: Available in many colors; solid-feeling and heavy. Cons: Susceptible to chips and cracks; relatively heavy weight may complicate undermount installations.

GLASS. Pros: Unique look; tolerant of high temperatures and temperature shocks. Cons: Can be severely damaged by hard impacts; limited number of manufacturers to choose from; may not be aesthetically compatible with all countertop options.

JSG OCEANA UNDERMOUNT

DUPONT CORIAN 850 DOUBLE SINK

ACRYLIC. Pros: Economical alternative to other sinks; lots of color options; solid composition means scratches can be buffed out. Cons: Sensitive to high temperatures; typically limited to undermount installations.

GLASS

Although they constitute a small niche, glass kitchen sinks exist. One manufacturer is Jeannette Specialty Glass/JSG Oceana, a company that uses a special borosilicate glass commonly found in cooking and refrigeration applications and in pharmaceutical laboratories. The company claims that the glass has a low coefficient of expansion, can take repeated temperature shocks from boiling water, and is highly resistant to nonfluorinated chemicals, so its surface retains its clear and lustrous qualities over time and after repeated cleaning. Although it's scratch resistant and can stand up to bumps and drops from normal use, like porcelain, it can break from blows by heavy objects. JSG Oceana glass sinks are available in top-mount and undermount configurations, but they also can be free-formed for high-end kitchens.

ACRYLIC

Acrylic sinks are light yet sturdy; come in a wide variety of colors, patterns, and shapes; and are less expensive than most other sinks. They are more vulnerable to scratches, however, and have a low luster when compared with quartz or granite composites. It's important to be careful where you put that hot pan; temperatures over 300°F can damage acrylic.

The material used in solid-surface counters, known under brand names such as Corian and Silestone®, also can be molded into sinks. Because the material is the same all the way through the sink profile, minor scratches can be buffed out. However, temperatures greater than 300°F may cause damage from melting.

NATURAL STONE

Stone sinks can make bold design statements. They are hewn from solid rock such as granite, marble, quartz, limestone, sandstone, onyx, travertine, or soapstone. Semiprecious materials such as fossil wood also can be used.

Although several manufacturers and artisans sell standard styles of natural-stone sinks, the crystalline structure and veining of the material makes each

GREEN MOUNTAIN SOAPSTONE DOUBLE BOWL

NATURAL STONE. Pros: Very durable; good sound-deadening properties. Cons: High price; may require sealing; heavy weight may complicate installation.

sink unique. Few materials are more durable than rock, but because all rock formations are porous, these sinks must be sealed before use. Also, many types of stone have natural pocks and imperfections that must be filled with stone dust and epoxy, matching the natural stone as much as possible.

EXOTIC METALS

Stainless steel isn't the only type of metal sink. For a distinctive look, consider more exotic metals such as copper, brass, nickel, and even titanium.

Copper has strong antibacterial and antiviral properties, even against *E. coli*, and because the surface oxidizes, slight scratches tend to "heal" themselves, although the patina can change.

High-quality brass or titanium sinks are actually a combination of stainless steel and either brass or titanium. A brass sink offers a warm, rich look, while titanium sinks come in three colors: anthracite, bronze, and gold. Beware of lower-quality brass sinks, which have coatings that can flake over time.

Depending on the material, exotic-metal sink prices range from slightly more than stainless steel for simple configurations of copper to thousands of dollars for high-end titanium or brass.

THOMPSON TRADERS MONTEROSSO

EXOTIC METALS. Pros: Durable; hygienic; can offer a unique handmade look. Cons: Some metals can change slightly in appearance with age; cost can be high.

Choose an Installation Style

Typically, sinks are installed either by dropping them into the hole cut in the counter or by mounting them under the counter. Manufacturers typically have specific instructions that need to be followed to the letter, especially in undermount installations.

DROP-IN

Drop-in sinks rest on top of the counter, making it more difficult to sweep crumbs and spills into the sink, but they are arguably the easiest to install. These sinks are fastened with either screw clamps that integrate with a factory-attached track or, in the case of heavy sinks, a bead of sealant between the countertop and the edge of the sink. A word of caution for screw-clamp installations: Overtightening the fastener will strip it out of the base material, twist off the head, bend the screw, or even break the sink. If it's an in-place installation, be sure to have a good light source when working.

UNDERMOUNT

Undermount, or rimless, sinks are gaining popularity, especially when used with granite, synthetic stone, or other materials that show the full-depth beauty of the countertop. However, they are more difficult to install and may require the use of special mounting brackets and tools (or, in the case of farmhouse sinks, often a solid platform). As a result, these sinks are often installed by the countertop fabricator. Don't use undermount sinks with laminate countertops because the slightest imperfection will expose the countertop's engineered-wood core to moisture, which can cause the wood to swell and the laminate to separate.

DROP-IN

Sealant secured

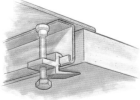

Screw clamps

UNDERMOUNT

Epoxy

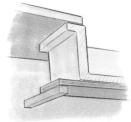

Brackets

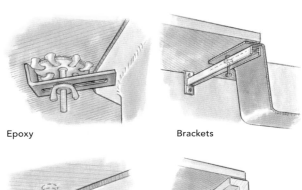

Inserts

Platform

Three reveal options

Cooktops from Simmer to Sear

BY SEAN GROOM

Cooktops have never been as popular as ranges, which combine stove and oven, perhaps because a separate cooktop and wall oven costs at least twice as much as a decent-quality range. Installation is also more costly with two distinct appliances. A separate cooktop offers several advantages, however. Freed of the burners, the oven can be put at a more comfortable height, and the cooktop can be placed anywhere in the kitchen. Installation heights can vary for comfort and can include space below for cabinets or for wheelchair access. Smooth-surface cooktops can integrate almost seamlessly into a countertop. Finally, having separate units allows you to pick cooktop features and oven features independently to match your needs exactly.

Choose the Fuel Type First

Today's market features three types of cooktop: gas burner, radiant electric, and induction. There are many reasons to choose one over another, but the detail that has the greatest impact on your cooking experience is heat response. You'll want to consider how finely you can tune the heat, how quickly the burners transfer heat to cookware, whether burners can cool rapidly and then return swiftly to high heat, and what the maximum and minimum heat-output settings are.

GLASS UPDATES A TRADITIONAL LOOK. While GE® offers traditionally designed gas cooktops with deeply recessed basins around the burners to contain spills, the company also makes "gas-on-glass" cooktops for a sleeker look. These cooktops are available with white or black glass and are easy to clean, assuming you don't allow liquids to boil over and run off the cooktop. The grates can be cleaned in the dishwasher, are fairly minimalist for good heat diffusion, and allow pots to slide easily between front and back burners. The 30-in. model shown here (PGP989DNBB) has four burners ranging from an 11,000-Btu high-output burner to a 5,500-Btu precise-simmer burner. This cooktop has a separate lockout knob to prevent unanticipated ignitions and an integrated 330-cfm downdraft exhaust.

THE POWER OF ONE

THE SLIM SIZE OF COOKTOPS makes them ideal stand-alone units for specialty cooking. Gaggenau, in particular, has carved out a niche with in-counter, single-element induction and gas burners, as well as steamers and electric grills.

Wok burners are popular stand-alone appliances and are available in gas or induction styles. In the gas category, Capital's 24-in. Power Wok (GRT-24WK) has a single 30,000-Btu gas burner and a grate that accommodates stockpots; Until recently Viking offered a similar unit (bottom photo at right) with a 27,500-Btu burner (VGWT240). If you don't cook with a wok enough to justify these products, consider purchasing a wok-ring adapter for a standard gas-burner grate.

Gaggenau's 3,500-watt induction wok burner (VI 411) doubles as a single-element induction cooktop.

If you're looking for added cooking capacity for holidays, a handful of portable induction burners by companies such as Fagor and Frigidaire are available. These 110-volt plug-in units typically have 1,300-watt to 1,800-watt high settings, so they aren't as powerful as in-counter devices.

No rule of thumb will guide you to a particular type of cookware or pot size with burner or element output. Generally speaking, higher-Btu burners heat a pot quicker. As important as heat output, though, is the physical size of the heating elements. For example, a 19,000-Btu gas burner is great for bringing a 12-in.-dia., 16-qt. stockpot to boil, but if the largest pot you use has a 7 in. or 8 in. dia., the flame pattern at the highest setting could be wider than the pot. Finally, look for burners or elements that accommodate specialty pots and pans you use frequently.

Next, Pick the Features

Once you've decided among gas, radiant, or induction, turn your attention to convenience features and appearance. The choices include timers and safety features. Some electric models even offer programs similar to those on a microwave.

Regardless of cooktop type, you should weigh two issues common to all cooktops. First, how easy is it to clean? Cleaning issues vary by cooking surface, so they're covered in the in-depth category discussions that follow. Second, what type of controls and location do you prefer? Some cooktops mount controls vertically on the front. While this location frees space on the cooktop surface, it eats up more under-cabinet space and positions knobs where they can be bumped while you work in the kitchen or where they can tempt children. Controls also can be mounted horizontally on one side of the burners or along the front edge. While twist knobs are de rigueur for gas burners, more expensive electric cooktops offer electronic touch controls that don't interrupt the smooth glass surface and typically have lockout features.

Gas: The Choice of Chefs

Gas is the serious cook's benchmark fuel for its nimble heating response. The flame on a gas cooktop seamlessly adjusts from steak-searing high to chocolate-melting low and back again. The open-grate system doesn't retain much heat, so the temperature transitions are nearly instantaneous.

Continuous grates let you slide cookware between burners; heavy cast iron provides even heating. Many grates are porcelain coated, and some can be cleaned in the dishwasher, although most manufacturers suggest soaking and hand scrubbing. Cleaning up spills with sealed burners on the full-size gas cooktops I researched means removing the grates and sponging out the depressed spill-collection areas.

Give serious thought to your ventilation choice if you are buying a gas-fueled cooktop (see "Breathe Easy with the Right Range Hood," on p. 212) because in addition to cooking odors and moisture, you'll want to remove the carbon dioxide, soot, and PCBs generated by gas combustion. If efficiency is a concern, it's worth noting that only between 35% and 40% of the combusted fuel's energy potential is used for cooking. Unlike the gas stoves of the old days, all the models shown here have electronic ignition rather than a standing pilot light, which cuts down on fuel consumption and pollutants.

While 30-in. and 36-in. models are the most common, gas cooktops are available in sizes ranging from simple four-burner 24-in.-wide units to 60-in.-wide cooktops. The largest units use the extra real estate for additional burners and/or specialty surfaces such as wok burners, griddles, or grills. Basic models are among the most economical cooktops on the market, but prices can exceed $3,000 for units with features that emulate the appearance or performance of restaurant-grade cooktops.

WANTED: SHORT-ORDER COOK

IF VIKING® WASN'T THE FIRST COMPANY to sell commercially inspired ranges and cooktops for homeowners, it has certainly made its name synonymous with the category. The units in Viking's premier Professional Series are technically range tops—deep stoves that slide into the counter—as opposed to thinner cooktops that fit into a cutout in the counter.

Viking's widest option (48 in.) is available in five different burner configurations. This model (VGRT548-4GQ), shown with an optional 8-in.-high back guard, has a griddle and a grill (each 12 in. wide) in addition to four 15,000-Btu burners. These burners ignite at any position on the dial, even the lowest setting—a nice feature that's not found on the cooktops of many brands that require twisting the dial past high to ignite before rotating it the other way to the desired setting. The ignition feature carries down to the D3 line of five-burner 30-in. and 36-in. cooktops.

If boiling water extinguishes the flame, this model (like many high-end gas cooktops) has automatic reignition, which relights the burner regardless of the knob position.

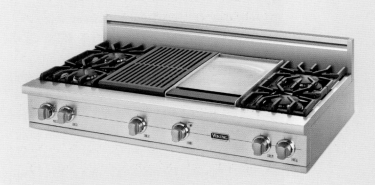

Radiant: Sleek and Easy to Clean

Electric elements used to mean unattractive, inexpensive, hard-to-clean coil burners. Although they're still used on entry-level ranges, they've largely been replaced with ceramic-glass-topped radiant elements. Electric cooktops are much more efficient than gas burners, and about 70% of the energy they consume is converted into cooking heat.

Radiant cooktops rely on a thin corrugated ribbon within an insulating "bowl" that directs heat upward. The element cycles on and off to maintain the desired temperature. Because glass is a poor heat conductor, the heat from the heating element warms the cookware without radiating far outward from the element. The roughly 30% heat loss comes from having to warm the glass before the pot.

Although a good electric cooktop can bring a pot of water to a boil faster than a gas cooktop, having the glass between the element and the pot makes for poor heat response. If you're warming a pot of milk on a gas cooktop and it's about to boil over, turning off the burner will stop the boiling almost instantly. On an electric cooktop, there's enough latent heat in the glass that milk will continue to boil.

Most radiant cooktops have at least one burner with a variable-size element that can operate at two

SET APART BY MORE THAN ITS SHAPE. If Steve Jobs had designed a cooking appliance instead of computers, it might look like this one from Gaggenau (CE 490). Forget a row of dials or touch keys: Move the single knob in the general direction of the element you wish to use, and twist it. Once the heating level is set, let go; a magnet in the knob centers it back in its cradle. Other functions are engaged with a combination of the knob and touch buttons.

One unique feature, called automatic boil-start control, lets you set the simmer temperature before heating begins; the cooktop brings the pot to a boil and then reduces heat to the simmer temperature. Combine this with cooking timers that automatically shut off each element, and cooking several dishes simultaneously becomes a lot easier.

The elongated rectangle—36 in. wide by 14 in. deep, including the stainless-steel trim—arranges the burners horizontally so that there's no reaching over hot pots. (The typical cooktop is between 21 in. and 22 in. deep.)

ELEMENTS OF ALL SHAPES AND SIZES

IF YOU LIKE THE TACTILE QUALITY of twisting a knob to adjust heat, GE offers several electric smooth-top models with knob controls. The 36-in. model (PP962BMBB) offers a great deal of flexibility. The central three-ring element adjusts among 6 in., 9 in., and 12 in., and from 1,050 watts at the smallest setting to 3,000 watts at the largest diameter. There is also a double-ring element (5 in. and 8 in.), and the two 7-in. elements on the left side have a bridge element between them. When both burners and the bridge element are turned on, an elongated cooking oval is created that can be used to accommodate large roasting pans or a griddle. The smallest element in this cooktop is a 120-watt zone designed to keep foods warm while the rest of the meal is being prepared.

As on many GE cooktops, a separate lockout knob for all the elements is intended to protect children and aging cooks from harm.

CONTROL AT THE TIP OF A FINGER. The matte-black graphite glass of Dacor®'s Electric Glide™ cooktop distinguishes this stove from the glossy finish on most others. Each of the four burners on the 30-in.-wide Discovery™ model (MET304) is a different size. The dual-size element expands from 5½ in. to 9¾ in., accommodating cookware ranging from a small butter-warming pot to a large stockpot. With the larger size activated, it's the most powerful burner on the cooktop at 2,400 watts.

The Electric Glide name comes from the touch controls. Each burner has its own control bar. By sliding your finger along the bar, you increase or decrease heat as indicated by a graduated light bar that changes color, height, and length as temperature increases. An accessory pop-up downdraft vent is also available.

or three different diameters. Look for a variety of element sizes that match an assortment of cookware sizes. Compared to the grate system on a gas cooktop, the smooth, sealed, glass cooking surface on an electric unit is minimalist and unobtrusive, and spills can be wiped away with a sponge—after the surface cools.

The surface does present a few potential problems, however. The glass can be scratched with abrasive cleaners, grains of sugar on the bottom of a pot, or even the rough surface of a cast-iron skillet. Blunt objects—a pepper mill, for instance—dropped from an overhead cabinet can crack the surface, and foods like sugar, sugar syrup, milk, and tomato sauce must be removed immediately. These items and some recalcitrant stains have to be scraped off with a razor blade held at 30° to the surface. (Cooktop manufacturers sell scrapers that make it easy to use a razor blade properly.)

Induction Magnetism Gets Things Cooking

The coolest feature of an induction cooktop is that elements don't generate heat. In fact, these cooktops won't work unless an appropriate piece of cookware is on the glass surface (more on that in a moment). An alternating current of electricity energizes a coil of copper wire beneath each heating area on the cooktop, creating a magnetic field. When a pot or pan with iron content or magnetic stainless steel is placed above the coil, the magnet excites electrons in the pan, causing them to vibrate. The friction of this agitation heats the pan and its contents. Because the friction is in the pan, the cooktop doesn't heat up. Marketing campaigns for induction cooking show pans that have been cut in half, revealing things like ice melting in the pan but not on the exposed portion of the element. Although you can touch the cooking surface right next to a boiling pot, it's important to recognize that the glass beneath cookware warms from its contact with the hot pot in the same way that coffee warms a mug; therefore, touching it can still burn you.

MAGNETS HEAT ONLY WHERE THE PAN IS. Frigidaire's 30-in. cooktop (FPIC3095MS) is one of the more affordable induction cooktops on the market. It has all the basics: 15 cooking settings per burner, a timer, cooktop lockout to prevent small hands from turning on the stove, and digital touch controls. Its largest element is 10 in. dia. and 3,400 watts. Although you shouldn't use a pan that extends more than ½ in. beyond the cooking zone, this cooktop, like all induction cooktops, automatically adjusts element size to the pan if it's smaller than the element.

Induction cooktops have even better heat response than gas, and control can be precise. There isn't any fiddling with a knob to adjust flame height. Push-button controls select the temperature, with up to 17 settings per element on the most flexible models.

Induction elements require cookware with ferrous content, so you may have to budget for new pots and pans in your kitchen renovation. Cookware manufacturers have begun adding an induction-compatible symbol to appropriate cookware. You can check your existing cookware or unlabeled new pots with a magnet. (It should stick.) To maximize efficiency, cookware bottoms should be flat. Cookware with an aluminum core is said to be best for taking advantage of induction's strengths.

Some people are put off by noises that can accompany the heating process. These can include a slight humming sound on high-heat settings or the sound of a fan in the cooktop cooling the electronics, but noises aren't that different from those made by a gas burner.

FROM ZERO TO BOIL IN HALF THE TIME

THIS 36-IN. BOSCH® 800-SERIES INDUCTION COOKTOP (NIT8665UC) is laden with features that make cooking easier, including built-in timers for each element, overflow detection that sounds an alarm and shuts off the cooktop, and AutoChef™ for frying foods. Using a special pan, this last feature monitors and regulates the temperature inside the pan according to a specific food type.

Bosch's 500-series midlevel induction cooktops feature almost all the same specifications as the more expensive 800 series, save for the AutoChef function. Unlike gas burners, induction elements are not continuously variable; you choose a set heating level. Like the Gaggenau, the Bosch cooktops have 17 heat levels for greater control.

The highest heating level on most induction cooktops is typically labeled with "boost" appended to an active verb. Called SpeedBoost by Bosch, the setting brings a pot to boil very quickly; Bosch claims to halve the time it would take with a radiant electric burner. These settings work by redirecting some of the power from the other element on the same side of the cooktop. Although it limits the high power setting on the other element, the fast boil time seems like a worthwhile trade-off.

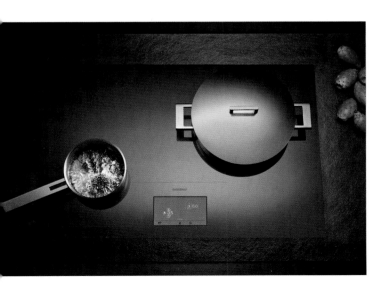

WORLD'S MOST FLEXIBLE COOKTOP? Of Gaggenau's four full-size induction cooktops, the full-surface induction unit (CX 491) has features that are out of this world, a phrase that might also apply to its price. Rather than consisting of several individual heating circles, the entire surface of the Gaggenau is capable of induction cooking. The cooking surface recognizes size, shape, and location of up to four pans, and it heats the areas under them. If you remove a pan, the element shuts off; return the pan to approximately the same position in less than 90 seconds, and the element returns to the previous setting. If you move the pan to a different place on the cooktop, you can transfer the timer information to the new hot spot with the touch of a finger. The cooktop cockpit is a small touch-screen display that you navigate like an iPhone®. You set the temperature by swiping a finger to scroll through the 17 heat settings.

Breathe Easy with the Right Range Hood

BY DEBRA JUDGE SILBER

With all the emphasis today on fresh food, you'd think that fresh air in the kitchen would deserve an equal amount of attention. As a rule, though, it doesn't. It's only after the kitchen layout is worked out, the appliances are selected, and much of the budget is earmarked that, well, yes, we realize we ought to do something about the steam, the grease particles, and the unhealthful gases generated by cooking.

According to manufacturer Vent-A-Hood®, the average home creates more than a gallon of cooking grease a year, not to mention the added hazard of nitrogen dioxide and carbon monoxide that are emitted from gas appliances. That's a nasty mix of stuff to leave lingering in your kitchen.

The good news is that today's ventilation equipment is up to the job like never before. Daniel Forest, the chairman of the certification committee of the Home Ventilating Institute®, which certifies range hoods, says that there has been "substantial improvement" in recent years in range-hood performance in terms of airflow, sound, and consumption of electricity. Still, when it comes to slick designs that push the boundaries of basic concepts—that steam rises, for instance—both range-hood manufacturers and consumers may discover that they need to compensate.

How Much Ventilation Do You Need?

Sizing a range hood correctly starts with a benchmark airflow in cubic feet per minute (cfm) based on the cooking appliance to be vented. Designers, manufacturers, and others vary slightly in how they arrive at that figure, but the formula suggested by Brian Wellnitz, Broan®'s marketing manager for kitchen ventilation, is nearly universal. For conventional gas appliances and all electric cooktops, the benchmark cfm is based on the appliance's width, with each linear foot requiring 100 cfm. The average 30-in. (2.5-ft.) range, then, would require a ventilation capacity in the area of 250 cfm. For larger professional appliances that generate 60,000 Btu or more, the basis becomes 1 cfm for every 100 Btu. Thus a 90,000-Btu cooktop should be matched with a hood capable of moving 900 cfm.

But considering only the cooking appliance would be a mistake. Wellnitz stresses that the benchmark number is a starting point for a hood of an "appropriate" size that should also take into account the hood design, its position, and the style of cooking done in the kitchen. "It's not just how many Btu," he says. "Do they cook with intensity, or do they cook gently?" If a grill is part of the mix, Wellnitz suggests at least an additional 200 cfm.

And while it's the designer's prerogative to reject the manufacturer's recommendation on how high to mount the hood over the stove—whether it's to provide a better view beneath an island hood or to avoid collisions with the cook's forehead—it's the designer's obligation to balance a higher hood with increased cfm. The rule of thumb here is 100 additional cfm for every 3 in. above the manufacturer's recommended height.

Problem: Ventilation Can Be Bad for You

While healthful indoor air requires adequate removal of the moisture, grease particles, and gases produced from cooking—particularly gas cooking—air quality is compromised when that removal draws in contaminants from fuel-burning water- and space-heating equipment as a result of negative air pressure. As energy efficiency places a premium on tight homes, the danger increases. For manufacturers, this means more emphasis on hood designs that do a better job of capturing smoke and steam, without relying on high cfm.

Sophie Piesse, a green architect in Carrboro, N.C., consults an HVAC (heating, ventilating, and air-conditioning) contractor when concerns arise about kitchen makeup air. "It's always better to look at the house as a whole, and get your makeup air through your HVAC system," she says. A little consumer education doesn't hurt either: "Just telling people about it helps. I tell them, 'Don't run the hood longer than you need to.'"

Broan, which manufactures a range of hoods under its own name and that of other brands, is anticipating a trend toward makeup air built in to the range-hood system in response to language in the *2009 International Residential Code* that calls for an interlocked makeup-air system on local ventilation devices rated above 400 cfm. Broan introduced a makeup-air damper that could be mounted in a separate duct and triggered by the kitchen-vent hood. "It's not the entire package," Wellnitz admits, "but it's the controlled interlock portion. What

(continued on p. 216)

NOTHING COMPROMISES range-hood performance like a poor installation. Most range-hood manufacturers offer training and technical assistance to installers in an effort to ensure that their products perform as promised in the field. The number-one cause of poor performance, manufacturers say, is improper ducting. Here's how to get it right.

- Vent the hood to the outdoors whenever possible so that odors and cooking gases can be removed completely from the home. Do not terminate a vent into an attic or chimney.
- Do not use flexible or corrugated duct, which will restrict airflow and reduce performance. Use only smooth galvanized-metal duct.
- The size (area) of the duct should be equal to or greater than that of the vent opening on the range hood. When combining multiple duct runs together, the area of the single duct, measured in square inches, must reflect the total area of the two ducts being combined.
- Make the duct run as short and straight as possible, with as few turns as possible. Avoid sharp-angled turns. Use smooth, gradual turns such as adjustable elbows or 45° angled turns to prevent turbulence or air dams. Never position two 90° elbows closer than 2 ft. within the duct system.
- Make sure dampers open and close freely. There is typically one in the duct located on or near the hood duct attachment and one in the exterior roof or wall cap. Do not use screen wire or spring-loaded doors on wall louvers or roof jacks.
- In very tight homes, it's beneficial to install a makeup-air damper to ensure there is an adequate supply of air when the hood is operating.

A VENT HOOD THAT WORKS

1. HEIGHT

To do its job, a vent hood has to be able to capture smoke and steam from the cooktop, without getting in the way of the cook. That often puts manufacturers at odds with designers and architects, who tend to hike up hoods (especially over islands) so that they don't interfere with sight lines or cooks' foreheads. This need not affect performance, as long as 100 cfm are added for every 3 in. the hood is raised above the recommended height.

2. CFM RATING

Most manufacturers recommend keying a hood's cfm rating to accepted benchmarks, then fine-tuning it based on the homeowner's style of cooking and any deviations from the recommended height (see "Height"). For most standard cooktops, the benchmark starts at 100 cfm for each linear foot of cooking surface; for professional-style appliances above 60,000 Btu, the rule of thumb becomes 1 cfm per 100 Btu.

3. LIGHTING

Most hoods today employ halogen lighting; Energy Star–rated hoods mostly use fluorescent. Although LEDs are used in some models, the technology tends to be too sensitive to heat. Multiple light levels, including night-light features, come in handy in most kitchens. Infrared warming lights, introduced on some of Jenn-Air®'s pro-style stainless hoods, are another option.

4. FILTERS

Baffle-style filters offer a professional look but are effective only at high speeds; mesh filters do a better job of collecting grease at lower speeds. Some manufacturers have developed combination filters that offer both. Broan's Evolution™ filter (below right) combines baffle and mesh; Zephyr offers a mesh filter in a decorative casing for hoods in which the filter is visible. Mesh filters typically come in stainless steel or aluminum; most are dishwasher safe. The easiest way to boost range-hood performance is to maintain the filters. "Throw them in the dishwasher," says Brian Wellnitz, marketing manager for Broan. "Clean the darn things"— ideally, every month or two.

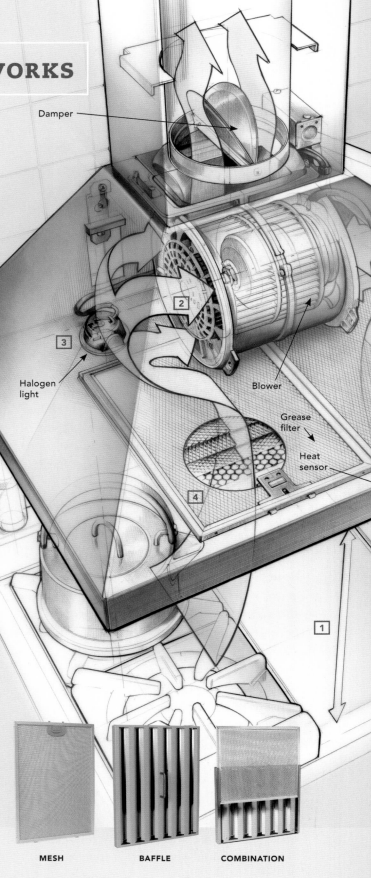

Damper

Blower

Grease filter

Heat sensor

Halogen light

MESH   BAFFLE   COMBINATION

5. CAPTURE AREA

For optimum performance, a wall-mount hood should overlap the cooking surface by 3 in. on each side and cover at least 50% of the front burners. Capture is often deficient in liners and built-in hoods, where the ventilation appliance is inserted in a plywood housing and does not extend over the full footprint of the cooktop. It's also compromised in many design-driven hoods.

Control panel

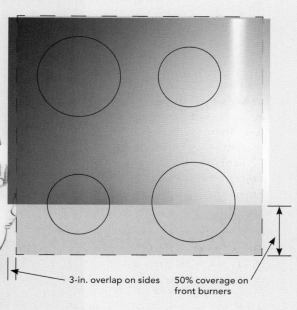

3-in. overlap on sides   50% coverage on front burners

6. ENERGY EFFICIENCY

To bear the Energy Star seal, a kitchen vent hood must have a fan of less than 500 cfm and fluorescent or LED lights as well as meet various performance standards.

7. CONTROLS

Multiple fan speeds are useful for air and noise control. A remote control is worthwhile on island hoods that may be mounted too high for users to reach onboard knobs comfortably. Some Zephyr models feature memory-touch controls, returning the hood to the last setting used; others feature a "clean air" control that activates the fan for 10 minutes every four hours to disperse lingering odors. On many hoods, heat-activated sensors automatically turn on fans or adjust fan speed based on temperature changes.

designers have to know is that these code languages will be adopted over the next year by local municipalities and that controlled makeup air is going to be a part of their life."

The Talk on Noise

When homeowners discuss kitchen ventilation, you're likely to hear about noise. The Kitchen-Aid® Architect® Series hood in Leslie Midgely's Texas kitchen clears the air well, but, says Midgely, "it's like a freight train on the loudest [setting]. Our kitchen and dining room are open, and folks always seem to congregate in the kitchen. You definitely have to yell over it."

Choosing a hood with multiple speed options is one way to increase the odds that your fan can do its job while still maintaining the peace, says Paul DeGroot, the architect who designed Midgely's kitchen. "If you do a lot of cooking, you have to go with at least two speeds. The low speed will be quiet, even though you won't be able to use it all the time." Broan's Wellnitz, meanwhile, suggests opting for the next-larger-size blower, because a large blower run on a low setting is typically quieter than a small blower run on high.

While motor and design improvements have made fans considerably quieter at normal speeds than they were 10 years ago, bets are still off at high speeds, when it's significantly more difficult to modulate the turbulence of moving air. Up to now, manufacturers have put their money on improving performance at low speeds because that's where most cooking is done, and it has paid off. Go back 15 years, says Wellnitz, and the average hood generated 2.5 sones (a measure of loudness) at low speed; today, it's down to 1 sone. "Over the past 10 years we've been working very hard to provide products that give quieter operation at normal or typical speeds," he says. "It's defeating in terms of cost to design something that's absolutely quiet at high speeds." Yet in the next decade, that's where he predicts hood designers will turn their attention, with advanced motor design, better hood insulation, and even noise-cancellation technology like that used on earphones favored by frequent fliers.

Until then, one of the best options is to remove the fan from the hood. An external blower not only distances a primary source of noise from the kitchen but also widens cfm options.

That's exactly what architect David Edrington of Eugene, Ore., does. "Particularly when the cooktop is on an island and one is cooking with a view, I like to mount hoods higher than in the specifications. The way I offset the reduction in efficiency is to use a larger fan motor in an outside unit—typically one above 1,000 cfm." The higher hood doesn't block the view, and the remote blower doesn't stifle kitchen communication. "Because conversation is an important part of my kitchens, I do it almost all the time," Edrington says.

Dealing with Less-Than-Ideal Conditions

Even dream kitchens have their rude awakenings: no exterior-wall access, inadequate room for a hood, or no alternative place to put the microwave, forcing it to double as both a cooking and venting appliance. The workarounds aren't new, but the fact that these situations keep cropping up has encouraged some manufacturers to improve on the solutions they offer. For the casual cook in a compromised kitchen, it's easier to live with the limitations than without any air-clearing at all.

RECIRCULATION

As long as there are apartment dwellers, oddly positioned cooktops, and cooks who won't surrender an inch of cabinet space, there will be recirculating, or, to use the preferred industry term, "duct-free" range fans. Because they don't meet the definition of ventilation as defined by ASHRAE 62.2—that is, they don't supply outdoor air or remove indoor air from a dwelling by natural or mechanical means—the Home Ventilating Institute does not consider them a substitute for kitchen ventilation, according to Daniel Forest, chair of the HVI certification com-

CONE OF SILENCE. The sound-silencing system on Jenn-Air's Euro-style stainless hoods combines insulation and filter design to minimize noise at high speeds.

mittee. He adds that there are currently no industry-accepted standards or tests to evaluate the performance of recirculation kits at capturing pollutants produced during cooking. Says Forest, "It is HVI's position that they should always be used in conjunction with an exhaust fan, of an adequate capacity, located in the kitchen."

Architect David Edrington steers clear of ductless range hoods when he can. "If it's an electric cooktop and my clients look like they'd be responsible enough to keep the filters clean—maybe," he says, after some consideration. "I would never do it in a gas-appliance situation."

Although Vent-A-Hood claims the first patent for a ductless hood in 1945, the company never brought the idea to market because, in the words of engineer Bob Seloff, "ductless range hoods didn't work then, and they don't work now." However, Vent-A-Hood has launched a new category of ductless range hoods called ARS (air recovery system). These hoods combine an active canopy, centrifugal blower, deep activated carbon bed, and accordion microfiber filter to scrub the air before releasing it out the top of the stack.

DOWNDRAFT

Like ductless hoods, downdraft ventilation is an option Austin architect Paul DeGroot would rather avoid. Why? Physics. "Downdrafts can't pull steam down. Steam rises," says DeGroot. "They're OK with odors, but they're just not in the right place to capture steam." Because they're drawing air from the level of the cooktop, there's interference with the heat source itself. "They work fine on electric and modestly well on residential-size gas cooktops,

although they affect the flames somewhat," says Edrington. "The ones that rise up do that less, but those just suck air. I don't think they're useful at all on commercial-style cooktops."

Jenn-Air, which introduced the downdraft ventilated range in 1965, hasn't abandoned the approach. If anything, it has upped the stakes by throwing recirculation into the mix with the introduction of a ductless downdraft cooktop. They've embraced the model for two reasons, according to Jenifer Golba, senior brand manager for Jenn-Air Cooking. First, designing the cooktop and venting system as an integrated unit boosts performance. Second, naysayers aside, customers want both features. Jenn-Air, along with other manufacturers, has also increased the height of its telescoping downdrafts to 14 in.—high enough to collect steam from the top of a medium-size stockpot.

RECIRCULATION

RETHINKING RECIRCULATION. Vent-A-Hood's ARS hoods send cooktop exhaust through stacked carbon and microfiber filters before expelling it.

DOWNDRAFT

UP IN SMOKE. Many telescoping downdrafts (such as this one from Jenn-Air) now rise 14 in. above the cooking surface.

MICROWAVE-VENT COMBINATIONS

Over-the-stove microwaves have two strikes against them as venting devices. First, their flat, rectangular bottoms are not designed to capture air and do not extend over the entire cooking surface. Second, the fan has more work to do. According to Brian Wellnitz, Broan's marketing manager for kitchen ventilation, 15% of the air in a microwave fan is being used to cool the magnetron. "The reality is, consumers buy them," Wellnitz says. "If you're going to use an over-the-range microwave, at least duct it. Some ventilation is better than no ventilation." For moderate cooking, a ducted microwave fan can do the job. Tammy Stone chose a Samsung SMH9187ST to vent her 30-in. Bosch gas cooktop, and it performs fine. "It has done a good job of venting smoke, which is what I use it most for," she says.

SOURCES

BROAN
www.broan.com

FABER
www.faberonline.com

JENN-AIR
www.jenn-air.com

KITCHENAID
www.kitchenaid.com

KOBE®
www.koberangehoods.com

NUTONE®
www.nutone.com

RANGECRAFT
www.rangecraft.com

VENT-A-HOOD
www.ventahood.com

ZEPHYR®
www.zephyronline.com

MICRO-VENT. Microwave units can offer adequate smoke and steam removal if vented outside.

EXPANDING THE DEFINITION OF HOOD

QUESTION: CAN A HOOD that takes your breath away with its style actually clear the air? Yes, say manufacturers, if it's matched to the right kitchen and cook.

Take Zephyr's modernistic Tilt design 1. "We're honest with people that this isn't your typical vent hood," company spokesman Arcadio Lainez says. "It's not for people doing stir-fry and wok cooking every night; this is for the more casual cook. We tell people the truth and let them buy the style they want."

Despite its angled projection, Tilt uses typical mesh filters to capture air between its panels. Other minimalist hoods use perimeter induction, where cooking air is collected at the edges of the hood's frame, allowing ultrathin designs.

Jenn-Air's Jenifer Golba maintains that her company's perimetric hood 2 performs as well as a traditional-style hood as long as the usual sizing benchmarks are adhered to, although she doesn't recommend it for professional-style ranges. "It's really about the cfm, not the design," she says.

Jerry Nast loves his 30-in. Zephyr under-cabinet hood 3. "It is very slim, unobtrusive, and sucks like a Hoover® Deluxe—in a good way," he says. "It looks great with our unfussy kitchen design, and we would buy it again."

But there's one company that may never abandon the true meaning of *hood*. Pioneer manufacturer Vent-A-Hood does make designer and custom hoods; however, resident engineer Bob Seloff says, "We do not compromise on the necessary capture space in order to deliver a look in place of a performing range hood."

How to Provide Makeup Air for Range Hoods

BY MARTIN HOLLADAY

When Cheryl Morris moved into her new home, she realized that the kitchen exhaust fan was probably too powerful. Whenever she turned on the 1,200-cfm fan, strange things happened. "It pulled the ashes out of the fireplace, halfway across the room, right up to my husband's chair," she says. Those dancing ashes demonstrate an important principle: Large exhaust fans need makeup air.

The Air That Fans Remove Has to Come from Somewhere

Most homes have several exhaust appliances. They can include a bathroom fan (40 cfm to 200 cfm), a clothes dryer (100 cfm to 225 cfm), a power-vented water heater (50 cfm), a woodstove (30 cfm to 50 cfm), and a central vacuum-cleaning system (100 cfm to 200 cfm). The most powerful exhaust appliance in most homes, however, is the kitchen range-hood fan (160 cfm to 1,200 cfm).

Although tightening up homes is a good way to make them more energy efficient, builders need to remember that plugging air leaks makes it harder for air to enter a home. Every time an exhaust fan removes air from your house, an equal volume of air must enter. If a house doesn't have enough random air leaks around windows, doors, and mudsills, makeup air can be pulled through water-heater flues or down wood-burning chimneys, a phenomenon called backdrafting. Because the flue gases of combustion appliances can include carbon monoxide, backdrafting can be dangerous.

One important way to limit backdrafting problems is to avoid installing a wood-burning fireplace or any atmospherically vented combustion appliance. Appliances in this category include gas-fired or oil-fired water heaters, furnaces, and boilers connected to old-fashioned vertical chimneys or flues. Instead, install sealed-combustion appliances with fresh-air ducts that bring combustion air directly to the burner. Most sealed-combustion appliances are practically immune to backdrafting problems.

Small exhaust fans—those rated at 300 cfm or less—usually don't cause backdrafting problems. Anyone planning to install a big fan (400 cfm or more), though, needs to provide a dedicated source of makeup air. As a stopgap measure, it's possible to open a window every time the range-hood fan is turned on, but this solution won't satisfy most homeowners. Moreover, builders who suggest this remedy may still be legally liable for future backdrafting problems.

A Ventilation System Isn't a Makeup-Air System

Most U.S. homes include a forced-air distribution system for heating or cooling. Just because your house has ducts, though, doesn't mean that you have a makeup-air system. Some new houses (especially tight ones) also have a mechanical ventilation system to bring fresh air into the house—for example, a heat-recovery ventilator (HRV), an energy-recovery ventilator (ERV), or an outdoor-air duct connected to the furnace's return-air plenum. If you're wondering whether your home's ventilation system can provide makeup air for your range hood, the answer is no.

Why not? First, most ventilation systems include dampers and controls that open according to the anticipated needs of the occupants; this ventilation

SMALL DUCTS SQUEEZE BIG FANS

IN THEORY, A MAKEUP-AIR DUCT should be at least as large as the duct connected to the range-hood fan. The sizing calculation is complicated, however, for several reasons. As an exhaust fan begins to depressurize a house, some of the necessary makeup air is inevitably drawn through cracks that exist in the building's envelope. This means that the air flowing through a makeup-air duct is only a fraction of the makeup air needed.

Also, there is a dynamic relationship between the airflow through an exhaust duct and the airflow entering a makeup-air duct. As the motorized damper in the makeup-air duct opens, some (but not all) of the necessary makeup air will begin flowing into the house through the duct. If the home's envelope is tight and the makeup-air duct is undersize, the exhaust fan won't be able to perform at its rated specification. In other words, a 1,200-cfm exhaust fan may be exhausting only 900 cfm. This happens because the volume of air leaving the house and the volume of air entering the house are always balanced. If the makeup-air duct in this example were larger, the exhaust fan would experience less resistance and might be able to ramp up to 1,100 cfm. These dynamic effects complicate duct-sizing calculations.

Broan recommends one 6-in. duct for a range hood up to 500 cfm, one 8-in. duct for a range hood rated at 501 cfm to 1,000 cfm, and two 8-in. ducts for a range hood rated at 1,001 cfm to 1,500 cfm.

schedule has nothing to do with the operation of a range-hood fan. Second, most mechanical ventilation systems provide only small quantities of fresh air—generally between 50 cfm and 100 cfm. That's much less than the amount of makeup air needed for a 600-cfm or 800-cfm range hood.

THREE WAYS TO PROVIDE THE MAKEUP AIR YOU NEED

THE IRC REQUIRES a dedicated makeup-air system for range hoods that are larger than 400 cfm. The necessary outside-air duct is usually connected to a wall or ceiling grille in the kitchen or directly connected to the return-air plenum of your furnace. As long as the duct dumps the makeup air into your home, however, it can dump the air almost anywhere.

Although an outdoor-air duct connected to a motorized damper solves the makeup-air problem, it can still lead to comfort complaints if the air isn't conditioned. This problem can be reduced by hooking the outdoor-air duct to your furnace plenum. If your house doesn't have a forced-air heating system, however, you'll need to investigate other solutions.

One solution is a powered makeup-air unit that tempers incoming air during the winter with electric-resistance heating coils. Such units include a supply-air fan wired to turn on when the kitchen exhaust fan is activated. Electro Industries has one such system (model EM-WH1025K), which includes a 10,000-watt heater and a blower, and can supply 632 cfm of makeup air while maintaining a 50°F temperature rise.

A 1,200-cfm range hood would need two of these units. In addition to their high upfront cost, these systems carry a severe energy penalty whenever they are turned on.

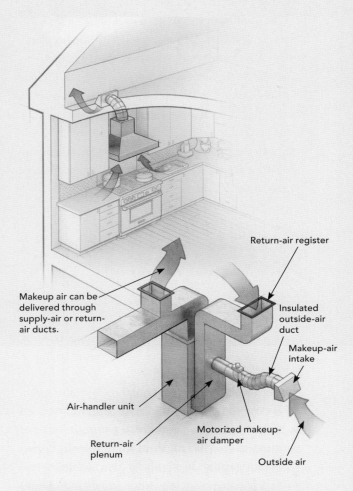

Makeup air can be delivered through supply-air or return-air ducts.

Return-air register

Insulated outside-air duct

Makeup-air intake

Air-handler unit

Return-air plenum

Motorized makeup-air damper

Outside air

MOTORIZED DAMPERS ARE TIGHT. Barometric dampers are bad for makeup-air ducts because they are leaky. Motorized dampers have a tight seal, and when installed in a makeup-air duct, they can be wired to open when a range-hood fan is turned on. Sources: www.Broan.com; www.Aprilaire.com

ADD MAKEUP AIR TO YOUR HVAC SYSTEM

As long as the outdoor-air duct brings air inside, it will be able to supply makeup air whenever the motorized damper is open and the range hood depressurizes your home. Outdoor makeup air can be ducted to the return plenum of a forced-air furnace. If the furnace is running, makeup air is discharged through supply registers. If the furnace is not running, makeup air can be pulled through return registers or supply registers, depending on which is closer to the range hood that is drawing the makeup air.

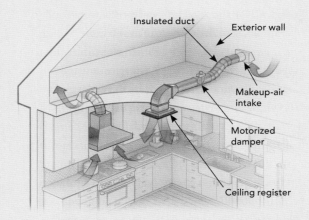

MAKEUP AIR FOR HOMES WITHOUT A FURNACE

In homes without forced-air ductwork, makeup-air ducts usually terminate in a ceiling- or wall-mounted grille in the kitchen. When introducing outdoor makeup air, be sure to choose a delivery location that won't lead to comfort complaints.

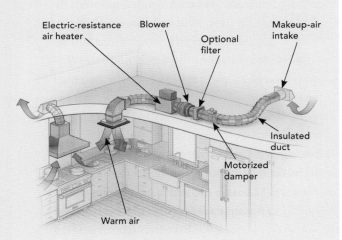

POWERED MAKEUP-AIR SOLUTIONS

You can add a heater and a blower to the through-wall solution, but it costs a lot to buy and a lot to operate. Makeup-air units with electric-resistance heaters are expensive and require large amounts of electricity to operate.

Some houses also include outdoor-air ducts that supply combustion air to appliances such as furnaces and boilers. In most cases, these outdoor-air ducts have been sized to meet the needs of only one appliance, so they can't be depended on to supply the makeup air for a range hood.

If you decide to install a makeup-air system for your range hood, you'll need a dedicated duct that introduces outdoor air into your house. (In most cases, this duct will be larger than a ventilation duct.) This makeup-air duct can be connected to your home's existing forced-air ductwork if you want, but it needs separate controls from those used to regulate your home's ventilation system.

Follow the Code, Not the Manufacturer's Advice

When I contacted four range-hood manufacturers recently to ask about makeup-air requirements, the quality of the answers ranged widely. The technical advisers at General Electric were the least informed, and four phone calls all elicited the same response: "What is makeup air?" A call to Broan was more fruitful, and a helpful representative advised, "If you start going above 300 cfm, then you might start considering makeup air, especially in a brand-new house that might be fairly airtight." Other manufacturers had answers somewhere in between: "We don't have any recommendations other than advising you to do whatever the code says."

According to section M1507.3 of the *2009 International Residential Code*, the minimum rating of a kitchen range hood is 100 cfm. Section M1503.4 of the code notes that you don't need a makeup-air system for a range hood rated at 400 cfm or less.

If your fan is larger than 400 cfm, however, you'll need a makeup-air system with a motorized damper and interlock controls. The code states, "Exhaust hood systems capable of exhausting in excess of 400 cfm shall be provided with makeup air at a rate approximately equal to the exhaust-air rate. Such makeup-air systems shall be equipped with a means of closure and shall be automatically controlled to start and operate simultaneously with the exhaust system."

TIGHT-HOUSE SOLUTION: A RECIRCULATING HOOD AND AN HRV

CODE REQUIREMENTS FOR KITCHEN VENTILA-TION vary widely from jurisdiction to jurisdiction. If your local building official is willing to accept the installation of a recirculating range hood that doesn't exhaust any air to the exterior, you can sidestep the makeup-air dilemma entirely. This approach has been pioneered by passive house builders, who usually try to avoid unnecessary exhaust fans or makeup-air supply ducts when they are building.

Passive house designers often specify a recirculating range hood connected to a replaceable charcoal filter. They also install an exhaust grille on the kitchen ceiling as far away from the stove as possible. The grille is connected to the exhaust duct of a heat-recovery ventilation (HRV) system. The exhaust grille is located away from the stove to limit the amount of filter-clogging grease reaching the HRV.

TWO FANS ARE BETTER THAN ONE

Some passive house builders have persuaded local inspectors to allow the installation of a recirculating range hood. A ceiling-mounted exhaust grille connected to an HRV removes kitchen air, and the HRV provides fresh air to another part of the living space.

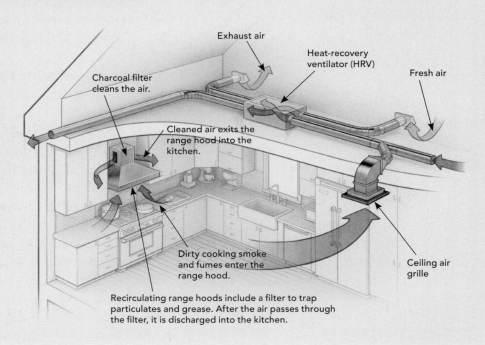

Exhaust air

Heat-recovery ventilator (HRV)

Fresh air

Charcoal filter cleans the air.

Cleaned air exits the range hood into the kitchen.

Dirty cooking smoke and fumes enter the range hood.

Ceiling air grille

Recirculating range hoods include a filter to trap particulates and grease. After the air passes through the filter, it is discharged into the kitchen.

If you are building a superinsulated house and, therefore, want to limit the number of penetrations in your building envelope, consider using a recirculating range hood rather than an exhaust fan. Combined with a ventilation appliance such as an HRV, this solution works well for some families. Those who do a lot of roasting and frying, however, may not find this solution satisfactory.

The bottom line is that powerful range hoods are great for getting rid of smoke from blackened redfish, but they are difficult to integrate into a tight house. It is best to avoid exhaust fans altogether, but if you can't live without one, be sure to provide plenty of makeup air. Backdrafting from combustion appliances can be deadly.

SMALL RANGE HOODS DON'T NEED DEDICATED MAKEUP AIR

BECAUSE THE SIZING GUIDELINES provided by range-hood manufacturers or kitchen-equipment dealers often result in the installation of oversize fans, some experts advise ignoring such guidelines. If you choose a residential-size (30-in.-wide) range, a fan rated at 160 cfm to 200 cfm will keep you out of trouble. One model you might consider is the Broan 40000 series fan; it's rated at 160 cfm.

THE SIMPLE WAY TO AVOID BACKDRAFTING. Choose a range hood with a small fan. Low-cfm fans won't depressurize your house and are quiet. Sources: www.Broan.com; www.GEAppliances.com; www.Whirlpool.com

WHY CAN'T RANGE-HOOD EXHAUST DUCTS BE DESIGNED TO RECOVER HEAT?

MANY MECHANICAL VENTILATION SYSTEMS are designed with a pipe-within-a-pipe system that allows heat to be exchanged between the outgoing and incoming air-streams. Range hoods can't do that for two reasons. First, the pipe diameters get big fast. If your range hood requires a 10-in.-dia. exhaust duct, then the duct-within-a-duct solution would require a 14-in. or 16-in. duct. It's hard to find that much room for ductwork in a house. Elbows compound the awkwardness.

Second (and the biggest problem with the pipe-within-a-pipe idea), the incoming cold air would cool the exhaust duct, encouraging the suspended grease in the exhaust air to congeal and moisture in the exhaust airstream to condense. The cooling effect of the incoming air makes an exhaust duct become dirtier than if it had stayed warm. This process is similar to what happens when woodstoves are vented to outdoor chimneys; cold flues become clogged with creosote much faster than warm flues.

CONTRIBUTORS

Rex Alexander is a cabinetmaker in Fenton, Mich.

Brent Benner runs The Roxbury Cabinet Company (www.roxbury-cabinet.com) in Roxbury, Conn.

Paul DeGroot (www.degroot-architect.com) is an architect who designs custom homes and additions in Austin, Texas.

David Edrington (edarchitect@qwestoffice.net) is an architect in Eugene, Ore. Thanks to architect John Hurst (john@johnhurstdesign.com) of Portland, Ore., for his first-rate kitchen-design insights.

Rick Gedney owns Kitchens by Gedney (www.gedneykitchens.com) in Madison, Conn.

David Getts (www.davidgettsdesign.com) is a cabinetmaker and designer in Seattle, Wash.

Scott Gibson, a contributing writer to *Fine Homebuilding*, lives in East Waterboro, Maine.

Sean Groom is a contributing editor to *Fine Homebuilding*.

David Hart is a full-time freelance writer and retired tile contractor from Rice, Va.

Nancy R. Hiller (www.nrhillerdesign.com) is a professional maker of custom furniture and cabinetry based in Bloomington, Ind. She specializes in period-authentic furniture and built-ins for homes and offices from the late-nineteenth through mid-twentieth centuries.

Jerri Holan, FAIA, is a California architect (www.holanarchitects.com) and author (http://sanfrancis-co.urbdezine.com) who specializes in rehabilitating older homes.

Martin Holladay is a *Fine Homebuilding* senior editor.

Katie Hutchison is an architect, design writer, and fine-art photographer in Warren, R.I. Find Katie Hutchison Studio at www.katiehutchison.com and at *House Enthusiast*, the online magazine she produces.

Joseph Lanza (www.josephlanza.com) designs and builds entire houses, as well as their parts, in Duxbury, Mass.

Mike Maines developed the system featured while working as a trim carpenter in Nantucket and Boston, Mass. He now designs kitchens and other residential projects at Fine Lines Construction in Freeport, Maine (www.finelines-maine.com).

John McLean (www.johnmclean-architect.net) is an architect in San Francisco.

Tom Meehan and his wife, Lane, own Cape Cod Tileworks, a three-story tile showroom in historic Harwich, Mass.

Michael Pekovich is the art director of *Fine Woodworking*.

Charles Peterson is a frequent contributor to *Fine Homebuilding*. His latest book is *Wood Flooring: A Complete Guide to Layout, Installation, and Finishing* (The Taunton Press, 2010).

Debra Judge Silber is the managing editor of *Fine Homebuilding*.

Gary Striegler is a builder in Fayetteville, Ark.

Matthew Teague builds furniture in Nashville and is the editor of *Popular Woodworking Magazine*.

Clair Urbain is a freelance writer in Fort Atkinson, Wis.

Dan Vos owns DeVos Custom Woodworking (www.devoswoodworking.com) in Dripping Springs, Texas.

Rob Yagid is a *Fine Homebuilding* design editor.

CREDITS

All photos are courtesy of *Fine Homebuilding* magazine © The Taunton Press, Inc., except as noted below:

The articles in this book appeared in the following issues of *Fine Homebuilding*:

pp. 5–12: How Much Will My Kitchen Cost? by John McLean, issue 183. Photos by Brian Pontolilo except for photo p. 6 by Charles Miller.

pp. 13–19: 10 Ingredients of a Great Kitchen by David Edrington, issue 183. Photos by Charles Miller. Kitchens designed by the author except for kitchens in photos p. 16 and left photo p. 18 designed by John Hurst.

pp. 20–22: Drawing Board: Opening up a small kitchen by Jerri Holan, issue 201. Drawings by Jerri Holan.

pp. 23–29: Getting Appliances to Fit Part 2 by David Getts, issue 215. Photo by David Chamberlain, Chamberlain Woodworking-Boulder. Drawings by Bob La Pointe.

pp. 30–40: Kitchen Remodeling for Any Budget by Paul DeGroot, issue 199. Photos by Brian Pontolilo. Drawings by Martha Garstang Hill.

pp. 41–46: A Kitchen for Cooks and Kids by Michael Pekovich, issue 199. Photos by Charles Miller except for photo p. 43 by Michael Pekovich. Drawings by Martha Garstang Hill.

pp. 48–53: 4 Quick Cabinet Upgrades by Gary Striegler, issue 214. Photos by Chris Ermides except for before photo p. 48 by Bryan Striegler.

pp. 54–61: A Buyer's Guide to Kitchen Cabinets by Scott Gibson, issue 191. Photos by Charles Miller except for right and left photos p. 54 and photos pp. 58-59 by Krysta S. Doerfler.

pp. 62–68: Installing Stock Cabinets by Rick Gedney, issue 223. Photos by Rob Yagid.

pp. 69–71: Master Carpenter: Installing cabinets in tight spaces by Brent Benner, issue 212. Photos by Charles Bickford.

pp. 72–79: A Faster, Easier Approach to Custom Cabinets by Mike Maines, issue 200. Photos by Rob Yagid. Drawing by Bob La Pointe.

pp. 80–87: Build a Kitchen Island by Rick Gedney, issue 232. Photos by Patrick McCombe except for photo p. 80 and top right photo p. 83 by Charles Bickford.

pp. 88–95: How to Install Inset Cabinet Doors by Scott Gibson, issue 226. Photos by Charles Bickford except for photo p. 89 and top right photo p. 93 by Nat Rea.

pp. 96–98: Upgrade to a Trash Drawer by Rex Alexander, issue 205. Photos by Charles Bickford. Drawing by Dan Thornton.

pp. 100–107: Amazing Countertops by Rob Yagid, issue 194. Photos by Krysta S. Doerfler except for bottom photo p. 101 courtesy of Totally Bamboo, left photo p. 102 courtesy of Klip Biotechnologies LLC., left photo p. 104 courtesy of ThinkGlass, right photo p. 105 courtesy of Vetrazzo, top right photo p. 107 courtesy of Alkemi, and top left photo p. 107 courtesy of Eleek Inc.

pp. 108–115: Making Wood Countertops by Dan Vos, issue 209. Photos by Brian Pontolilo except for bottom photo p. 109 by Dan Vos. Drawing by Dan Thornton.

pp. 116–121: Tiling a Backsplash by Tom Meehan, issue 167. Photos by Lindsay Meehan.

pp. 123–125: Drawing Board: Secrets to an uncluttered kitchen by Katie Hutchison, issue 213. Drawings by Katie Hutchison.

pp. 126–133: Off-the-Shelf Kitchen Storage Solutions by Debra Judge Silber, issue 207. Photos courtesy of the manufacturers.

pp. 134–141: Design the Perfect Pantry by Paul DeGroot, issue 223. Photos by Brian Pontolilo except for photo p. 141 by Samuel Pontolilo. Drawings by Paul De Groot.

pp. 142–149: A Clever Kitchen Built-In by Nancy R. Hiller, issue 193. Photos by Kendall Reeves. Drawings by Bob La Pointe.

pp. 150–152: Maximize Pantry Storage by Rex Alexander, issue 185. Photo by Dietrich Floeter. Drawings by Bob La Pointe.

pp. 153–160: A Built-In Corner Seating Nook by Joseph Lanza, issue 225. Photos by Charles Bickford. Drawings by John Hartman.

pp. 162–174: Flooring Options for the Kitchen by Matthew Teague, issue 207. Photos by Rodney Diaz except for photo p. 162 courtesy of Carlisle Wide Plank Floors, bottom photos p. 163, and photo p. 167 courtesy of Armstrong, photo p. 164 courtesy of Wilsonart, photos p. 165, and bottom photo p. 168 by Krysta S. Doerfler, left photo p. 166 courtesy of Forbo Flooring, top photo p. 168 and right photo p. 171 by Charles Bickford, left photo p. 170 by Henry Biber, courtesy of Acanthus Inc. Concrete Stain Design, top photo p. 171 courtesy of Planium, and left photo p. 174 by Joseph Kugielsky. Drawing by Don Foley.

pp. 175–178: For Great Tile Floors, Layout is Everything by David Hart, issue 214. Photo by Sandor Nagyszalanczy. Drawings by Bob La Pointe.

pp. 179–185: Save Time with a Prefinished Wood Floor by Charles Peterson, issue 213. Photos by Rob Yagid except for bottom left photo p. 185 by Dan Thornton. Drawings by Dan Thornton.

pp. 187–196: Kitchen Lighting Design by Matthew Teague, Kitchen & Bath Planning Guide 2008. Photos courtesy of the manufacturers except for photo p. 187 by Susan Teare, photo p. 188 by Brian Vanden Brink, kitchen photo p. 189 by Randy O'Rourke, fixture photos p. 190 by Krysta S. Doerfler, bottom right photo p. 191 by Joe DeMaio, bottom photo p. 192 by Jennifer Cheung, top right photo p. 193 and top left photo p. 194 by Charles Miller, and photos p. 195 by Justin Fink.

pp. 197–204: Choose the Right Kitchen Sink by Clair Urbain, issue 231. Photos courtesy of the manufacturers, except bottom left photo p. 198 by Patrick McCombe. Drawings by Dan Thornton.

pp. 205–211: Cooktops from Simmer to Sear by Sean Groom, issue 231. Photos courtesy of the manufacturers.

pp. 212–219: Breathe Easy with the Right Range Hood by Debra Judge Silber, issue 215. Photos courtesy of the manufacturers except for photo p. 213 by Joseph Kugielsky and photos p. 214 by Dan Thornton. Drawings by Bruce Morser.

pp. 220–225: How to Provide Makeup Air for Range Hoods by Martin Holladay, issue 232. Photo p. 220 by Charles Miller, photo p. 222 and top left photo p. 225 courtesy of Broan, bottom left photo p. 225 courtesy of Whirlpool, and right photo p. 225 courtesy of Kaplan Thompson Architects. Drawings by John Hartman.

INDEX

If you like this book, you'll love *Fine Homebuilding*.

Read *Fine Homebuilding* Magazine:

Get eight issues, including our two annual design issues, *Houses* and *Kitchens & Baths*, plus FREE tablet editions. Packed with expert advice and skill-building techniques, every issue provides the latest information on quality building and remodeling.

Subscribe today at:
FineHomebuilding.com/4Sub

Discover our *Fine Homebuilding* Online Store:

It's your destination for premium resources from America's best builders: how-to and design books, DVDs, videos, special interest publications, and more.

Visit today at:
FineHomebuilding.com/4More

Get our FREE *Fine Homebuilding* eNewsletter:

Keep up with the current best practices, the newest tools, and the latest materials, plus free tips and advice from *Fine Homebuilding* editors.

Sign up, it's free:
FineHomebuilding.com/4Newsletter

Become a FineHomebuilding.com member

Join to enjoy unlimited access to premium content and exclusive benefits, including: 1,400+ articles; 350 tip, tool, and technique videos; our how-to video project series; over 1,600 field-tested tips; monthly giveaways; tablet editions; contests; special offers; and more.

Discover more information online:
FineHomebuilding.com/4Join